D1195681

Informal Entente

INFORMAL ENTENTE

The Private Structure of Cooperation in Anglo-American Economic Diplomacy, 1918-1928

Michael J. Hogan

University of Missouri Press
Columbia & London, 1977

Copyright © 1977 by The Curators of the University of Missouri
Library of Congress Catalog Card Number 76–45829
Printed and bound in the United States of America
University of Missouri Press, Columbia, Missouri 65201
All rights reserved

Library of Congress Cataloging in Publication Data

Hogan, Michael J   1943–
    Informal entente.

    Bibliography: p. 229
    Includes index.
    1.   United States—Foreign economic relations.
2.   Great Britain—Foreign economic relations.   3.   United States—Foreign
relations—20th century.   4.   Great Britain—Foreign relations—1910–1936.
I.   Title.
HF1455.H54   338.91'172'4073   76–45829
ISBN 0–8262–0217–9

An earlier version of Chapter 2 appeared as "The United States and the
Problem of International Economic Control: American Attitudes Toward
European Reconstruction, 1918–1920," in the *Pacific Historical Review*
(February 1975).

An earlier version of Chapter 8 appeared as "Informal Entente: Public Policy
and Private Management in Anglo-American Petroleum Affairs, 1918–1924,"
in the *Business History Review* (Summer 1974).

Library
I.U.P.
Indiana, Pa.
337. 73042   H678i

c.1

To Virginia

Acknowledgments

Professor Lawrence E. Gelfand of the University of Iowa suggested the area of inquiry that led to this study. His advice and encouragement during the period of research and his helpful criticism of the manuscript can never be fully repaid. Thanks is also due to Professor Ellis W. Hawley of the University of Iowa for his enthusiasm, searching criticism, and many thoughtful suggestions. Dr. Robert Van Meter of the State University College, New Paltz, New York, and Professors Carl Parrini of Northern Illinois University, Joan Hoff Wilson of California State University, Sacramento, Melvyn Leffler of Vanderbilt University, and David Burner of the State University of New York, Stony Brook, all provided much useful advice and encouragement during various stages of research and writing. So did many friends who read portions of this manuscript or otherwise provided helpful assistance, including Nina Noring of the Department of State, Lane Moore of the National Archives, and Robert Humphrey of the University of Iowa.

I owe an important intellectual debt to other historians, a few of whom should be mentioned here. Significant studies on foreign policy by Parrini, Wilson, William Appleman Williams, and N. Gordon Levin, Jr., were useful in conceptualizing my own topics, especially the problems involved in government-business relations and the theme of cooperation that runs throughout American policy. In addition, I have benefited from the work on domestic history by a diverse collection of "neo-institutional," "New Right," and "New Left" historians who, in different ways, stress what Ellis Hawley has called "the quest for order rather than the pursuit of liberal democracy" as the major theme in recent American history. In particular, works by Williams, James Weinstein, Murray Rothbard, and Hawley were helpful in pointing up the corporatist tendencies of many private and public decisionmakers. Studies by Robert Wiebe provided a useful view into the growth of bureaucratic management and the business community's search for stability. And Louis Galambos, Grant McConnell, Robert Cuff, and Hawley stimulated many insights into the preoccupation of public and private planners with economic efficiency, their emphasis on scientific management and voluntarism, and their attempts to organize cooperative arrangements for rationalizing business activity in both war and peace.

I am also indebted to the staff members of the Herbert Hoover Presidential Library, the Library of Congress, the National Archives, the Baker Library, and the Public Record Office for their cooperation and friendly service. I owe a special debt to Mr. and Mrs. Everett N. Case of Van Hornesville, New York, for their kind assistance with the Owen D. Young papers.

Most important, I thank my wife, Virginia, and our children, Christopher, David, Joseph, and Ann for their warm encouragement and loving company.

M. J. H.
Austin, Texas
November 1976

Contents

CHAPTER 1

Introduction

This study focuses on American efforts to control and regulate international economic development after the First World War and particularly on American attempts to reconcile narrow national ambitions with the goals of a broader multinationalism. For Americans, the problem of restoring peace was compounded by the need to reform prewar commercial policies and practices and to do so in a way that would encourage constructive and efficient development without risking new political and military conflicts. And then, as now, many spoke hopefully of cooperative action as the key factor in any equation for permanent peace. In theory, cooperative action would help to avoid future wars by submerging competitive behavior and special interests in common programs to promote a stable and expanding prosperity in which all nations could share according to their needs.

The central question concerned how this cooperative order was to be organized, especially in view of the public antipathy toward new political entanglements. And the answer is that Americans hoped to institutionalize cooperation through private programs organized by business and financial leaders and fostered by limited and carefully delineated government action. Thus, while government officials could not interfere with private decisionmakers in arranging particular business transactions, they could enforce the ground rules for economic activity, protect private interests abroad, provide helpful information, and, most important, work with business leaders to develop the cooperative mechanisms that could achieve peace and prosperity.

This reliance upon cooperation among private American and multinational interests stemmed from three interrelated ideas held by Americans. One was the notion that economic and financial power must be consciously guided toward maximum efficiency and growth. The second was the belief that failure to develop cooperative integration and regulation in an interdependent world had generated and would continue to generate the destructive competitive behavior that produced world wars. And the third was the conviction that excessive statist intervention in the economy would introduce a "political" element that was both wasteful and conducive to international conflict. This left the management of the international economy in private hands, especially in a private leadership that was believed to be interested in maximum efficiency and international peace.

This approach, of course, conformed with American tradition, with the distinctly private character of the American political economy, and, equally important, with parallel developments in the domestic economy. Here, as Robert Wiebe argues, "new middle class" managers were already deeply engaged in a vast "experiment in bureaucratic order" prior to the First World War.[1] Here also, as Alfred Chandler points out, small competitive units were being rapidly displaced by large aggregations of industrial power characterized by bureaucracies of organizational personnel committed to rationalizing economic and administrative procedures.[2] At the same time, as Louis Galambos and Grant McConnell note, private officials from related industries were working through cooperative structures to achieve market integration and development, stabilize economic activity, eliminate reckless competition, and regularize business practices.[3] And while Robert Cuff argues that the kind of business-government cooperation organized through the war boards was rapidly terminated at the end of hostilities, Galambos, McConnell, and Ellis W. Hawley all show that the practice of business cooperation and informal government-business collaboration remained an important feature in attempts to stabilize and rationalize the domestic economy in the postwar decade.[4]

1. Robert H. Wiebe, *The Search for Order, 1877–1920*, p. xiv.
2. Alfred D. Chandler, Jr., "The Beginnings of 'Big Business' in American Industry," pp. 1–30. See also Alfred D. Chandler, Jr., *Strategy and Structure: Chapters in the History of the Industrial Enterprise*.
3. Louis Galambos, *Competition & Cooperation: The Emergence of a National Trade Association*; Grant McConnell, *Private Power & American Democracy*.
4. Robert Cuff, *The War Industries Board: Business-Government Relations During World War I*, see especially pp. 241–64; Galambos, *Competition & Cooperation*, pp. 54–138; McConnell, *Private Power & American Democracy*, especially see pp. 60–69; Ellis W. Hawley, "Herbert Hoover, the Commerce Secretariat, and the Vision of an 'Associative State,' 1921–1928," pp. 116–40. See also Ellis W. Hawley, "Herbert Hoover and American Corporatism, 1929–

In operation, so it seemed, this system of private-public collaboration and industrial cooperation could produce a new economic order, organized around self-regulating economic groups and led by responsible private officials supposedly committed to public goals. Under it, business collectivism and self-government, rather than state regulation or natural market forces, would assure order, stability, and progress. And they would do so without sacrificing such old virtues as voluntarism, individualism, and equal economic opportunity. The result, in other words, would be a healthy blend of traditional ideals and the new cooperation, a blend that in many ways came closer to corporatist prescriptions than the old laissez-faire principles.

In the postwar era, Secretary of Commerce Herbert Hoover became the central figure in efforts to implement this American brand of corporatism. Through scientific management and voluntary cooperation, he believed, industrial leaders could overcome the business cycle, increase efficiency, and raise living standards. Cooperation between enlightened labor and management leaders, he argued, could increase productivity, eliminate waste, avoid industrial violence, and afford workers the kind of meaningful participation in vital decisions, which was essential for industrial democracy. New scientific methods and voluntary cooperation among farmers, too, could eliminate price-depressing surpluses, stimulate diversification, and raise real farm income. The government certainly was to play a part in regulating economic activity; but if successfully employed, voluntary cooperation and scientific management would alleviate pressure for the kind of rigorous state intervention that fostered waste and bureaucratic inefficiency. Instead, Hoover believed, the government's role would be that of coordinator, educator, and sponsor of voluntary programs.[5]

In the international arena as well, Hoover and others were convinced that American and multinational businessmen could bal-

1933," in Martin L. Fausold and George T. Mazuzan, eds., *The Hoover Presidency: A Reappraisal*, pp. 101–19; Hawley's essay in J. Joseph Huthmacher and Warren I. Susman, eds., *Herbert Hoover and the Crisis of American Capitalism*, pp. 3–34; and Ellis W. Hawley, "Techno-Corporatist Formulas in the Liberal State, 1920–1960: A Neglected Aspect of America's Search For a New Order."

5. See Robert H. Zieger, "Herbert Hoover, The Wage-Earner, and the 'New Economic System,' 1919–1929"; Joan Hoff Wilson, "Hoover's Agricultural Policies, 1921–1928"; and Ellis W. Hawley, "Herbert Hoover and Economic Stabilization, 1921–1922."

ance self-interest and cooperation in such a way as to achieve stability and prosperity for all. Here too, it seemed that cooperative action conformed with the interrelated character of the modern world economy. Together with enlightened business self-regulation, it could alleviate destructive economic conflict, allow disinterested private experts to regulate the international economy on a business basis, and avoid preferential and state-sponsored programs that were economically wasteful and politically dangerous.

In both the domestic and international spheres, therefore, public policy became largely a private responsibility, a transformation justified in the name of scientific management, rationalized development, business efficiency, and disinterested administration. This transformation did not go uncontested, however. In both spheres, advocates of the new "cooperative competition" worked to maintain their programs against spokesmen for an older, competitive individualism, on the one hand, and champions of government ownership, or at least rigorous government regulation, on the other. The domestic controversies surrounding McNary-Haugenism, Muscle Shoals, and the antitrust activities of the Justice Department and the Federal Trade Commission were matched internationally by similar battles over the competitive, cooperative, or statist management of foreign loans, European economic reconstruction, resource development, and international communications. Naturally, the results often represented a blend of these competing ideologies; new cooperative programs coexisted with competitive initiatives and expanded governmental activities.

The extent to which Americans succeeded in implementing the cooperative formula internationally also depended upon their readiness, and the readiness of their foreign counterparts, to sacrifice privilege and traditional principles for the sake of cooperative action. In particular, the American vision of private, multinational cooperation required new working arrangements with Great Britain, for international economic disputes were in most cases Anglo-American controversies involving efforts by both nations to adjust their relationship to the new realities of the postwar era. For their part, the British had to open areas of the world formerly under their domination and accept the intrusion of powerful American interests into their prewar managerial hegemony in international finance, resource development, and communications. Yet, despite the sacrifices entailed, they were willing to make the necessary adjustments. Already the war had weakened their grip on the international economy, making it imperative to yield to the more vigorous American bankers and industrialists who commanded the resources needed to underwrite European recovery and finance modernization in other areas of the international economy. For the British, moreover, cooperation would also avoid unprofitable competition and, equally important, strap their American associates with a share of the responsibility for maintaining world order and protecting vested interests, both British and American.

Cooperation involved important concessions on the American side as well. Decisionmakers had to adopt a reciprocal policy in Latin America, abandon early attempts to construct independent economic systems, and accept cooperative arrangements with the British. Additionally, they often found their defense of the Open Door at variance with "business realities," especially the economic need to organize cooperation through multinational monopolies. Yet, in such cases the desire to extend the economic stake of the United States abroad combined with the desire to organize cooperative arrangements at the private level to make compromise possible. This compromise was achieved by reshaping the principle of equal opportunity to fit the economic merits of each case as defined by private officials, thus preserving the ban on state management, stimulating American expansion, and widening the pattern of multinational, especially Anglo-American, cooperation that underlay much of what happened in the postwar decade.

This interpretation differs from other accounts of foreign policy during the Wilson, Harding, and Coolidge administrations. Until recently, historians viewed American policy after the war as a utopian search for the illusionary normalcy of some prewar era. Influenced by the events of later decades, particularly Axis aggression and Western appeasement in the 1930s, they condemned Wilsonian diplomacy as hopelessly moralistic and criticized the Harding and Coolidge administrations for failing to accept the political responsibilities that would have guaranteed world peace and stability. At the same time, they attacked Republican policymakers for abandoning Wilsonian economic internationalism in favor of neo-mercantilism or economic nationalism. In particular, they condemned the Republicans' support of the high tariff and their alleged intransigence on the debt question as unrealistic departures from progressive foreign policy and as ruinous to United States and world prosperity alike.[6]

This older interpretation, however, has been largely abandoned. Instead, other historians have begun to reassess the postwar period and, in doing so, have discovered a large degree of continuity in the foreign policies of the Wilson, Harding, and Coolidge administrations. Viewing the world as an interrelated system of national economies, they argue, Americans did not abandon wartime involvement for isolationism but envisioned a new era with the United States deeply involved in the world economy. To be sure, these revisionists point out, Americans hoped to implement their programs without new political entanglements. But this should not conceal their hard-headed approach to such critical problems as war debts and reparations, nor their efforts to restructure the international order in line with American ideals and interests. This new order was to avoid the pitfalls of both prewar imperialism and Bolshevik revolution. Instead, it was to be founded on a "community" among the capitalist countries, one rooted in shared interests, common dedication to democratic values, and respect for the principles of liberal capitalism.[7]

6. See for example Hans Morgenthau, *In Defense of the National Interest: A Critical Examination of American Foreign Policy*; George F. Kennan, *American Diplomacy, 1900–1950*; Robert E. Osgood, *Ideals and Self-Interest in America's Foreign Relations*; John D. Hicks, *Republican Ascendancy, 1921–1933*; Dexter Perkins, "The State Department and Public Opinion," in Gordon A. Craig and Felix Gilbert, eds., *The Diplomats, 1919–1939*, vol. 1, pp. 282–308; Selig Adler, *The Uncertain Giant, 1921–1941: American Foreign Policy Between the Wars*; and L. Ethan Ellis, *Republican Foreign Policy, 1921–1933*.

7. See William Appleman Williams, *The Tragedy of American Diplomacy*; N. Gordon Levin, Jr., *Woodrow Wilson and World Politics: America's Response to War and Revolution*; Arno J. Mayer, *Wilson vs. Lenin: Political Origins of the New Diplomacy, 1917–1918*; Arno J. Mayer, *Diplomacy of Peacemaking: Containment and Counterrevolution at Versailles, 1918–1919*; Carl P. Parrini, *Heir to Empire: United States Economic Diplomacy, 1916–1923*; and Joan Hoff Wilson, *American Business & Foreign Policy, 1920–1933*. Along with Williams, Parrini, and Wilson, other historians have begun reassessing the economic foreign policies of the Harding and Coolidge administrations. See Benjamin Rhodes, "Reassessing 'Uncle Shylock': The United States and the French War Debt, 1917–1929," pp. 787–803; Melvyn Leffler, "The Origins of Republican War Debt Policy, 1921–1923: A Case Study in the Applicability of the Open Door Interpretation," pp. 585–601; Frank C. Costigliola, "The Other Side of Isolationism: The Establishment of the First World Bank, 1929–1930," pp. 602–20; and Robert H. Van Meter, Jr., "The United States and European Recovery, 1918–1923: A Study of Public Policy and Private Finance" (Ph.D. dissertation). See also Joseph Brandes, *Herbert*

Although belonging largely to the revisionist camp, the following work differs in important ways from these recent studies. In the first place, such accounts have failed to discern the important patterns of cooperation and compromise that emerged in Anglo-American affairs during the postwar period. Specifically, significant studies by Carl Parrini and Frank Costigliola focus largely on Anglo-American rivalry immediately after the war or at the end of the 1920s and ignore the wide area of cooperation and collaboration that existed in the middle years of the decade. Moreover, dealing mainly with financial and commercial matters these works lose sight of the Anglo-American rapprochement worked out in such vital areas as cable, radio, and petroleum policy.[8] To be sure, there was tension involved as each nation struggled to protect its interests and extend its influence abroad. But at middecade at least both the British and American governments had acquiesced in private arrangements that resolved many disputes on a cooperative basis.

Secondly, revisionist historians have not carefully defined the character of the cooperative formula envisioned by most American policymakers and business officials. Parrini, Joan Hoff Wilson, N. Gordon Levin, and others, have noted the American vision of a great power "community" founded on the Open Door and led primarily by the United States. Moreover, William Appleman Williams took the lead in revisionist efforts to demonstrate a parallel between this vision and Hoover's programs at home.[9] But to my knowledge, no one has elevated the cooperative theme to a level of central importance, outlined its application to a wide variety of problems, or taken note of the many conflicts between those who favored private and cooperative programs and the advocates of state management or competitive action.

Burton Kaufman's important new work, with its emphasis on the

Hoover and Economic Diplomacy: Department of Commerce Policy, 1921–1928. Brandes's book is in many ways a transitional work. It had an important impact on subsequent revisionist historians, particularly their view of Herbert Hoover's central role in formulating American economic foreign policy. At the same time, however, it continued to view American policy as a kind of neo-mercantilism.

8. Parrini, _Heir to Empire_; and Frank C. Costigliola, "The Politics of Financial Stabilization: American Reconstruction Policy in Europe, 1924–1930" (Ph.D. dissertation).

9. Parrini, _Heir to Empire_; Wilson, _American Business & Foreign Policy_; and William Appleman Williams, _The Contours of American History_, see especially pp. 425–39.

influence of the "German model" of increased efficiency, organization, and government involvement on American plans for the promotion of overseas trade, pays scant attention to the lingering
impact of the competitive tradition. He notes without much elaboration the tension between those policymakers who favored a
religious duplication of the German model and those who preferred
a modified system founded on private enterprise tempered by government coordination of foreign-trade activity and a generous
policy toward private combinations. And he concludes that governmental "leadership in coordinating and integrating foreign
trade" forms the major theme in the American program for overseas expansion.[10] For Americans, however, the strong appeal of the
German model, symbolized by legislation such as the Federal Reserve Act, the Webb-Pomerene Act, and the Edge Act, was always
severely limited by their view that excessive government intervention was economically and politically dangerous. And this is
true not only in trade and financial policy, to which Kaufman's
work is largely confined, but also in radio, cable, and raw-material
policy.

It is important to recall in this connection the Wilson administration's rapid disbandment of the elaborate system of government
controls after the armistice. Even the Central Foreign Trade Committee, which was established in 1919 to coordinate governmental
foreign-trade policy, met only once. And as to the government-
controlled merchant fleet, the Merchant Marine Act of 1920 looked
toward a peacetime fleet under private ownership. This is not to
say that Wilson was a spokesman for classical laissez-faire liberalism. New forms of public-private cooperation were devised, and
historians generally agree that government played an increasing
role in economic affairs after the First World War. Yet, Kaufman's
uncomplicated emphasis on new governmental intrusion glides
past the efforts of public and private leaders to reconcile nineteenth-century verities with twentieth-century realities, efforts that
constitute a central theme in recent United States history. Repeatedly rejecting both state capitalism or management and destructive competition, they relied on private officials to organize
cooperative structures that could guarantee efficiency, eliminate

---

10. Burton I. Kaufman, *Efficiency and Expansion: Foreign Trade Organization in the Wilson Administration, 1913–1921*, see especially pp. 206–54;
the quote is from p. 248. See also Burton I. Kaufman, "The Organizational
Dimension of United States Economic Foreign Policy, 1900–1920," pp. 17–44.

waste, avoid destructive competition, and limit government intrusion. Involved here is a familiar American dilemma; that is, how to preserve the traditional values associated with localism, privatism, individual initiative, and competition in the face of modern trends toward concentration, centralization, and government involvement. Kaufman's account disregards the significance of this dilemma and, in particular, the weighty arguments for limiting government involvement in economic affairs.

Nor do those accounts that take note of the American reliance on private action, particularly the works by Parrini and Robert Van Meter, fully appreciate its central significance in American ideology and policy. Still other accounts tend to see it as the product of a governmental surrender to private interests rather than as a major feature of public policy. In Wilson's work, for example, one often loses sight of the fact that both government and business leaders considered excessive state intervention to be wasteful and inefficient, incompatible with the private character of the American political economy, and a threat to world peace.[11]

Similarly, revisionist studies fail to show how American officials tried to reconcile the tension between independent action and cooperation in United States policy. As Wilson points out, this tension provided the dynamic element in much of American economic diplomacy; and, in part, she is correct in arguing that policy moved back and forth between nationalism and internationalism, depending upon which approach best enhanced American interests. Yet, her concept of "independent internationalism," like Parrini's emphasis on efforts to construct an independent financial and commercial apparatus, reduces the notion of cooperation to a mere tactical device for gaining independent objectives.[12] This obscures the fact that cooperation itself was often an important policy objective, one that leading business and government officials considered necessary for peace and prosperity in a world of modern technology and economic interdependence. They believed it was possible to replace competitive action with cooperative programs through which the interests of each nation could be realized.

In this connection, revisionist works often interpret the policy of equal opportunity as mere leverage for unilateral aggrandizement.

---

11. Parrini, *Heir to Empire*; Van Meter, "The United States and European Recovery"; and Wilson, *American Business & Foreign Policy*.

12. Wilson, *American Business & Foreign Policy*, see especially pp. xvi–xvii; and Parrini, *Heir to Empire*, see especially pp. 101–37.

And while it was that, it is important to remember that because American leaders viewed the world as an interdependent economic unit, they understood that prosperity and progress at home required stability and development abroad. Accordingly, they tried to conceive of American ambitions as being realized within the framework of a larger interrelated community. In many cases, they accepted the principle of equal opportunity for themselves, opening the large domestic market and areas in the world under American control to foreign interests in exchange for reciprocal concessions abroad. Obviously, this exchange often came out as opportunity only for the great powers and their largest private firms. But it did involve more than sheer expediency. It allowed policymakers to interpret the various restrictions entailed not as a violation of the Open Door but as a realistic application of that principle, one that fulfilled their desire for cooperation, avoided destabilizing economic conflict, accommodated contemporary business and political realities, and conformed with their faith in private management.

This approach often entailed an important modification of the traditional definition of the Open Door—a modification that revisionist historians and others have not noted. A central feature of liberal economic theory, the Open Door concept originally envisaged a world of free trade with economic progress the result of equal competition in world markets. Yet, just as combination, cooperation, and bureaucratic administration were displacing individual enterprise and natural market forces as the dynamic and integrative factors in the domestic sphere, so also multinational collaboration and managerial regulation were replacing nationalism and competition in the world economy. Naturally, a tension remained in American policy between contemporary processes and the older conception of the Open Door. But more often than not public officials found it necessary to redefine traditional principles because of business insistence upon order, stability, and progress through cooperation.

Although this "search for order" and the resulting emphasis on bureaucratization and specialization have been the subject of important works dealing with American efforts to rationalize economic activity at home, only lately have diplomatic historians begun to trace the organizational, institutional, and corporatist elements in the economic foreign policy of the United States.[13] These

13. See in particular Wiebe, *The Search for Order*; and Louis Galambos,

accounts, however, focus on the organizational impulse toward an improved foreign trade and investment structure in the United States and thereby give new stress to the more competitive aspects of American policy.[14] And yet, cooperationists at both the public and private levels were busy extending the "organizational dimension" to the international arena as well, fostering collaboration among private, multinational interests and helping to organize new cooperative institutions like the China financial consortium, the South American radio consortium, and the Middle Eastern oil consortium for the bureaucratic and managerial regulation of the world economy.

This study is not a comprehensive survey of economic diplomacy in the postwar era. Certain areas have been largely ignored, particularly tariff and commercial policy where American interests were more competitively organized.[15] Instead, my work, which focuses on Anglo-American affairs, deals only with selected areas in which the ideology and policies of "cooperative competition" were important. The second chapter outlines the ideological setting at the end of the war, specifically the contending European and American programs for reconstructing Europe. It argues that Wilsonians advocated the cooperative, private financing of recovery on a basis outlined by multinational financial experts. The third and fourth chapters treat Republican reconstruction policy. This policy, they argue, was a basic extension of the Wilsonian program and was implemented only after there emerged an Anglo-American financial entente founded on cooperative financial efforts among private and semigovernmental banking institutions and on a willingness at the government level to compromise on the critical problems of war debts and reparations. The fifth chapter studies the attempt by banking, commercial, and government officials to organize, at both the domestic and international levels, voluntary and cooperative structures for managing foreign lending. The par-

---

"The Emerging Organizational Synthesis in Modern American History," pp. 279–90.

14. See especially Kaufman, *Efficiency and Expansion* and "The Organizational Dimension of United States Foreign Policy"; and Burton I. Kaufman, "Organization for Foreign Trade Expansion in the Mississippi Valley, 1900–1920," pp. 444–65. See also Joan Hoff Wilson, *Ideology and Economics: U. S. Relations with the Soviet Union, 1918–1933*. Wiebe, of course, also pioneered in analyzing the organizational aspects of American foreign policy; see Wiebe, *The Search for Order*, pp. 224–85.

15. Wilson, *American Business & Foreign Policy*, pp. 65–100; and Parrini, *Heir to Empire*, pp. 212–47.

ticular focus is on the successful Anglo-American financial collaboration in China, the difficulty in accommodating different functional groups within a cooperative framework, and the problems involved in regulating private lending without rigorous government controls. Chapters six through nine discuss cable, radio, oil, and resource policy, stressing how cooperation or competition, government ownership or private management, equality of opportunity or monopoly constituted the controversial issues involved in formulating American policy. They emphasize the rejection of statist schemes, private and governmental attempts to organize cooperation among American interests, and the importance of business considerations and reciprocity in fostering multinational, especially Anglo-American, cooperation. The last chapter reviews American policy in an attempt to evaluate the program for cooperative multinationalism.

CHAPTER 2

The United States and European Reconstruction

The Ideological Setting at the End of the War

For American officials in 1918, the interrelated nature of the modern world demanded participation by the United States in reconstructing the international economy. Yet, they believed that this demand could be satisfied without sacrificing the traditional policy of political noninvolvement. Rejecting both isolationism and political entanglement, they also turned away from either thoroughgoing laissez-faire or preferential and state-sponsored commercial policies. These alternatives, so it seemed, were either inadequate to solve postwar problems or incompatible with American tradition. Instead, they favored private, cooperative programs, which would operate within the framework of equal commercial opportunity. Such programs, according to their argument, would eliminate preferential practices that hampered trade and would allow business experts to exercise their talents, organize the world economy on the basis of efficiency and productivity, and avoid governmental "paternalism" that fostered instability and conflict. Already applied in the domestic sphere, this approach emerged internationally during the early debate over European reconstruction—a debate that matched American hopes for European self-help, private management, and German reintegration against the state-sponsored and preferential plans of the Allied powers.

I

For many Wilsonians, the economic origins of the war lay in the failure of the European powers to accept the basic law of economic interdependence and to maintain an open international market. The well-being of all nations, explained Norman Davis, required the free exchange of goods and services. But instead, the European powers had often pursued aggressive and state-sponsored policies designed to obtain "exclusive access" to sources of "raw materials and preferential markets for the sale of their products." Germany was considered the "signal though not the only example" of this European policy of "commercial imperialism." Not satisfied with "her fair share of trade," argued Shipping Board Chairman Edward Hurley, Germany, by the use of state-supported cartels and combinations, had aggressively extended her commercial enterprises throughout the world in direct conflict with the far-flung interests of British business. With each country struggling for exclusive control of a larger share of the world market, commercial competition between British and German interests, backed by their respective governments, had escalated into political and military conflict.[1]

As Americans viewed it, moreover, the European belligerents were apparently determined to renew the policy of commercial imperialism after the war. In September 1914, Imperial Chancellor Theobald von Bethmann-Hollweg had announced Germany's postwar plans. He called for the creation of a great central European economic unit (*Mitteleuropa*) under German domination and the expansion of Germany's African colonies (*Mittelafrika*) by partitioning the African possessions of France, Great Britain, and Portugal.[2] And at the Paris Economic Conference of 1916, representatives of the Entente Powers had approved a postwar plan that included government control over major aspects of the domestic economy, regulation of foreign competition, restrictions on enemy shipping, and preferential tariff and raw-material arrangements among the Allied countries.[3]

1. Speech by Norman H. Davis, n.d., Norman H. Davis Papers, box 15; Edwin F. Gay, chief of the Bureau of Planning and Statistics, "Economic Defensive: Strategic 'Key' Resources and the 'Master Key' Shipping, Summary," 11 June 1918, Record Group 32, "General Records of the United States Shipping Board," "Subject-Classified General File," 34514 (hereafter cited as RG 32 with file and number); Commissioner William B. Colver, Federal Trade Commission, to President Woodrow Wilson, 16 November 1918, Woodrow Wilson Papers, Series 2, box 188; Edward N. Hurley to Wilson, 2 March 1918, RG 32, "Subject-Classified General File," 34514. See also Hurley to Bernard Baruch of the War Industries Board, 21 May 1919, Record Group 40, "General Records of the Department of Commerce," "Office of the Secretary," file, 77270 (hereafter cited as RG 40 with file number).

2. Fritz Fischer, *Germany's War Aims in the First World War*, pp. 98–119.

3. American Ambassador in Paris to the Secretary of State, 22 June 1916, in U.S. Department of State, *Papers Relating to the Foreign Relations of the United States, 1916*, Supplement, pp. 974–77 (hereafter cited as *Foreign Relations*. For a further analysis of the Paris resolves and the extent to which

In view of these European pronouncements, one group of officials in the Wilson administration favored similar policies for the United States. The "best way to fight combination is by combination," Secretary of State Robert Lansing had declared in June 1916. And in November, Henry P. Fletcher, soon to be the State Department's new minister to Mexico, had suggested an "American Economic League" consisting of the United States and the Latin-American republics and designed to protect the commercial gains made by the United States in South America during the war.[4] Other plans for a countervailing combination under United States leadership would be forthcoming at the end of the war, including financial control over the public finances of South American governments, domination of radio and cable communications in the Western Hemisphere, and control over raw-material resources in South America through government-supported cartels.[5]

For other officials in the Wilson administration, however, such policies would be detrimental to American trade and world peace. Secretary of Commerce William Redfield called for a moderate commercial policy, and while interpreted otherwise by business leaders, he did not consider this recommendation at variance with the goal of an expansive foreign commerce.[6] Redfield repeatedly affirmed his department's determination to capture foreign markets

they were discussed and implemented in the Allied countries during the war see "Economic Reconstruction"—a report prepared by the Bureau of Foreign and Domestic Commerce and enclosed in an unsigned letter to the Secretary of Commerce, 19 June 1918, Record Group 151, "General Records of the Department of Commerce," "Bureau of Foreign and Domestic Commerce," file, 880 (hereafter cited as RG 151 with file number); William MacDonald, "Great Britain and the Economic War," pp. 117–19; and National Foreign Trade Council, *European Economic Alliances: A Compilation of Information on International Commercial Policies After the European War and Their Effect Upon the Foreign Trade of the United States*, pp. 7–16, 23–24.

4. Robert Lansing to Wilson, 23 June 1916, in *Papers Relating to the Foreign Relations of the United States: The Lansing Papers, 1914–1921*, vol. 1, pp. 311–12; Henry P. Fletcher to Lansing, 13 November 1916, Record Group 59, "General Records of the Department of State," file, 611.0031/138 (hereafter cited as RG 59 with file number).

5. See chapters 5, 6, 7, and 9.

6. According to Mark Osmand Prentiss of the Board of Managers of the Council on Foreign Relations, "American businessmen. . . were filled with dismay and discouragement" by Redfield's position, especially his announcement that the United States did not intend to "hog" all postwar trade. See *New York Times*, 2 December 1918, p. 6. The Council on Foreign Relations reacted by sending a questionnaire to the secretary soliciting a more detailed statement of his position. See Lindsay Russell, Richard Washburn Child, and Mark Osmand Prentiss to Redfield, 29 November 1918, RG 40, file, 78075.

for American trade but pointed out his opposition to an economic "offensive" that went beyond the "normal resumption of our international trade." Such an offensive, he argued, would undermine European recovery, make it impossible for the Allies to repay their war debts, and prevent the wider expansion of American commerce on a reciprocal basis. "We must not be put in the position of even seeming to hold down the progress of American commerce," he warned B. S. Cutler of the Bureau of Foreign and Domestic Commerce, "whereas our purpose is to guide it into a more secure and larger field than would be had by excessive activity now." At his request, the Bureau of Foreign and Domestic Commerce prepared a memorandum cautioning American businessmen to go slowly in their postwar efforts to expand foreign commerce, allowing time for the economic situation in Europe to develop more clearly. But Redfield decided to withhold the statement from publication after Assistant Secretary of State Frank Polk warned that it might "increase the discontent" in the business community over the secretary's apparent anti-export attitude.[7]

Rather than a state-sponsored and preferential policy, Redfield and others envisioned some form of multinational economic cooperation in the postwar era. Already in 1916, Col. Edward House had suggested that Great Britain, France, and Germany join the United States in "some sort of tentative understanding" for regulating and protecting the capital invested in developing "the waste places of the earth." And Walter Hines Page, America's wartime Ambassador in London, had recommended close Anglo-American cooperation as the cornerstone for a wider system of multinational collaboration in managing the world economy.[8]

This cooperation was to be founded on equal commercial opportunity rather than preferential policies. Assuming that commercial imperialism generated conflict, it followed for these Wilsonians that the Open Door "dovetailed with peace." A "just and contin-

---

7. For Redfield's views see Redfield to Jason Neilson, 29 November 1918, Redfield to the Council on Foreign Relations, 10 December 1918, RG 40, file, 78075; and Redfield to B. S. Cutler, 8 January 1919, RG 40, file, 78288. On the proposed memorandum see Redfield to Frank Polk, 8 January 1919, enclosing draft memorandum by the BFDC, n.d., Polk to Redfield, 16 January 1919, and Redfield to Cutler, 21 January 1919, all in RG 40, file, 78288.

8. See Charles Seymour, ed., *The Intimate Papers of Colonel House*, vol. 1, pp. 240–41, 264–67; Ray Stannard Baker, ed., *Woodrow Wilson: Life and Letters*, vol. 5, pp. 25–26, 28–29, 31, 42–44; and Burton J. Hendrick, ed., *The Life and Letters of Walter H. Page*, vol. 1, pp. 194–95, 210–13, 215–17, 270–83.

uing peace," explained Bernard Baruch of the War Industries Board, "must include a just and equal access to the raw materials and manufacturing facilities of the world." Otherwise, "the resulting industrial inequalities" would cause "dissatisfaction and revolution within countries or force wars to relieve intolerable conditions."[9] And the League of Nations could help to enforce the ground rules for peaceful economic expansion. The League, noted William Culbertson of the Tariff Commission, could regulate competition on the basis of the Open Door and encourage world growth by protecting investments in economically underdeveloped regions. Redfield, Hurley, and Secretary of the Treasury William Gibbs McAdoo emphasized similar themes, seeing the League as an agency for preventing "bitter [rivalry] for commercial supremacy" and for resolving international disputes that might arise from the investment of capital abroad. In operation, they believed, League controls would offer incentive for investment, stimulate economic development, and facilitate the peaceful expansion of trade.[10]

Yet, the Open Door represented only part of this postwar vision. Cooperationists in the Wilson administration hoped to avoid the kind of state-sponsored programs and dangerous political entanglements that, in their opinion, had characterized European policy in the prewar period. Instead, they wanted to organize multinational economic cooperation at the private level—cooperation based on business rather than political considerations and freed of excessive government intervention. In many ways, this program was to parallel their earlier efforts to foster responsible collaboration among American producers in regulating economic activity both at home and abroad. In the prewar period, for example, they had attempted to organize export industries for the cooperative promotion of foreign trade. President Woodrow Wilson openly admired Germany's success in expanding its foreign commerce by developing cooperative promotion programs and increasing in-

9. Cordell Hull, *The Memoirs of Cordell Hull,* vol. 1, pp. 81–82; and Baruch to Wilson, 23 October 1918, Wilson Papers, Series 2, box 186.
10. William S. Culbertson diary, 2 September 1919, William S. Culbertson Papers, box 4; Edward N. Hurley Diary, 24 October 1918; Hurley to Wilson, 12 December 1918, attached to entry for 15 December 1918, Hurley Diary; speech by William Gibbs McAdoo in New York City, 26 May 1919, William Gibbs McAdoo Papers, box 564; Chairman Lindsay Russell, Council on Foreign Relations, to Redfield, 1 March 1919, and Redfield to Russell, 3 March 1919, RG 40, file, 78075.

dustrial efficiency through scientific management and innovative technology. The "encouragement of trade associations" and greater efficiency in production, he believed, would also help to make the United States "an important factor in the world's markets." Accordingly, he had supported a recommendation by the Federal Trade Commission that exporters be exempted from the antitrust laws, and the result in 1918 was the Webb-Pomerene Act, allowing private interests to combine voluntarily in the export trade.[11] The measure, as Secretary Redfield saw it, adapted the German model to American traditions. It permitted cooperative action through open associations instead of the closed system of state-supported cartels that was "justly felt to be a source of complaint in German commercial activities."[12]

In the domestic sphere, cooperationists had made similar efforts to stimulate the kind of enlightened collaboration and business self-regulation, which would rationalize economic activity and alleviate the need for excessive government intervention. During Redfield's tenure, the Commerce Department had become a leading promoter of trade associations, industrial cooperation, and business self-regulation under the auspices of a friendly government. At the same time, the Federal Trade Commission was encouraging the spread of scientific management and associational activities, while supervising business behavior according to the ground rules laid down in the Clayton Act. After the armistice, such an approach seemed all the more promising in view of the successful wartime collaboration among business interests and between them and the government. This had fortified the cooperationists' faith in the ability of progressive businessmen to regulate their own affairs without excessive state interference.[13]

11. Wilson to Hurley, 12 May 1916, in Ray Stannard Baker and William E. Dodd, eds., *The Public Papers of Woodrow Wilson*, vol. 2, pp. 167–68 (this letter was drafted by Hurley for Wilson's signature); Cleona Lewis, *America's Stake in International Investments*, p. 186; Martin J. Sklar, "Woodrow Wilson and the Political Economy of Modern United States Liberalism," p. 36; Carl P. Parrini, *Heir to Empire: United States Economic Diplomacy, 1916–1923*, pp. 8–9, 27–31; Burton I. Kaufman, "The Organizational Dimension of United States Economic Foreign Policy, 1900–1920," pp. 22–29, 41; and Gabriel Kolko, *The Triumph of Conservatism: A Reinterpretation of American History, 1900–1916*, p. 276.

12. Redfield to Hurley, 28 May 1918, RG 40, file, 77270.

13. Kolko, *The Triumph of Conservatism*, pp. 275–76; Grant McConnell, *Private Power & American Democracy*, pp. 59–64; Robert H. Weibe, *Search*

As a result, Bernard Baruch and other representatives of the private sector within the war government refused to extend the planning and regulatory functions of such agencies as the War Industries Board during the postwar transition. Baruch counted on economic expansion abroad, informal business-government collaboration, and cooperation organized at the private level to guarantee a stable and orderly transition. In the Commerce Department, Redfield followed a similar course; he appointed a Business Advisory Board made up of former dollar-a-year men and established the Industrial Cooperation Service to foster the spread of associational activities in the business community.[14]

In the domestic arena, however, spokesmen for the cooperative approach were soon opposed by defenders of the antitrust tradition and by advocates of government-sanctioned business monopoly. The debate revolved around the Commerce Department's short-lived Industrial Board. Originally, the Board was to cooperate with businessmen in achieving voluntary and orderly price reductions to levels at which government-purchasing agencies would agree to buy. This plan, it was hoped, would inspire consumer confidence, accelerate purchases, and achieve price stabilization without a postwar recession. On this basis, President Wilson approved the plan and, in February 1919, established the Industrial Board under the chairmanship of George N. Peek. Along with his business supporters, however, Peek was soon attempting to stabilize prices at prevailing high levels. Voluntary price reductions, he believed, might generate additional price competition, lead to still further reductions, and cause serious deflation. To prevent this, he now favored industrial price-fixing agreements approved by the government through the Board. Fuel Administrator Harry Garfield and Secretary of Commerce Redfield defended the Board's action, but many government agencies considered it an unwarranted departure from the original emphasis on voluntary cooperation and a dangerous violation of the antitrust laws. The resulting acrimony

for Order, 1877–1920, pp. 220, 293–301; and Robert F. Himmelberg, "Business, Antitrust Policy, and the Industrial Board of the Department of Commerce, 1919," p. 13.

14. Grosvenor B. Clarkson, Industrial America in the World War: The Strategy Behind the Line, 1917–1918, pp. 475–88; Robert D. Cuff, The War Industries Board: Business-Government Relations During World War I, pp. 241–64; and Himmelberg, "Business, Antitrust Policy, and the Industrial Board," p. 14.

led Wilson to abolish the Board in May 1919, stymied attempts to replace the war boards with a new system of voluntary and cooperative business self-regulation, and undermined efforts to deal effectively with the serious deflation in prices that hampered the American economy in the postwar period.[15]

Cooperationists faced similar problems internationally. Here too, they favored economic cooperation institutionalized at the private level, paralleled by government-business collaboration, and free of oppressive government interference. After the war, they recommended this approach as the basis for European reconstruction. But as in the domestic sphere, they faced challenges, both from Allied leaders committed to state-sponsored and preferential programs and from domestic advocates of a larger role for the government.

II

The Allied threat to the cooperationists' vision, surfacing first at the Paris Economic Conference in 1916, reappeared in the summer and fall of 1918, this time in the shape of Allied proposals to transform wartime cooperation into preferential postwar commercial arrangements. British officials offered a series of suggestions for an Anglo-American commercial alliance that included the pooling of raw materials and shipping and the joint development of underdeveloped regions.[16] At the same time, and with support from the French government, they initiated a second series of proposals for continued inter-Allied economic cooperation in reconstructing the European economy. To institutionalize this new alliance and assure Allied leadership, they wanted to transform the economic agencies of the wartime coalition into semipermanent reconstruction and relief councils. These councils were to have administrative control over American and Allied resources, regulate neutral and enemy

15. This story can be followed in Himmelberg, "Business, Antitrust Policy, and the Industrial Board," pp. 1–23.

16. Colville Barclay, for the British Ambassador, to Lansing, 12 June 1918, RG 59, file, 611.4131/58; Hurley to Wilson, 7 September 1918, Wilson Papers, Series 2, box 183; Chandler P. Anderson, Counsel for the War Industries Board, diary, 1 May and 16 May 1918, Chandler P. Anderson Papers, box 2; Richard Crawford, commercial adviser for the British Embassy, to Polk, 15 October 1918, in *Foreign Relations, 1918*, Supplement 1, vol. 1, pp. 612–14. See also in this connection Philip B. Kennedy, "British Trade Attitude Towards the United States," 22 November 1918, RG 151, file, 413.1.

competition, control enemy shipping, and organize commercial and raw material arrangements among the victors. Execution of the entire program, therefore, assumed that the Associated Powers would continue to regulate their domestic economies and foreign trade.[17]

Believing in an economically interdependent world, Wilson was determined that the United States should cooperate in European recovery. "Europe is our best customer," he announced in 1919. "We must keep her going or thousands of our shops and scores of our mines must close." But he opposed cooperative action based on special intergovernmental arrangements among the victors. For him, such arrangements would hamper German recovery, encourage economic disintegration in Europe, and foster the spread of bolshevism.[18] Accordingly, he rejected all proposals to transform wartime cooperation into preferential postwar economic arrangements and sought to keep American resources free from Allied manipulation. When Hurley reported a suggestion by Lord Reading to pool British and American shipping, for example, Wilson termed the idea an "extraordinary proposition," told Hurley he would not "make special arrangements with any one nation," and emphasized his determination "to deal upon the same terms with all."[19]

He also turned down all suggestions to utilize the inter-Allied economic councils as relief and reconstruction agencies. Many of the American experts associated with these agencies had endorsed the Allied proposals. For them, the institutional arrangements worked out during the war provided ready-made structures

17. Joseph Cotton, Food Administration representative in Europe, to Herbert Hoover, food administrator, 30 October and 8 November 1918, in Suda Lorena Bane and Ralph Haswell Lutz, eds., *The Organization of American Relief in Europe, 1918–1919*, pp. 30–32, 39–40; "Resolution Approved by the British War Cabinet, November 13, 1918," in James A. Salter, *Allied Shipping Control*, p. 329; Raymond Stevens and George Rublee, Shipping Board representatives in Europe, to Gay and Hurley, 16 November 1918, RG 59, file, 800.88/217; and Oscar Crosby, Treasury Department representative in Europe, to McAdoo, 25 October 1918, Record Group 39, "General Records of the Department of the Treasury," "Bureau of Accounts," World War Material, box 99, Inter-Ally Councils (hereafter cited as RG 39).

18. Woodrow Wilson, "Address to Congress on the High Cost of Living," 8 August 1919, in Baker and Dodd, eds., *Public Papers of Woodrow Wilson*, vol. 5, p. 569. See also N. Gordon Levin, Jr., *Wilson and World Politics: America's Response to War and Revolution*, pp. 125–53.

19. Hurley to Wilson, 7 September 1918, and Wilson to Hurley, 9 September 1918, Wilson Papers, Series 2, box 183.

through which trained, experienced, semigovernmental experts could manage pressing economic problems on a scientific basis. This procedure, in turn, would expedite recovery and help to develop the kind of permanent cooperative mechanisms that were needed for the objective management of long-range economic problems.[20]

To policymakers in Washington, however, it seemed that the Allies intended to transform the inter-Allied bodies into political rather than scientific councils. As a result, on Wilson's instructions, they limited American participation on such agencies after the armistice and, so far as possible, withdrew American representation altogether.[21] Baruch ordered his representatives on the Interallied Munitions Council and the Allied Maritime Transport Council to withdraw from all program committees and return to Washington as soon as possible. The administration, he explained, had considered the "advantages" of continuing the inter-Allied councils, but the objection seemed to be "the danger of limiting independence of action and also of departing from the general policy of equality of treatment and no economic barriers."[22] The Treasury Department also terminated its representation on the Interallied Council on War Purchases and Finance.[23] And Food

20. See for example Cotton to Hoover, 30 October and 8 November 1918, in Bane and Lutz, eds., *Organization of American Relief*, pp. 30–32, 39–40; Leland Summers, War Industries Board representative in Europe, to Baruch, 8 November 1918, enclosed in Baruch to Wilson, 12 November 1918, Wilson Papers, Series 2, box 187; L. P. Sheldon, War Trade Board representative in Europe, to Vance McCormick, chairman of the War Trade Board, 15 November 1918, in *Papers Relating to the Foreign Relations of the United States: Paris Peace Conference, 1919*, vol. 2, pp. 732–33 (hereafter cited as *Foreign Relations: Peace Conference*); Stevens and Rublee to Gay and Hurley, 16 November 1918, RG 59, file, 103.94/730; Paul Cravath, Treasury Department representative in Europe, to Russell Leffingwell and Albert Rathbone, assistant secretaries of the Treasury, 22 November 1918, RG 59, file, 102.1/1451; and Summers to Baruch, 25 November 1918, RG 59, file, 103.94/774.

21. According to Anderson, the decision to withdraw support from the councils came directly from Wilson. See Anderson diary, 16 November 1918, Anderson Papers, box 2.

22. Draft telegram from Baruch to Alexander Legge and Leland Summers, 16 November 1918, Anderson Papers, Correspondence File, box 33. The draft was not sent because it displayed a willingness to discuss the matter if Summers and Legge thought withdrawal from the councils inadvisable. Instead, a substitute cable was dispatched stating definitely that American participation should be wound up. See Anderson diary, 16 November 1918, Anderson Papers, box 2.

23. Crosby to Tasker H. Bliss, 26 and 27 December 1918 and 21 January 1919, Tasker H. Bliss Papers, World War Material, Personal File, box 76,

Administrator Herbert Hoover instructed his London agent to block Allied plans to transform the Food Council into a general reconstruction and relief agency.[24] Sailing for Europe after the armistice, he told Hurley of his decision "to stand firmly against any attempt at British control, either of food distribution or of shipping." For his part, Hurley recalled Wilson's instructions to "stand firm" and assured Hoover of his determination to do so.[25]

Hoover and others did want to cooperate in organizing food relief for Europe, particularly as a barrier against the spread of bolshevism. But they favored creating a new relief agency, which would be separate from existing Allied councils and under the day-to-day control of an American director-general. This agency was to control enemy shipping and the distribution of food supplies, but it would not have independent control over food resources nor the capital to finance their purchase and distribution. Rather, food would be purchased directly from the food administrations of the Associated Powers with credits arranged separately by their treasuries. This plan contrasted sharply with Allied proposals for a semipermanent general economic council that would handle relief work along with its larger responsibilities, for the management of food relief by existing inter-Allied bodies, and for the formation of a new relief agency with administrative control over the world's food resources, including American supplies and prices.[26]

The American plan was designed to facilitate relief without entangling American resources in preferential and semipermanent commercial and political programs. As House pointed out, it would do so by separating relief from the "very keen struggle" for "selfish trade advantage" that would arise after the armistice. With Hoover as director-general, it also would guarantee independent American control of the large food and capital reserves to be contributed by

file 11; Bliss diary, 28 December 1918, Bliss Papers, box 65; Crosby to McAdoo, 27 December 1918, RG 59, file, 800.51/127; Crosby to Wilson, 17 January 1919, Wilson Papers, Series 5–B, box 9; Crosby to Secretary of the Treasury Carter Glass, 18 January 1919, RG 39, box 104, Peace Commission. Crosby and Bliss were the American representatives on the Council on War Purchases and Finance.

24. Hoover to Cotton, 14 November 1918, in Bane and Lutz, eds., *Organization of American Relief*, pp. 32–33.

25. Hurley Diary, 16 November 1918.

26. The negotiations over food relief can be followed in Bane and Lutz, eds., *Organization of American Relief*, pp. 26–147. See also Levin, *Wilson and World Politics*, pp. 139–40; and Arno J. Mayer, *Diplomacy of Peacemaking: Containment and Counterrevolution at Versailles*, pp. 257–83.

the United States and give Wilson sufficient latitude to avoid undesirable intergovernmental commitments. As Hoover and Davis
notified the Allies, only such an arrangement could satisfy the "in-
stinctive desire" of the American people "for separation from European entanglements" and assure their support for relief.[27]

In late December 1918, the Allies accepted the American plan,
with slight modifications, and created the Supreme Council of
Supply and Relief. At the Paris Peace Conference the following
February, they incorporated this agency into the newly formed
Supreme Economic Council. In organizing the SEC, the American
delegates at the conference hoped to foster increased efficiency
and greater coordination in distributing the shipping, food, and
financial resources needed to relieve Europe. Specifically, they
wanted specialists from the Allied countries to manage resource
allocation and use, thus undermining the kind of political control
exercised over European relief by the French military under the
armistice terms. On Wilson's insistence, moreover, the SEC's authority pertained only to relief and reconstruction matters pending
peace. Like the Supreme Council of Supply and Relief, it reflected
his desire to forge temporary and purely economic arrangements
that avoided undesirable political commitments.[28]

Regarding the long-range reconstruction of Europe, officials in
the United States Treasury Department wanted to avoid new intergovernmental programs that might promote state management
or impair their domestic stabilization plans. Since rapid termina-
tion of government loans to Europe might injure the American export trade during the period of transition, they did agree to provide
some temporary and limited credit. Once this was provided, however, both Congress and the Treasury Department intended to
cease government lending and return international finance to private channels. Treasury officials took the position that Allied countries possessed sufficient assets to attract private long-term credits

27. Bane and Lutz, eds., *Organization of American Relief*, pp. 26–147.
Quotations are from House to Wilson, 8 November 1918, and "Statement
Furnished by Messrs. Hoover and Davis to the Committee Appointed by the
Allied Premiers to Consider Relief Matters," London, 10 December 1918, in
Bane and Lutz, pp. 34–35, 82–84.

28. Minutes of a Meeting of the Council of Ten, 8 February 1919, in *Foreign Relations: Peace Conference*, vol. 3, pp. 934–35; Seth P. Tillman, *Anglo-
American Relations at the Paris Peace Conference of 1919*, p. 263; H. W. V.
Temperley, ed., *A History of the Peace Conference at Paris*, vol. 1, pp. 296–
300; and Nina J. Noring, "American Coalition Diplomacy and the Armistice,
1918–1919" (Ph.D. dissertation), pp. 177–99.

Library
I.U.P.
Indiana, Pa.

without special inter-Allied economic arrangements based on new loans or debt cancellation. Such arrangements, they believed, would impose an excessive tax burden on the American public, hamper efforts to liquidate the war debt at home, and promote serious inflation.[29] Equally important, they assumed that governmental financing of world recovery would encourage a trend toward "policies of centralization" abroad. And their program of "retrenchment" was designed to undermine state management and to support those elements, particularly in England, that favored ending government controls.[30]

Following the policy of the Treasury Department, the American delegates at Paris attacked all Allied proposals for new intergovernmental financial arrangements as tantamount to drawing a "blank check" on American taxpayers.[31] In April 1919, Baruch dismissed a suggestion by Robert Cecil of the British delegation to create a select committee for examining methods of financing recovery, including government subsidies.[32] When Cecil responded that private resources would not be sufficient to underwrite reconstruction, both Baruch and Davis agreed that some temporary assistance from the United States Treasury would be desirable to meet immediate needs but insisted that private resources were adequate for all further requirements.[33]

Later that same month, the American delegates also rejected the British plan drafted by John Maynard Keynes. It called for a guarantee by Associated and neutral governments on bonds to be issued by the enemy states. The proceeds from the sale of these bonds

29. McAdoo to Crosby, 22 November 1918 and 7 December 1918, McAdoo to House, 11 December 1918, Glass to Wilson, 19 December 1918, and Glass to Davis, 15 January 1919, in *Foreign Relations: Peace Conference*, vol. 2, pp. 535–40, 544–46; Paul Abrahams, "American Bankers and the Economic Tactics of Peace," pp. 572–83; and Robert H. Van Meter, Jr., "The United States and European Recovery, 1918–1923: A Study of Public Policy and Private Finance," pp. 26–46, 64–104.

30. Crosby to McAdoo, 13 November 1918, and McAdoo to Crosby, 22 November 1918, in *Foreign Relations: Peace Conference*, vol. 2, pp. 533–36.

31. Davis to Wilson, 2 February 1919, and Baruch to Wilson, 4 February 1919, Wilson Papers, Series 5–B, box 13.

32. Baruch to Cecil, 12 April 1919, in Ray Stannard Baker, *Woodrow Wilson and World Settlement*, vol. 3, pp. 332–34. For the origins of Cecil's proposal, see ibid., pp. 331–32, and "Summary of a Memorandum by Lord Robert Cecil on the Economic Situation of Europe," n.d., Davis Papers, box 16a.

33. Cecil to Baruch, 14 April 1919, in Baker, *Wilson and World Settlement*, vol. 3, p. 335; Baruch to Davis, 30 April and 2 May 1919, and Davis to Baruch, 1 May 1919, Davis Papers, box 46.

could then be used for reparation payments and to finance reconstruction.[34] For the Americans, however, the plan would substitute excessive indemnities and new assistance from the Treasury Department for European initiatives, especially in German reconstruction. Throughout the conference they had struggled for a fixed indemnity within Germany's capacity to pay. This, they believed, would leave Germany with sufficient capital to begin reconstruction, insure that private investors would be willing to invest in German recovery, and expedite general reconstruction by reintegrating a revitalized Germany into the economic fabric of an interrelated European community.[35] Keynes's proposal, on the other hand, seemed to them tantamount to a guarantee by the United States on private American loans to underwrite Allied reparation demands on Germany. As Wilson wrote Lloyd George, it amounted to the United States supplying Germany with "new working capital" to replace that taken by the Allies in reparations.[36]

If implemented, or so the Americans believed, the Keynes Plan would also prejudice the Treasury Department's domestic stabilization program. Under a key feature of the proposal, enemy bonds purchased by the Allies could be transferred to the United States in payment for war debts. Yet, with an "excessive" reparation bill assessed Germany and the United States the main guarantor of German bonds, the American delegates viewed this provision as an attempt to shift the heavy burden of European indebtedness to American shoulders. "It is the same old game they have been working on all through the Conference," complained Vance McCormick, "to get the United States to underwrite their war debts."[37] Further, if issued in the American market the enemy bonds would compete with Liberty Loan bonds for buyers. This would strain

34. A copy of the Keynes Plan is attached to Lloyd George to Wilson, 23 April 1919, in Baker, *Wilson and World Settlement*, vol. 3, pp. 336–38.

35. For concise statements of the American view on reparations see Norman Davis, "Personal and Confidential Observations of Mr. Norman Davis to the President on the Subject of the German Reply to the Allied Conditions of Peace, with Particular Reference to the Reparation Clauses, Paris, June 1st, 1919," and Norman Davis, "Peace Conference Notes," n.d., Davis Papers, box 16a. See also "Stenographic Report of a Meeting Between the President, the Commissioners, and the Technical Advisers of the American Commission to Negotiate Peace, June 3, 1919" in *Foreign Relations: Peace Conference*, vol. 11, pp. 197–222.

36. Wilson to Lloyd George, 23 April 1919, in Baker, *Wilson and World Settlement*, vol. 3, pp. 344–46.

37. Vance McCormick Diary, 25 April 1919.

American financial resources, interfere with the Treasury Department's efforts to finance the war debt, and risk serious inflation. For these reasons, then, they rejected the proposal.[38]

They also turned back a suggestion in June to perpetuate the Supreme Economic Council as an intergovernmental agency for postwar planning. McCormick considered it another attempt by the British to "hold us down to [their] level in trade."[39] Wilson warned the Allies about "banding together in an economic union against the Central Powers" and would only agree to permit the SEC to suggest possible means whereby economic discussions might be continued after the conference. But when that agency later recommended a new international economic council, officials in Washington refused to participate until the Senate ratified the peace treaty.[40] And for Hoover, perpetuating such inter-Allied agencies would redivide Europe into separate economic and military camps. Accordingly, he notified the SEC that the United States considered all economic arrangements arising from the war terminated and would not contemplate new proposals that were limited to a "particular block [sic] of nations."[41]

Instead of these Allied proposals, the American delegates at Paris were only interested in stimulating European recovery through private programs. From their point of view, it was time to "cut out" governmental "paternalism" and allow private initiative to assert itself.[42] As a result, they launched a full-scale assult on

38. Wilson to Lloyd George, 23 April 1919, in Baker, *Wilson and World Settlement*, vol. 3, pp. 344–46. See also Davis to Rathbone, 24 April 1919, Rathbone to Davis, 28 April 1919, Albert Strauss, assistant secretary of the Treasury, to Davis and Thomas Lamont, 28 April 1919, Davis and Lamont to Rathbone and Leffingwell, 29 April 1919, Leffingwell to Davis, 2 and 6 May 1919, all in Davis Papers, box 16a; Leffingwell and Rathbone to Davis, 26 April 1919 and Leffingwell to Davis, 28 April 1919, Russell C. Leffingwell Papers, Letterbooks, vol. 28.

39. McCormick Diary, 9, 10, 22, 23 June 1919; and Minutes of the Supreme Economic Council, 10 and 23 June 1919, in *Foreign Relations: Peace Conference*, vol. 10, pp. 344–56, 414–27.

40. Minutes of a Meeting of the Council of Four, 28 June 1919, in *Foreign Relations: Peace Conference*, vol. 6, pp. 741–43. Minutes of the 26th Meeting of the SEC, 10 July 1919, in *Foreign Relations: Peace Conference*, vol. 10, pp. 450–51; Hoover and John Foster Dulles to Wilson, n.d., Hoover-Wilson Correspondence, Herbert Hoover Papers (hereafter cited as HHP,); and Lansing to House, 21 August 1919, Robert Lansing Papers.

41. Hoover to Wilson, 11 April 1919, HHP, Hoover-Wilson Correspondence; and Minutes of a Meeting of the SEC, 30 June 1919, in *Foreign Relations: Peace Conference*, vol. 10, pp. 434–35.

42. McCormick Diary, 10 June.

governmental interference with trade promotion, including the
wartime blockade.[43] The "prime object," Baruch explained, "should
be to set the world going" by abolishing commercial restrictions.[44]
This seemed especially desirable since economic "inequality and
[commercial] barriers were among the causes of the war." Indeed,
he believed that "no greater use" could be made of American resources than to force the elimination of all such barriers on the continent.[45] Wilson agreed that it was "perfectly legitimate" to consider
whether the Allies were "cooperating" in a "satisfactory" way before extending temporary relief and reconstruction credits.[46] And
when reports reached the American delegates that the British and
French were exacting preferential oil concessions from Rumania
in exchange for loans, they made American assistance to the Rumanian government conditional upon its agreement to guarantee
equality of opportunity.[47] In June, moreover, Davis offered to re-
fund the interest on the Allies' debt in return for their recognition
of the Open Door principle.[48]

This desire to end wartime controls and trade restrictions did not

43. For a brief treatment of United States blockade policy see Noring,
"American Coalition Diplomacy," pp. 219–25.

44. Baruch to Wilson, 12 February 1919, Davis Papers, box 61.

45. Baruch to Wilson, 7 May 1919, in Baker, *Wilson and World Settlement*,
vol. 3, pp. 347–51.

46. Wilson to Davis, 15 April 1919, Wilson Papers, Series 5–B, box 28.
Wilson did not hesitate to use American resources as leverage at the Peace
Conference. During debate over the Adriatic question, for example, he in-
structed the Treasury Department to withhold additional credits from Italy.
And Italian officials also believed that the Wilson administration was behind
their failure to gain private loans from Wall Street. See Wilson to Davis, 15
April 1919, Wilson Papers, Series 5–B, box 28; Davis to Wilson, 16 and 18
April 1919, Wilson Papers, Series 5–B, box 29; Wilson to Davis, 19 April 1919,
Wilson Papers, Series 5–B, box 30; Wilson to Glass, 3 May 1919, Wilson
Papers, Series 5–B, box 37; Davis to Glass, 6 May 1919, M. Stringher to Vic-
tor Orlando, 7 May 1919, enclosed in Davis to Wilson, 13 May 1919, Glass to
Davis, 10 May 1919, Wilson Papers, Series 5–B, box 36; "Notes on Informal
Conversation between Mr. Henry White and M. Tittoni, on July 4, 1919,"
Lansing Papers; and Henry White to Lansing, 29 July 1919, Henry White
Papers, Paris Peace Conference File, box 44.

47. Minutes of the American Economic Group, 15 March 1919, Davis
Papers, box 46; Davis to Joseph Grew, secretary general, American Commis-
sion to Negotiate Peace, 12 April 1919, Davis to Rumanian Prime Minister
Bratiano, 15 and 25 April 1919, Lansing to the State Department, 16 April
1919, and Bratiano to Davis, 17 May 1919, Record Group 256, "General
Records of the American Commission to Negotiate Peace," "Paris Peace Con-
ference," file, 871.51/34, 31a, 50; and Davis to Wilson, 7 May 1919, Wilson
Papers, Series 5–B, box 35.

48. Davis to Wilson, 7 June 1919, Wilson Papers, Series 5–B, box 43.

mean that American officials would rely strictly on individualistic initiatives or economic competition to stimulate European recovery. Their program for European reconstruction combined demands for a moderate reparation settlement, European self-help, and the abolition of preferential trade barriers with an emphasis on cooperative arrangements among multinational financial experts in organizing economic rehabilitation on a business basis. The question was not whether the United States would cooperate, as Assistant Secretary of the Treasury Russell Leffingwell put it, but whether the Allies could "interest American businessmen" in sound "business transactions."[49]

In May 1919, Thomas Lamont and Davis, on Wilson's suggestion, elaborated this program in a memorandum endorsed by the President's chief economic advisers. Couched in the rhetoric of economic interdependence, it attributed "American prosperity in the last decade" to the "growth of its export trade" with Europe. Economic instability in Europe, therefore, would cause "serious business and industrial depression" in the United States. And this, in turn, would generate "industrial and political revolutions" that could not be contained on the continent. Under these circumstances, it was "inconceivable" that the United States would not provide the aid necessary to restore Europe. Following the policy of the Treasury Department, however, the memorandum called for continued but limited government loans, while relying on the "normal channels of private enterprise" for long-term reconstruction credits. This long-term financing was to be organized by private experts on a cooperative, multinational basis. The memorandum specifically envisioned a European committee of "private bankers and men of affairs" that would coordinate a "general scheme of credits" with a "country-wide investment group" in the United States. The latter group would consist of the major banks and commercial houses acting under the "general approval of the United States Treasury." Such a mechanism, it was argued, would "enlist the combined judgement and responsibility of the business man and the banker," assure "unity of action," and provide a system of regulation institutionalized at the private level and overlaid by informal business-government consultation.[50]

49. Leffingwell to Davis, 6 May 1919, Record Group 56, "General Records of the Department of the Treasury," "Office of the Secretary, General Correspondence," box 83 (hereafter cited as RG 56 with box number).

50. Lamont to Wilson, 15 May 1919, enclosing "Observations Upon the

United States participation in the scheme would also require a European readiness to meet certain basic conditions. In order to "command the confidence of American investors," there would have to be responsible fiscal and monetary reforms in the borrowing nations. All credits would have to be applied only to reproductive industrial and commercial projects. Discriminatory "tariffs or secret trade understandings" would have to be eliminated. Preferential industrial and banking concessions could not be exacted by the lending institutions. And the Allied governments would have to agree to a liberal reparation settlement that would leave Germany with sufficient assets to begin its own reconstruction.[51]

Although the Allied and Associated powers did not act on this plan at Paris, similar proposals were soon forthcoming. Reflecting the earlier efforts to promote cooperation among domestic producers, important bankers and government officials tried to organize American investors for the cooperative financing of European recovery. In doing so, however, they now were ready to abandon the policy of the Treasury Department and to seek direct assistance from the government. In the background was a growing concern that prolonged financial instability in Europe would foster social unrest on the continent and drastically curtail the American export trade. In the summer and fall of 1919, Hoover called for government-business collaboration in launching a foreign-investment program that would draw largely upon private capital but operate with the assistance and approval of the War Finance Corporation. The WFC already was authorized to assist American exporters on a temporary basis, and Hoover considered it a likely agency to coordinate the massive undertaking, instill confidence in private investors, and guarantee equitable distribution of American resources.[52] At the same time, Frank Vanderlip, former president of the National City Bank of New York, was campaigning for a gov-

European Situation: Possible Measures to be Taken," in Baker, *Wilson and World Settlement*, vol. 3, pp. 352–62. In his cover letter Lamont notes that McCormick, Baruch, Davis, and Hoover had approved the memorandum. A copy of the memorandum in the Davis Papers, box 16a, is initialed by McCormick and Baruch as well as Davis and Lamont. The text of the memorandum was also cabled to the Treasury Department. See Lamont to Leffingwell, 29 May 1919, RG 56, box 277.

51. "Observations Upon the European Situation . . . ," in Baker, *Wilson and World Settlement*, vol. 3, pp. 352–62.

52. Robert H. Van Meter, Jr., "Herbert Hoover and the Economic Reconstruction of Europe, 1918–1921."

ernment-supported financial consortium that could cooperate with similar institutions abroad in financing European recovery.[53]

More important, Henry Davison of J. P. Morgan & Co. suggested a powerful investment trust to finance the movement of American commodities needed abroad. This it could do by issuing its own debentures to the American government and investment public against credits established in Europe and secured by options on the property of European buyers. Davison's plan found support from Sens. Walter Edge of New Jersey and Robert Owen of Oklahoma. Senator Owen, in particular, wanted the government to purchase a specified number of debentures issued by the proposed trust. This, he hoped, would inspire public confidence in the enterprise and allow the combine to tap the resources of private American investors. In turn, this would provide the capital needed to sub-sidize European purchasing power and underwrite the American export trade. Without this assistance, he warned, "a large part of [the] foreign market for our surplus products" would be lost, "caus-ing a very serious recession of prices due to overproduction."[54]

Following a report by the Bureau of Foreign and Domestic Com-merce on American foreign trade during the fiscal year ending in June 1919, Secretary of Commerce Redfield also began attacking the Treasury Department's ban on state financing. According to the report, the value of American exports totaled an astounding $7.25 billion—an increase of $1.33 billion over fiscal 1918. Exports, however, exceeded imports by a whopping $4 billion. The unpaid balance on account, Redfield argued, reflected a severe European credit stringency that had to be relieved. Otherwise, he warned, American export industries would have to shut down or, worse, prices would collapse due to the "congestion of products" lacking foreign outlets. Because of unstable conditions in Europe, he be-lieved that private investors would not underwrite European needs without government assistance. Accordingly, he urged Wilson to

53. Frank A. Vanderlip to House, 29 April 1919, Davis Papers, box 16a; Franklin Mott Gunther, American Chargé d'Affaires, The Hague, to Norman Davis, 28 July 1919, enclosing a copy of Vanderlip's "Memorandum in Re-gard to an International Loan, May 1, 1919," Davis Papers, box 46; and Frank A. Vanderlip, *What Happened to Europe?*, pp. 177–88.

54. Concerning the activities of Henry Davison and Sen. Walter Edge, see Van Meter, "The United States and European Recovery," pp. 115–20. For Owen's views see Owen to Wilson, 16 July 1919, Wilson Papers, Series 2, box 190; and Owen to Wilson, 16 November 1919, RG 40, file, 79161.

support limited government financing, endorsed the Davison scheme, and demanded an open discussion by the whole administration and not, "if you will pardon my so saying, [by] the Treasury Department alone."[55]

For officials in the Treasury Department, however, the Davison proposal was going to extremes. In June 1919, Secretary of the Treasury Carter Glass complained about Davison's pessimistic pronouncements on European economic conditions and urged the President to postpone a final decision on future financial assistance until the Treasury Department had presented its views.[56] In subsequent memoranda, he ticked off the measures for temporary government assistance already instituted, argued that private resources could meet all additional demands, and complained that further action by the Treasury Department would depreciate the value of the dollar, shift the tax burden of foreign countries to the American people, and encourage American industries to believe that high wartime profits could be maintained without reducing prices, discovering new markets, and developing new methods of export financing.[57]

For similar reasons, Glass later vetoed a proposal for an international exchange conference recommended by Senator Owen and endorsed by the Commerce Department. According to Owen, the conference could devise means for bringing the dollar into line with European currencies and preventing drastic fluctuations in foreign-exchange rates. As he saw it, this would alleviate serious impediments to foreign commerce, stimulate the flow of American capital abroad, eliminate surplus production in the United States, and help underwrite European recovery. But for Glass, the conference would promote false hopes of continued advances by the Treasury Department—advances that would prop up depreciated European currencies at the expense of the dollar, increase the cost of living at home, and put the government "into debt for the purpose of subsidizing the export trade."[58]

55. Redfield to Wilson, 29 and 31 July 1919, Wilson Papers, Series 4, box 484, file, 4647; and Redfield to Owen, 3 June 1919, RG 40, file, 79161.

56. Glass to Davis, 24 June 1919, Leffingwell Papers, Letterbooks, vol 31. Davis forwarded a copy of Glass's cable to Wilson on 25 June. See Davis Papers, box 11.

57. Glass to Wilson, 25 August and 11 September 1919, Wilson Papers, Series 2, boxes 192 and 193 respectively.

58. Owen to Wilson, 6 November 1919, and Acting Secretary of Commerce E. F. Sweet to Wilson, 14 November 1919, RG 40, file, 79161; and

The bankers, however, were not so averse to a larger governmental role in organizing recovery. In November 1919, a group of American and European bankers met in Amsterdam to petition for a government conference on reconstruction. The Treasury Department refused to sanction official participation by the United States and repeated the usual injunction against new government lending or multilateral discussion of war debts. Instead, the officials in the Treasury Department insisted that United States policy rested on the "deep-seated conviction" that "private initiative should be restored and government control and interference removed."[59] And when the bankers presented their petition to the Treasury Department anyway, Glass delivered a chilly rebuttal, reminding them that the key to recovery lay in Europe—through an adjusted reparation schedule, enlightened fiscal and commercial policies, and reliance on private initiative.[60]

In 1920, moreover, the Treasury Department refused to send an American delegation when the government conference on reconstruction finally met at Brussels under the auspices of the League of Nations. In this case, fresh British and French initiatives for debt adjustment undermined a tentative decision by the Wilson administration to attend the meeting.[61] Aware of congressional opposition

---

Glass to Wilson, 11 November 1919, RG 56, box 47, file, Exchange Stabilization. The Federal Reserve Board was also unenthusiastic about the Owen proposal. See W.P.G. Harding, governor of the Federal Reserve Board, to Joseph Tumulty, 18 November 1919, Wilson Papers, Series 2, box 193.

59. Glass to Rathbone, 13 November 1919, RG 39, box 104, file, Peace Conference; Davis to Paul Warburg, 26 November 1919 and 7 January 1920, and "Memorandum Concerning Warburg Memorial," n.d., RG 39, file, Warburg Memorial; Davis to Rathbone, 2 December 1919, RG 39, box 105, file, Reconstruction-European; Russell C. Leffingwell, "Memorandum of Statements made by Mr. Warburg, January 8th and 9th, Concerning His Proposed Memorial," 10 January 1920, Leffingwell Papers, Letterbooks, vol. 39.

60. Glass to Homer Ferguson, president of the United States Chamber of Commerce, 28 January 1920, Leffingwell Papers, Letterbooks, vol. 40.

61. For the British and French proposals see Ronald C. Lindsay, British Embassy, to Leffingwell, 9 February 1920, enclosing Chancellor of the Exchequer to Leffingwell, n.d., Davis Papers, box 48; Robert Skinner, American consul, London, to the Secretary of State, 13 February 1920, enclosing a clipping from the Morning Post, 12 February 1920, RG 59, file, 841.51/248; Celier to Davis, 25 May and 24 June 1920, Davis Papers, box 26; and "Confidential Conversations with Diplomats, July 1, 1920," Davis Papers, box 9. Prior to the last of these initiatives, Treasury Secretary D. F. Houston, with President Wilson's approval, had undertaken to consult congressional opinion on the possibility of authorizing an official delegation. See Houston to Wilson, 30 April 1920, and Wilson to Houston, 3 May 1920, Wilson Papers, Series 2, box 196.

to cancellation, the Treasury Department responded that debt adjustment would not enhance Europe's ability to finance reconstruction. Only a revised reparation agreement, the department contended, together with responsible fiscal policies would reestablish Europe's credit. Sound credit, in turn, would attract private investment and facilitate recovery. And with recovery underway, the Allied countries would possess the resources to meet their debt obligations.[62]

Despite this opposition to state financing, through new government loans or debt cancellation, Treasury officials did support cooperative financial efforts that went beyond the usual strictures of laissez-faire capitalism. As in the Lamont-Davis memorandum, this cooperative approach was to be organized by private experts and founded on a business basis. For example, when Senator Edge reshaped the Davison scheme to eliminate government subsidies, both the Treasury Department and the Federal Reserve Board had supported the new proposal. Passed by Congress in December 1919, the Edge Act substituted an unspecified number of private, federally chartered investment cooperatives for Davison's proposed government-subsidized investment trust, thereby preserving the ban on state financing in favor of largely private and cooperative programs.[63] And when informed that the League would convene the government conference on reconstruction as suggested in the Amsterdam petition, Assistant Secretary of the Treasury Davis had recommended instead a meeting of private multinational financial experts to study the issues involved. Such experts, he asserted, would be uncommitted to government policies and free to make objective business recommendations.[64]

This reiteration of the American formula did not move the Allies. And with the Treasury Department opposed to multilateral discussion of the debt question at Brussels, the League conference accomplished little of consequence.[65] Still worse, the Allies refused

62. See for example Houston to Lindsay, 1 March 1920, Leffingwell Papers, Letterbooks, vol. 41.

63. For details on banking legislation see Lewis, *America's Stake in International Investments*, p. 195; and Kaufman, "The Organizational Dimension of United States Economic Foreign Policy," pp. 41–43.

64. Davis to Rathbone, 3 April 1920, in *Foreign Relations, 1920*, vol. 1, pp. 90–91; Davis to Rathbone, 27 March 1920, Leffingwell Papers, Letterbooks, vol. 42a; and Davis to Rathbone, 11 April 1920, RG 39, file, Warburg Memorial.

65. For developments at the Brussels Conference see Brand Whitlock,

to consider appeals for a reasonable reparation settlement. As Americans saw it, the heavy indemnity payments demanded contradicted Wilson's hope for German reintegration, undermined the confidence of investors, and undercut the private approach to European recovery. "The economic rehabilitation of Europe," Davis lamented, was "an impossibility" until the reparation question had been "constructively settled" and German recovery was underway. By demanding more than Germany could pay, he concluded, Allied policy was "as logical" as "plucking all the feathers from a bird and then turning it loose to fly."[66]

These developments, together with the Senate's attack on the Versailles treaty, dealt a severe blow to the American plan. For as Davis and others saw it, the treaty structure, particularly the League of Nations and the Reparation Commission, would complete the unfinished work of the peace conference, amend the reparation terms, and stabilize Europe for private investment.[67] Secretary Glass was amazed that the Senate did not understand a situation so "critical in every respect" and "so patent to every businessman" in the United States. Europe, he warned, was on "the verge of catastrophe, political, economic and social." Should it collapse, America's "war expanded exports" would falter, industry and commerce would stagnate, and "social disorder" would spread from Europe to the United States. Europe could not be fortified, however, until "definite action" by the Reparation Commission and ratification of the treaty had removed the "political" rather than "commercial or credit risk" that was deterring private investors. With this risk eliminated, he predicted, European and American businessmen could then "lay the basis of credit in sound

American Ambassador to Belgium, to the Secretary of State, 6 October 1920, in *Foreign Relations, 1920*, vol. 1, pp. 100–102.

66. Davis to Wilson, 4 December 1920, Davis Papers, box 67; and statement attached to "Memorandum of a Conversation Between the French Ambassador and Mr. Norman Davis, January 31, 1920," Davis Papers, box 9.

67. See for example Davis to John Maynard Keynes, 19 March 1920, Davis Papers, box 32. After publication of Keynes's famous *Economic Consequences of the Peace*, Davis and Keynes exchanged views on the book as well as the treaty. Davis was upset by Keynes's criticism of United States policy at the peace conference, especially his description of Wilson, and for a time considered publishing a rebuttal. A draft of this rebuttal remains in his papers, box 32. See also Davis to Tumulty, 25 February 1920, Davis Papers, box 32. For his part, Keynes wrote Davis that he did not believe that the treaty contained "within itself effective provisions for its own modification." See Keynes to Davis, 18 April 1920, Davis Papers, box 32.

business transactions."[68] Like the Allied position on war debts and reparations, therefore, the Senate's action was undermining the private approach to European reconstruction.

For cooperationists like Davis, the League could provide a protective umbrella for the machinations of private commerce and investment. And it could do so without entangling the United States in European intrigues and alliances. Indeed, it was the instrument of American political independence in an economically interdependent world. It did not represent a "departure" from the "traditional principle of avoiding entangling alliances." Rather, it was the "only practical means" in an "industrial era of advancing the ideals and policies of our forefathers," discharging the "moral obligations" of the United States, and safeguarding American interests "without becoming entangled in European affairs or future wars."[69] The Senate, however, was jeopardizing this opportunity. As a result, concluded Secretary of State Bainbridge Colby, the Bolsheviks felt vindicated in their view that rivalry among the developed capitalist countries made meaningful and permanent cooperation impossible.[70]

III

When Wilson left office in 1921, the debate over European recovery remained deadlocked. Suspicious of Allied motives and convinced that state-sponsored and preferential policies provided the economic underpinnings of war, he had withdrawn from the inter-Allied councils, tried to organize European relief on a temporary basis, attacked continued governmental restraints on trade, and refused to accept new intergovernmental schemes to finance reconstruction at the expense of the American taxpayer and with-

68. Glass to Wilson, 25 August 1919, Wilson Papers, Series 2, box 192; and Glass to Wilson, 13 August 1919, Wilson Papers, Series 2, box 191. This last letter is based on a memorandum prepared by Assistant Secretary of the Treasury Leffingwell and dated 13 August 1919. See Leffingwell Papers, Letterbooks, vol. 33. Moreover, the letter was apparently a response to a request by Wilson for an analysis of the impact of the Senate's delay in ratifying the treaty. Similar analyses were also written by Secretaries Houston and William B. Wilson. See Houston to Wilson, 13 August 1919, and William B. Wilson to Woodrow Wilson, 30 August 1919, Wilson Papers, Series 2, box 191.

69. Norman H. Davis, "Address Before the Bond Club of New York City," 1 April 1921, Davis Papers, box 15; and Davis to McAdoo, 20 November 1923, Davis Papers, box 40.

70. Bainbridge Colby Press Release, n.d., Bainbridge Colby Papers, box 8.

out German reintegration. Instead, cooperationists in the Wilson administration had sought to prevent future conflicts by promoting the League of Nations, eliminating preferential trade policies, and returning economic affairs to private and cooperative management. From their point of view, this program conformed with the inter-related nature of the modern world and, if implemented, would stimulate constructive investment and promote recovery without the kind of state capitalism or excessive government intervention that undermined private initiative and transformed economic arrangements into dangerous political entanglements. But Allied leaders, together with some American bankers and government officials, held out for government assistance, and, as a result, the debate over European recovery was to continue into the Republican era.

CHAPTER 3

The Republicans
and the Policy of Continuity

European Reconstruction and the
Anglo-American Creditor Entente

Until recently, the policy of the Republican administrations toward war-torn Europe has received negative treatment by historians. Concentrating on the debt issue, one camp concludes that United States policy was shortsighted, economically naive, and the product of American inexperience in world affairs.[1] Others insist that the "Shylock" image of the United States is exaggerated but remain critical of American officials for waiting until the French occupied the Ruhr Valley before taking the initiative and for failing to integrate the debt and reparation settlements into a comprehensive program designed to stabilize the European and world economies.[2] Still others place United States reconstruction policy in the context of Anglo-American competition for leadership of the international economy.[3] Yet, the narrow focus on the debt question has obscured the broader American program for European re-

1. See for example Harold G. Moulton and Leo Pasvolsky, *War Debts and World Prosperity*; Dexter Perkins, "The State Department and Public Opinion," in Gordon A. Craig and Felix Gilbert, eds., *The Diplomats, 1919–1931*, vol. 1, pp. 282–308; John D. Hicks, *Republican Ascendancy, 1921–1933*, pp. 135–42; and Ellis L. Ethan, *Republican Foreign Policy, 1921–1933*, pp. 191–201.

2. See Benjamin Rhodes, "Reassessing 'Uncle Shylock': The United States and the French War Debt, 1917–1929"; Robert K. Murray, *The Harding Era: Warren G. Harding and His Administration*, pp. 360–67; Joan Hoff Wilson, *American Business & Foreign Policy, 1920–1933*, pp. 123–29; see also Melvyn P. Leffler, "The Origins of Republican War Debt Policy, 1921–1923: A Case Study in the Applicability of the Open Door Interpretation." Leffler breaks somewhat with the conventional approach by insisting that Republican intransigence on the debt issue did not stem from an ignorance of economic realities but from an awareness of the intense public hostility to the higher taxes that would result from debt cancellation.

3. See in particular Carl P. Parrini, *Heir to Empire: United States Economic Diplomacy, 1916–1923*; and Frank Costigliola, "The Politics of Financial Stabilization: American Reconstruction Policy in Europe, 1924–1930," pp. 1–243.

covery. And the emphasis on British and American conflict has ignored the pattern of cooperation and compromise that developed in Anglo-American affairs and the importance of this to the temporary resolution of the German issue in 1924.

Although repudiating Wilson's League of Nations, Republican policymakers continued to advocate private programs for European recovery. By permitting private experts to devise schemes based solely on economic considerations and financed through normal banking and commercial channels, they believed it was possible to avoid the waste, instability, and political conflict inherent in the modified mercantilism favored by the Allies. They offered this program of private action, along with an emphasis on European self-help and German reintegration, as the basis for reconstruction. Its adoption, however, would come only after the emergence of an informal Anglo-American financial entente and after a decision by both the British and United States governments to bind reparations and war debts together in a general settlement. This entente, together with deteriorating conditions in Europe, made possible a fragile accommodation among the victorious powers on the German issue. To be sure, there were areas of conflict and discontent involved, and the Anglo-American accord reached between 1923 and 1925 would falter a few years later.[4] But these factors should not conceal the important compromises made, nor the public and private cooperation that arose in Anglo-American affairs at middecade.

I

Sharing the Wilsonian assumptions of economic interdependence, Republican policymakers could agree that European rehabilitation was of "daily importance to every worker or farmer" in the United States. In a world that had become "little more than a great neighborhood," President Coolidge explained, "our common sense must tell us, if our self-interest did not, that our prosperity, our advancement, our portion of good fortune, must largely depend upon the share that shall be allocated to our neighbors."[5] This did not mean that European recovery must be purchased at

4. See Chapter 10.
5. Secretary of Commerce Herbert Hoover to Secretary of State Charles Evans Hughes, 30 August 1921, HHP, Commerce, Official File, box 284; and "Address by President Coolidge before the Chicago Commercial Club," 4 December 1924, HHP, Commerce, Official File, box 235.

the expense of American prosperity. New Treasury Department loans or debt cancellation, for example, might expand trade temporarily, but they would also impose an increased tax burden on the American public—a burden neither Congress nor the public would tolerate.[6] The real route to mutual expansion lay through the settlement of interstate indebtedness, the ending of commercial discrimination, the stabilization of internal economies, and, most important, the adjustment of reparations in a fashion that would permit German reconstruction, thereby stimulating general recovery on the Continent. Such reforms, it was insisted, would encourage generous private assistance and promote recovery without resort to new governmental programs based on Treasury loans or debt cancellation. "Cessation of inflation," Secretary of Commerce Herbert Hoover explained, "implies balanced budgets, reduction in land armament, adjustment of internal and external debt, etc." After such reforms in Europe, he continued, it would be possible for the United States to "extend the use of [its] banking capital." Otherwise, American investors would be simply "pouring money down an infinite sink."[7]

For Republicans, financial assistance to Europe should be arranged through private and cooperative programs organized by financial experts uncommitted to the political policies of their governments. This paralleled their attempt to extend Wilson's policy of encouraging responsible collaboration among private business leaders in regulating economic change. During the Republican ascendancy, Secretary Hoover became the philosopher for this program of "cooperative competition." Applied domestically, he believed, it could create a "new economic system, based neither on the capitalism of Adam Smith nor upon the Socialism of Karl Marx." Instead, it would produce a "third alternative"—one that preserved and stimulated individual initiative through cooperative endeavors that avoided "violent" economic conflict, rationalized economic behavior, raised living standards, and allowed the kind of enlightened action that was needed to solve contemporary economic problems. And given these results, there would be less pressure for government intervention in the economy—intervention

6. Leffler, "Origins of Republican War Debt Policy," pp. 585–601.
7. Hoover to Sen. Charles Curtis, 26 January 1922, HHP, Commerce, Official File, box 121. See also Hoover to Hughes, 4 January 1922, with enclosure, RG 59, file, 550.E1/3.

that, in his view, would politicize economic affairs and cause bureaucratic inefficiency, oppression, and paternalism.[8]

Accordingly, Hoover continued to mobilize competitive domestic interests into cooperative associations tied informally to the government and directed by broad-minded business leaders, equipped with professional expertise and supposedly dedicated to fulfilling their triple trusteeship to owners, workers, and the community at large. Under his tutelage, for example, export industries were organized along commodity lines; the result by 1922 being some 70 associations, representing approximately 150,000 firms. This private structure was then paralleled by the division of the Commerce Department into commodity branches, which were headed by experts usually chosen by the trade committees. And together, the commodity divisions, the trade associations, and the foreign representatives of both industry and the Commerce Department worked to promote the efficient management of foreign business. "The whole operation," according to Hoover, was "one of cooperation and service to industry and commerce."[9]

For the Republicans, these same principles could be applied internationally as well. Moving from the theme of cooperation among domestic functional groups to cooperation among multinational interests, Coolidge told the Chicago Commercial Club in 1924 that if American businessmen wished to serve themselves,

8. Hoover, "Speech before the Federated American Engineering Societies," 19 November 1920, HHP, Commerce, Official File, box 60. See also Hoover, "Speech on Combinations," 12 October 1920, HHP, Commerce, Official File, box 60; Herbert Hoover, *American Individualism*, pp. 32–47; and Herbert Hoover, *The New Day*, pp. 9–44.

9. For a sample of Hoover's views on the enlightened businessman see his address at a dinner given to Owen Young by the businessmen of New York City, 11 December 1924, HHP, Commerce, Personal File, box 75. Concerning his efforts to organize export industries, see Hoover, "The Future of Our Foreign Trade," 16 March 1926, and "Adjusting the Department of Commerce to Our Export Needs," unsigned, 6 May 1922, HHP, Commerce, Personal File, box 24; Hoover memorandum for President Warren G. Harding, 15 June 1923, HHP, Commerce, Official File, box 235; and Joseph Brandes, *Herbert Hoover and Economic Diplomacy: Department of Commerce Policy, 1921–1928*, pp. 5–21. For Hoover's program in the domestic sphere and the collectivist tendencies among American industries during this period see Grant McConnell, *Private Power & American Democracy*, pp. 64–68; Louis Galambos, *Competition & Cooperation: The Emergence of a National Trade Association*, pp. 68–138; and Ellis W. Hawley, "Herbert Hoover, the Commerce Secretariat, and the Vision of an 'Associative State.'"

they must cooperate with their foreign counterparts in "raising the standards of human welfare everywhere." The "major proportion of foreign trade," Hoover elaborated, was a "cooperative effort among nations to secure the greatest total output and total consumption."[10]

Yet, this cooperation was best arranged by private officials who were skilled in scientific management and free of excessive governmental impediments. Hoover insisted that government action lacked the efficiency of "business and individual initiative" and was subject to "every political pressure that desperate foreign statesmen" could invent. This pressure, in turn, escalated the risk of political and military conflict. Whenever the government entered economic affairs, he concluded, the resulting process became one of "inflation, waste, and intrigue."[11] Accordingly, while desiring to cooperate in European recovery, Republican officials shared the Wilsonian view that the Allies prevented a truly economic settlement by insisting on political schemes that would hamper market recovery and integration. And unwilling to involve the United States in political complications on the continent, they would reject these schemes and reassert the American formula.

II

In August 1921, Hoover and Gov. Benjamin Strong of the New York Federal Reserve Bank drafted the first Republican proposal for managing European reconstruction based on the American formula. It would authorize Strong to discuss with European central bankers the economic and financial issues underpinning the restoration of eastern Europe. Wary of political solutions, Hoover called for a program "divorced from political origin and action" and proceeding "through the healing power" of "private finance and commerce." This could work, he thought, if conditioned upon the elimination of all "economic barriers which defeated the flow of goods and services." To this Strong added that adequate collateral and responsible fiscal reforms by the borrowing governments would also be necessary.[12]

10. Coolidge address, 4 December 1924, HHP, Commerce, Official File, box 235; and Hoover, "The Future of Our Foreign Trade," 16 March 1926, HHP, Commerce, Personal File, box 24.

11. Herbert Hoover, *The Memoirs of Herbert Hoover*, vol. 2, pp. 13–14.

12. Hoover to Hughes, 30 August 1921, enclosing draft of a letter from President Harding to Benjamin Strong, 30 August 1921, and Strong to

Secretary of State Charles Evans Hughes, however, reacted unfavorably to the proposal. He worried that making assistance dependent upon internal financial reforms would involve the central bankers in complicated political discussions. Worse, authorizing Strong to participate in such a conference would be tantamount to an administration endorsement. This meant that its recommendations would be viewed as political proposals emanating from government officials. And instead, he insisted that any scheme devised should be "initiated and undertaken as a private enterprise" and without "governmental sanction." Yet, this stipulation revealed the broad consensus at the base of his disagreement with Hoover. For Hoover, who believed that his proposal would avoid "the pitfalls of international political life," clearly thought of the quasi-governmental officials who would constitute the bankers' committee as experts rather than politicians.[13]

This agreement became clear when Hoover joined Hughes in refusing to sanction participation by the United States in a new government conference on reconstruction that met at Genoa in March 1922. The Allied Supreme Council had called the conference to investigate ways of stimulating recovery, including the commercial reintegration of Russia into Europe.[14] As Americans saw it, however, European plans for the meeting were largely political rather than economic. According to Ambassador Richard Washburn Child in Italy, it was becoming "clearer daily that the economic agenda" for Genoa would be "overshadowed by political interests."[15] State Department officials seemed especially worried that Soviet delegates invited to the conference would use the opportunity to offer preferential economic concessions in Russia as a bribe for Western recognition—a strategy the British were encouraging.[16]

For his part, Hoover feared that political panaceas rather than

---

Hoover, 1 September 1921, HHP, Commerce, Official File, box 284.

13. Hughes to Hoover, 1 September 1921, RG 59, file, 800.51/312; and Hoover to Hughes, 30 August 1921, enclosing draft of a letter from Harding to Strong, 30 August 1921, HHP, Commerce, Official File, box 284.

14. Ambassador George Harvey, London, to Hughes, 6 January 1922, in *Foreign Relations, 1922,* vol. 1, pp. 384–85.

15. Child to Hughes, 30 January 1922, in *Foreign Relations, 1922,* vol. 1, pp. 389–98.

16. Assistant Secretary of State Fred Dearing to Hughes, 12 January 1922, and Robert Skinner, American consul general, London, to Hughes, 20 January 1922, in *Foreign Relations, 1922,* vol. 1, pp. 386–88.

economic solutions would be discussed at Genoa. Like other American officials, he believed that a constructive reparation settlement and enlightened fiscal policies were the keys to financial stabilization on the Continent. Accordingly, he wanted the Genoa conference to deal with these problems and, in January 1922, outlined his objectives in a memorandum for President Warren Harding. The memorandum envisaged European arms reduction, a reasonable reparation settlement, and German loans to finance reconstruction in France and Belgium. In addition, it called for private assistance from American investors in stabilizing European currencies—provided the countries involved balanced their budgets, eliminated preferential trade barriers, and established responsible central banks. This program, he argued, could win support from the expert economists and businessmen on the Continent. And if implemented at Genoa, it would promote "peace and growing good will," save Europe from "social chaos," rehabilitate European export markets, and end the "artificial competition" that American producers suffered from European commodities that were subsidized by depreciated currencies. When European plans for the conference were revealed, however, Hoover withdrew his support for United States involvement. Russian participation and the absence of the reparation question from the conference agenda, he now declared, betrayed the "political" rather than "economic" character of the meeting. Although certain that the United States should attend a "real honest-to-God economic conference," he urged Harding to postpone the meeting until the "economic air" had cleared and a "real conference" could be convened.[17]

Hughes agreed. In the State Department, economic advisers Arthur Young and Arthur Millspaugh wanted the Secretary to reserve United States policy on Russia, government loans, and war debts and appoint an official delegation to the conference. But Hughes decided against formal participation and dispatched Ambassador Child as an unofficial observer instead. Without mentioning reparations, he wrote the Italian Ambassador in Washington that vital issues were absent from the Genoa agenda, making the conference primarily "political" rather than "economic." The

17. Hoover to Harding, 4 January 1922, HHP, Commerce, Official File, box 91; Hoover to Hughes, 4 January 1922, enclosing "Memorandum on the Major Questions Before the Proposed Economic Conference," 4 January 1922, RG 59, file, 550.E1/3; Hoover to Harding, 23 January 1922, HHP, Commerce, Official File, box 21; and Dearing to Hughes, 23 January 1922, RG 50, file, 550.E1/75.

United States, he explained, could not "become involved in European political questions" and he urged the Allies to convene a conference of private financial experts to consider the reparation question. Such a conference, he argued, would address the "root" problem and receive warm support in the United States.[18]

At Genoa, the British advocated multinational cooperation in a financial consortium that would subsidize continental recovery under British leadership. Their program called for a central syndicate of private industrial and financial institutions to provide capital for the restoration of European trade. The syndicate was to act through affiliated national companies and, from the standpoint of the British, would be especially useful in reestablishing Germany's vital prewar trade with eastern Europe and Russia. Germany's profits on this trade, together with her share of the proceeds accruing from the syndicate's operations, could then be used to finance reparations and attract large foreign loans. Already in 1921, Lloyd George had recommended this scheme in discussions with French and German officials.[19] During a meeting at Cannes in January 1922, the Allies had also endorsed the plan in principle.[20] And at the same time, Montagu Norman, Governor of the Bank of England, had broached the idea in correspondence with Benjamin Strong.[21]

Despite their tentative support, French officials remained uneasy about the commercial reintegration of Russia and disagreed with a British demand that shares in the consortium be subscribed in

18. Arthur N. Young to Dearing and Arthur Millspaugh, 7 January 1922, RG 59, file, 550.E1/144; Hughes to Harding, 8 November 1922, and Harding to Hughes, 9 November 1922, Warren G. Harding Papers (microfilm edition, roll 144); and Hughes to the Italian Ambassador, 8 March 1922, and Hughes to Child, 24 March 1922, in Foreign Relations, 1922, vol. 1, pp. 392–94.

19. "British Secretary's Notes of Meetings Between Mr. Lloyd George and Mr. Briand, London, December 19, 20, 21, and 22, 1921," in Foreign Office, Documents on British Foreign Policy, 1919–1939, First Series, vol. 15 (London, 1967), pp. 764–85, 788–800 (hereafter cited as Documents on British Foreign Policy).

20. Parliament, Parliamentary Papers, 1922, Cmd. 1621, "Resolutions Adopted by the Supreme Council at Cannes"; Foreign Office memorandum, "The Cannes Conference: Proposals for Establishing Better Economic Conditions in Europe Approved by the Supreme Council at Cannes, January 10, 1922," Record Group 371, "General Records of the Foreign Office," Foreign Office file: C868/458/62 (hereafter cited as F.O. with file number).

21. Montagu Norman, governor of the Bank of England, to Strong, 20 December 1921, 6 February and 8 March 1922, Benjamin Strong-Montagu Norman Correspondence.

sterling. The latter would tie the central syndicate to London, enhance Britain's financial position on the Continent, and leave French investors with substantial losses should the value of the franc later appreciate. From Genoa, Ambassador Child took a similar position. The proposal, he claimed, would benefit the British at American expense; it would enable them "to manage" American investment in eastern Europe and Russia, to "capture the trade" that resulted, and to leave the United States "the bare interest rates." Indeed, they regarded the United States "as gullible enough" to put its "gold surplus out through British controlled pipelines." The proposed syndicate, he concluded, would allow the British to regulate American capital, which could be either "dribbled into Europe without exactions" or funneled in through "any consortiums which fall under British control and management."[22]

Given these French and American reservations, the proposed consortium did not take hold at Genoa. Nor did the conference produce an alternative scheme for restoring Europe. The Economic Committee avoided all discussion of reparations, war debts, and new government loans. And a recommendation of the Finance Committee to have a central bankers' conference to draw up a monetary convention that would facilitate an early return to the gold standard across Europe won only temporary support from some American policymakers and bankers.[23] In April, Hoover noted its similarity to his earlier proposal for a central bankers' meeting and endorsed the conference as a further step towards achieving exchange stabilization. For James Logan, the assistant American representative on the Reparation Commission, the large gold holdings and related currency position of the United States also required official participation. In May, Strong urged the idea upon the Federal Reserve Board. And when Norman arrived in Wash-

---

22. "British Secretary's Notes of Meetings of British and French Financial Delegations, Paris, December 30 and 31, 1921," in *Documents on British Foreign Policy*, First Series, vol. 15, pp. 806–30; Child to Hughes, 19, 21, and 29 April 1922, RG 59, file, 550.E1/200, 226; Child to Hughes, 5 May 1922, RG 59, file, 800.51/325; and Child to Harding, 22 May 1922, with attached memorandum, Harding Papers, microfilm edition, roll 231. For the Genoa proposal see also John Gregory to the Foreign Office, 19 April 1922, F.O. file: C6281/458/62.

23. James Logan, assistant American representative on the Reparation Commission, to Assistant Secretary Leland Harrison, 28 April 1922, enclosed in Logan to Henry Fletcher, Undersecretary of State, 1 May 1922, Henry P. Fletcher Papers, General Correspondence, box 8; and Henry Clay, *Lord Norman*, p. 137.

ington for discussions with American officials, he supported Strong's efforts and, along with Strong, drew up a draft agenda for the conference.[24]

Subsequently, however, American officials became suspicious of British plans for the proposed conference. Under British direction, the Finance Committee at Genoa had urged the central bankers to discuss methods for coordinating their domestic credit policies in order to regulate the international movement of metallic reserves and avoid wide fluctuations in the commodity value of gold. Although endorsing an eventual return to gold parity, the committee had also urged the bankers to temporarily establish a gold-exchange standard. Under this, certain designated central banks, including the Bank of England, would maintain their reserves in gold, but others would hold their reserves partly in gold and partly in foreign exchange claims on the designated banks.[25]

For the British, this system would economize the use of gold, make Britain a major depository of the world's metallic reserves, and increase the value of the pound. But for Strong, the responsibility on central bankers to coordinate their credit policies and the large foreign-dollar holdings that would result under the gold exchange proposal might impair the Federal Reserve Board's primary obligation to maintain monetary stability in the domestic market. At the same time, Hughes probably remained suspicious of a quasi-governmental conference, especially one where the debt question might be subject to multilateral discussion. During their meetings with the Federal Reserve Board, both Strong and Nor-

24. Harrison to Hughes, 26 April 1922, and Hoover to Hughes, 22 April 1922, RG 59, file, 550.E1/203; Logan to Harrison, 28 April 1922, Fletcher Papers, General Correspondence, box 8; Charles Hamlin Diary, vol. 6, 2, 3, 8, 9, and 12 May 1922, Strong to Norman, 15 May, 14 and 27 July 1922, and Norman to Strong, 15 July 1922, Strong-Norman Correspondence. See also Clay, *Lord Norman*, p. 138.

25. Parliament, *Parliamentary Papers*, 1922, Cmd. 1650, "International Economic Conference, Genoa: Resolutions and Reports," and Cmd. 1667, "Papers Relating to the International Economic Conference, Genoa"; Gregory to the Foreign Office, 20 April 1922, F.O. file: C5759/458/62; "International Economic Conference, Genoa. British Empire Delegation Draft Proposals for an International Gold Standard Monetary Convention," 10 April 1922, F.O. file: C5838/458/62; Ralph Wigram to Miles Lampson, 2 May 1922, F.O. file: C6587/458/62; "Summary of the Financial, Economic, and Transport Resolutions of the Genoa Conference," 13 May 1922, F.O. file: C7217/458/62; and R. G. Hawtrey of the British Treasury, "The Genoa Currency Proposals," 4 February 1925, Records of the British Treasury, file, T172/1499B (hereafter cited as Treasury Papers with file number).

man had endorsed a temporary moratorium on debt payments, and
the question of debt adjustment was listed on their draft agenda
for the conference. Such action threatened to violate United States
policy against multilateral discussion of the debt question and at
the very time when a British delegation would be in Washington
to arrange, bilaterally, the funding of the British debt to the United
States.[26]

Moreover, the proposal for a central bankers' conference was
displaced by another suggestion more in tune with the private approach of United States policy. On April 4, the Reparation Commission had agreed to appoint a committee of private financial
experts to consider and report on the conditions necessary for Germany to attract a large foreign loan. At the time, Germany was
about to default on the schedule of indemnity payments drawn up
at London in May 1921. As a result, one American official explained,
it had become impossible for the Allies "to maintain the rich flow
of juice from the German lemon." Following the suggestion of
British representative John Bradbury, therefore, the Reparation
Commission had agreed to consider a moratorium on payments if
Germany stabilized its currency and reformed its fiscal policies.
The bankers, led by J. P. Morgan of the United States, were to cer-
tify the reforms necessary to insure private assistance. This proposal, then, was essentially what American leaders had in mind when
they held that European reconstruction should rest solely on economic considerations as determined by private financial experts,
should proceed through normal banking channels, and should be
founded on Europe's initiative in resolving its own economic difficulties.[27]

Once appointed, the committee decided early that the key to
private assistance for Germany lay in a reasonable adjustment of
reparations. Unless indemnity payments were revised downward,
they argued, private, especially American, bankers would refuse
the risk of German investment. Yet, the French had opposed em-

26. In addition to the last citation in the preceding note see Frank C.
Costigliola, "Anglo-American Rivalry in the 1920's"; Stephen V. O. Clarke,
Central Bank Cooperation, 1924–1931, pp. 34–38, 40–41; Clay, *Lord Nor-
man*, pp. 138–39; Hamlin Diary, vol. 6, 9 May 1922; Strong to Norman, 15
May and 7 September 1922, and Norman to Strong, 9 August 1922, Strong-
Norman Correspondence.

27. Procès-Verbal of the Reparation Commission, 28 March, 4, 18, and
25 April 1922, F.O. file: C5419/C6007/C6407/C6721/192/62; Logan to
Harrison, 17 May 1922, and Logan to Ambassador Alanson Houghton, Germany, 17 May 1922, Fletcher Papers, General Correspondence, box 8.

powering the committee with the authority to examine the London schedule of payments. And when the bankers appealed to the Reparation Commission for a revision of their instructions, the French representative again voted against it. Thus, the bankers considered it impossible to proceed and instead published a report critical of the French position.[28]

Despite the committee's failure, the Harding administration did not abandon its policy of European initiative and private management. In early October, Hughes discussed the possibility of recalling the adjourned bankers' committee with Lamont of Morgan & Co. For the information of J. P. Morgan, who was then in Italy, he also dispatched the substance of his proposal to Ambassador Child in Rome. At the same time, he presented his plan to the French government, instructing the American Ambassador in Paris to secure French approval for a "practical businesslike solution" by "financiers of the highest distinction." He also approached the French Ambassador in Washington, urging that the Allies enlist "authoritative financial opinion through a meeting of important financial men." Such men, he argued, if free to work "without restrictions by instructions from foreign offices," would produce a financial plan that governments could accept "as inevitable." If a "professional man, or a man of highest authority in finance or business were approached for his opinion upon a question relating to his profession," his answer would be "as clear as crystal." By "virtue of his own integrity and prestige," he could offer no reply "except that which corresponded to his intellectual conviction based upon his experience and knowledge."[29]

The French, however, rejected this proposal. On December 21,

28. Procès-Verbal of the Reparation Commission, 6 and 7 June 1922, F.O. file: C8833/192/62; John Bradbury to the Foreign Office, 7 June 1922, and Lord Hardinge, British Ambassador, Paris, to the Foreign Office, 8 June 1922, F.O. file: C8375/C8285/99/18; Foreign Office, "Memorandum Respecting the Reparation Situation," 14 June 1922, F.O. file: C8534/99/62; Logan to Harrison, 9 June 1922, Fletcher Papers, General Correspondence, box 8; "Report of the Loan Committee to the Reparation Commission," Fletcher Papers, General Correspondence, box 9; Fletcher to Hughes, 6 June 1922, Harding Papers, microfilm edition, roll 234.

29. Lamont to J. P. Morgan, 16 October 1922, Thomas Lamont Papers, Series 2, file, 108–13; J. P. Morgan; Hughes to Ambassador Myron Herrick, Paris, 8 and 17 October 1922, and "Memoranda by the Secretary of State of Conversations with the French Ambassador, November 7 and December 14, 1922," in Foreign Relations, 1922, vol. 2, pp. 165, 168–70, 178–80, 187–92; Hughes to Child, 18 October 1922, RG 59, file, 462.OOR296/–.; and "The Dawes Plan" [Beeritz Memorandum], Charles Evans Hughes Papers, box 172.

the French Ambassador informed Hughes that his government opposed reconvening the experts' committee. Specifically, it would not agree to a downward revision of reparations unless its share of indemnities was increased and its debt to Great Britain reduced. Further, the Allied Premiers were scheduled to meet in January 1923, and the French opposed new suggestions until they had exhausted other alternatives for making Germany meet its obligations.[30]

Speaking before a meeting of the American Historical Association in New Haven, Connecticut, one week later, Hughes reacted by blasting the French position and reaffirming United States policy. War debts, he insisted, were not a factor in reconstruction as they did not affect Germany's capacity to pay. The "crux" of the problem was reparations, and the "key" to its solution lay in Europe, not America. The situation called for a settlement "upon its merits," and this required taking reparations "out of politics" and allowing men "of the highest authority in finance" to devise a "financial plan" that "would be accepted throughout the world as the most authoritative expression obtainable." Governments, he argued, could assist by liberating these experts "from any responsibility to Foreign Offices and from any duty to obey political instructions." This would insure a solution "prompted only by knowledge and conscience."[31]

III

Although the French rejected this proposal, an emerging Anglo-American financial entente did make its implementation possible. The first step in this new rapprochement was an informal consensus on the problems of war debts and reparations. In August 1922, the British government had issued the Balfour note. In it, the Foreign Secretary lamented Great Britain's inability to cancel all debts due the British Treasury, including reparation payments, because of United States demands for repayment of the British debt. The note was widely interpreted as a last-ditch effort to pressure the United States into a general cancellation. Yet, while

30. "Memorandum by the Secretary of State of a Conversation with the French Ambassador, December 21, 1922," in *Foreign Relations, 1922*, vol. 2, pp. 195–96; and Leffler, "The Origins of Republican War Debt Policy," p. 598.

31. The pertinent portions of Hughes's address are printed in *Foreign Relations, 1922*, vol. 2, pp. 199–202.

it was that, the statement also declared Great Britain's determination to fund its American obligations and called upon England's debtors to negotiate debt settlements with the British Treasury. Debt payments to Great Britain, however, were to be reduced to amounts sufficient for the British to cover their obligations to the United States.[32]

The United States matched this compromise. In this case, official American denunciation of all proposals for cancellation concealed the flexibility that the Harding administration tried to maintain. Important officials in both the banking community and the government appreciated the connection between the heavy European debt, the success of American exports, and the reconstruction of Europe. As a result, they did favor a reasonable settlement of all debts that were owed to the United States Treasury. Initially, Hoover had favored a moratorium on interest payments or cancellation of the prearmistice debts. But when warned that Congress would be less flexible, he became more intransigent and, in October 1922, delivered a scathing attack on European proposals for cancellation. Yet, despite this and similar attacks on American bankers who wanted to remit part of the principal due, he still hoped to achieve a remission by scaling down interest rates and spreading payments over a number of years. Mellon and Hughes, too, had hoped to gain from Congress a broad and flexible authority for the Treasury Department to negotiate funding agreements. This would separate the debt issue from congressional politics, place it on a business basis, and give the Treasury Department freedom to maneuver in negotiating with debtor countries.[33]

Congress had refused to cooperate in these schemes, however, and had passed legislation that placed funding negotiations under a special agency, the World War Foreign Debt Commission. The funding act also fixed interest rates at a 4¼ percent minimum and the time for repayment of all principal and interest at a twenty-five year maximum. Officially, then, it denied the administration any

32. See Foreign Office, *British and Foreign State Papers, 1922*, vol. 16, pp. 198–201, (hereafter cited as *British State Papers*).

33. Hoover to Hughes, 4 January 1922, RG 59, file, 550.E1/3; Hoover, "The Repayment of European Debts to Our Government," 16 October 1922, HHP, Commerce, Official File, box 336; Hoover, *Memoirs*, vol. 2, pp. 177–78; Wilson, *American Business & Foreign Policy*, pp. 124–26; and Leffler, "The Origins of Republican War Debt Policy," pp. 588–89. See also Lamont to E. C. Grenfell, 20 February 1922, Lamont Papers, Series 2, file, 111–13, Morgan, Grenfell & Co.

freedom in dealing with debt matters, a fact that Hughes never tired of pointing out in his conversations with Allied Ambassadors.[34]

Still, in practice, the commission never followed the congressional guidelines. It adopted a capacity-to-pay principle, applied it in bilateral negotiations, and then secured modification of the congressional terms after completing each funding agreement. The average interest rate on these agreements fell well below 4¼ percent, and the time allowed for repayment was extended from twenty-five to sixty-two years. On these or similar terms, the debts of thirteen nations, constituting about 90 percent of all indebtedness to the United States, were funded by 1927. And the result was an over-all cancellation of approximately 50 percent of the combined debt, if calculated on the original 5 percent interest fixed on the loans.[35] It "must be clear," Lamont remarked in 1925, "that although our Senators have yelled about collecting the last red cent out of the continental nations, yet when it has come to actual settlement, the adjustment has been very lenient."[36]

Of all the settlements, the British funding arrangement was the first one of importance. By late 1922, British and American officials had come to believe that a settlement of the British debt would permit a degree of Anglo-American solidarity on the debt question and encourage stabilization in Europe. "I have always felt that the position of the British and the American Governments as to the Continental indebtedness is just the same," Eliot Wadsworth, Assistant Secretary of the Treasury and Secretary of the World War Foreign Debt Commission, told Lamont in September 1922. "What we have long wanted was the opportunity of sitting down to talk [with the British] on the same side of the table." For their part, influential segments of London's financial community thought an Anglo-American debt agreement would foster European recovery, "pave the way towards greater stability of the exchanges,"

34. Moulton and Pasvolsky, *War Debts and World Prosperity*, pp. 71–78; Leffler, "The Origins of Republican War Debt Policy," pp. 591–95; and "Memorandum by the Secretary of State of a Conversation with the French Ambassador, November 7, 1922," in *Foreign Relations, 1922*, vol. 2, pp. 178–80.

35. Moulton and Pasvolsky, *War Debts and World Prosperity*, pp. 81–108. According to Lamont, the "most sensible" people in Washington always expected that the Debt Commission would follow such a course. See Lamont to Grenfell, 20 February 1922, Lamont Papers, Series 2, file, 111–13, Morgan, Grenfell & Co.

36. Lamont to Robert Cecil, 17 December 1925, Lamont Papers, Series 2, file, 87–2, Lord Robert Cecil.

and revive "general trade." And equally important, explained E. C. Grenfell, it would bring the United States and Great Britain "nearer together" and then "the rest of the world would have a combination to whom they would have to pay attention."[37]

Motivated by these sentiments, British and American officials began negotiations for funding the British debt in January 1923. The Americans favored an arrangement based on sixty-two annual installments with a sliding 3 to 3½ percent interest rate; terms substantially better than allowed under the funding act. Indeed, as the British delegation reported early in the negotiations, the "atmosphere" in Washington seemed conducive to a favorable settlement. President Harding, explained Ambassador Geddes, had told press reporters that neither he nor the American commissioners, including Hoover, Hughes, and Mellon, expected an agreement within the terms prescribed by Congress. Instead, the commission was to negotiate the best settlement possible, whereupon the President would urge Congress to approve. And as Norman explained, the American commissioners were anxious to recommend the "most lenient" terms that Congress would accept.[38]

Accordingly, the British delegation considered the results "good." The American proposal exceeded anything "the [British] Treasury believed to be possible a few months ago" and represented a "vast improvement on terms offered us under [the] United States funding act." Indeed, "taking all things into consideration," the entire British delegation "strongly" recommended acceptance. Washington's proposal signified a "tremendous advance in American opinion," explained Chancellor of the Exchequer Stanley Baldwin, head of the British delegation; and unless accepted, "we cannot expect improvement in general financial conditions." Still worse, if the British government rejected what he considered "the best terms we can" get, it could not "escape appearing as a defaulter."[39]

Despite these recommendations, Prime Minister Bonar Law balked at endorsing the settlement. He viewed the terms as still too harsh and worried that acceptance would provoke criticism of the

37. Lamont to Grenfell (quoting Eliot Wadsworth), 27 September 1922, Grenfell to Lamont, 16 October 1922, Lamont Papers, Series 2, file, 111–14, Morgan, Grenfell & Co.; and Clay, *Lord Norman*, pp. 174–75.

38. Geddes to the Foreign Office, from the Chancellor of the Exchequer for the Prime Minister, 8, 10, and 13 January 1923, and Geddes to the Foreign Office, 10 January 1923, F.O. file: A261/A245/A273/A244/136/45; and Clay, *Lord Norman*, pp. 178–79.

39. Baldwin to Bonar Law, 13 and 15 January 1923, F.O. file: A273/A313/136/45; and Clay, *Lord Norman*, p. 178.

government in Parliament. By this time, moreover, the French had invaded the Ruhr and, in his opinion, this action could destroy any hope of reparation transfers by Germany and, concomitantly, hamper efforts by the continental Allies to liquidate their debts to the British Treasury. And this, in turn, would make it difficult for the British to meet their American obligations. At a meeting in mid-January, the Cabinet tentatively supported this position and summoned the British delegation back from Washington to present its case.[40]

Subsequently, opinion shifted in favor of a settlement. From Washington, Ambassador Geddes endorsed the American proposal. Great Britain, he argued, could not win more generous terms, and any breakdown in the negotiations now would delay a settlement until after the American elections in 1924 when, in all probability, conditions would be less favorable. More important, he added, "if we fail to settle now, [the] dawning recognition of Anglo-American unity of ideals and interest over wide fields [of] international affairs will suffer a temporary eclipse and we shall slip back to where we were two or even three years ago." In London, the British delegates presented similar arguments to the Cabinet while policymakers in the Foreign Office contemplated the advantages of a prompt settlement. "By preventing a breach with the U. S.," noted Maurice Peterson of the American Department, "we prevent the encouragement which such a breach cannot fail to give" Great Britain's continental debtors. An immediate settlement would take advantage of a "more propitious moment" in American politics "than we are likely to have again for some years to come." And most important, it would expedite American involvement in efforts "to arrive at a world economic settlement, including reparations."[41]

At a meeting on 31 January 1923 the Cabinet, apparently convinced by these and other arguments, reversed its original opposition and agreed to accept in principle the terms outlined earlier by the British delegation. The Foreign Office instructed Ambassador

40. Bonar Law to Baldwin, 13 (two cables), 15, 16, 17, and 23 January 1923, F.O. file: A273/A313/A335/A345/A440/136/45; and Conclusions of a Meeting of the Cabinet, 15 January 1923, Cabinet Papers, 2(23)3 (hereafter cited as Conclusions of the Cabinet).

41. Geddes to the Foreign Office, 26 January 1923, F.O. file: A521/136/45; Conclusions of the Cabinet, 30 January 1923, 4(23)2; Foreign Office minute by Peterson, 16 January 1923, F.O. file: A313/136/45; and minute by Ronald C. Lindsay, Assistant Undersecretary of State, 16 January 1923, F.O. file: A313/136/45.

Geddes to confide this information to the Department of State. In mid-February, the British delegation returned to Washington, where an agreement was reached along the lines suggested by the Americans.[42] And despite some regret that it was not lenient enough, the settlement was endorsed in London as paving the way towards greater Anglo-American cooperation. Regardless of his "personal opinion" about "what would have been the best" arrangement, Robert McKenna of the Joint City and Midland Bank and a leading advocate of a more generous proposal "spoke strongly in favor" of the agreement. Reminding Lamont of his warm feelings on the friendly "private relationship between Americans and British," he thought it "of vital importance to the world that the public relationship between the two countries should be not less good." Accordingly, it was "far more" important to dispose of a "possible cause of irritation than to haggle over" a "little more or a little less."[43]

Like their American counterparts, the British hoped that an Anglo-American funding arrangement would "facilitate the settlement of other Inter-State War Debts" and permit Anglo-American cooperation on the German issue. And indeed, one result was a kind of creditor alliance between the two countries. As stated in the Balfour note, Great Britain's decision to settle with the United States was matched by demands upon its debtors to negotiate funding agreements with the British Treasury. The British accepted the principle of bilateral debt negotiations and both the British and United States governments agreed to partial cancellation, with the British passing on to their debtors all savings won in their American negotiations.[44] As will be seen, moreover, both governments exploited their claims on the continental allies to promote a new solution to the reparation imbroglio.

IV

The British funding agreement eliminated, temporarily at least, a source of irritation and tension between the British and American

42. Conclusions of the Cabinet, 31 January 1923, 5(23)1; Foreign Office to Geddes, 31 January 1923, Baldwin to Geddes, 31 January 1923, F.O. file: A636/136/45.

43. Robert McKenna to Lamont, 12 March 1923, Lamont Papers, Series 2, file, 96–13, Great Britain. See also Lamont to Grenfell, 26 January 1923, Lamont Papers, Series 2, file, 111–15, Morgan, Grenfell & Co.

44. Clay, *Lord Norman*, p. 174; Moulton and Pasvolsky, *War Debts and World Prosperity*, pp. 83–86, 92–93, 113–14.

governments and represented the first block in an incipient structure of Anglo-American cooperation. It provided new incentive for
efforts, already underway, to devise the kind of European stabilization scheme that could insure reparation and debt transfers now
needed by the British to liquidate their newly funded debt and to
guarantee cooperative action by American banks in financing
European recovery. Shortly after the debt negotiations ended, Foreign Secretary Lord Curzon was telling American Ambassador
George Harvey that it was now "very desirable that our two Governments should keep in touch with each other about the [repara-
tions] matter." For his part, Harvey explained that the attitude of
the United States toward Great Britain had been metamorphosed
by the "settlement of the debt question; that a more favorable atmosphere had never prevailed between the two countries since the
end of the revolution; and that any suggestion emanating from
London would be assured of a most friendly reception."[45] Indeed,
concurrent with the debt negotiations, British and American officials, in both the public and private spheres, were working on the
related problems of reparations and reconstruction, and their efforts in both cases would forge still additional links in the emerging
Atlantic partnership.

45. Curzon to Geddes, 19 February 1923, F.O. file: C3188/1/18.

CHAPTER 4

The Policy of
"Disinterested Statesmanship"

Private Management and the
Atlantic Partnership

The pattern of Anglo-American cooperation, still inchoate in 1923, assumed well-rounded proportions over the next two years. Funding of the British debt and the resulting creditor entente permitted a united Anglo-American front on the reparation problem. To be sure, the Harding and Coolidge administrations publicly opposed a comprehensive settlement based on a mutual reduction of war debts and German reparations. But this formal opposition, and the tendency of subsequent historians to condemn American truculence, does not gainsay the readiness of American leaders, informally at least, to join the British in linking reparations and war debts in a general downward revision. Of equal importance was the confluence of British and American policy on the private approach to European recovery favored by the United States. This process, emerging since 1920, received fresh stimulus from the British funding agreement and reached final fusion in the successful launching of the Austrian and German stabilization schemes of 1923 and 1924. These successes, in turn, cleared the way for an Anglo-American program to return pound sterling to the gold standard, a program at once elemental to the American formula for world stabilization and symbolic of the full flowering of the Atlantic partnership.

I

Since Versailles, important British officials, like their American associates, had come to appreciate that excessive reparation payments by Germany would impair European recovery. In addition, such payments could be met only if Germany had a substantial export surplus and this, as they saw it, would hamper British traders and threaten British labor. Instead, they wanted to restore Ger-

many's credit in order to attract the private financial assistance that
would expedite German recovery. And this, they now insisted, required a reasonable adjustment of the indemnity issue. During the
reparation debates of 1920 and 1921, however, they had usually
found French claims at odds with their desire to fix reparation payments at a sum within Germany's capacity to pay. Already in 1920,
one official in the Foreign Office complained that the British were
being reviled by the French press because of their "lenient attitude"
on German reparations.[1]

To the chagrin of French authorities, the British were moving
toward the American position. In 1922, for example, it was John
Bradbury, Britain's representative on the Reparation Commission,
who took the lead in sponsoring the unsuccessful investigation by
the bankers' committee into the conditions necessary for Germany
to attract private financial assistance. Following this failure the
British championed a German request for a moratorium on the
bulk of reparation payments in 1922 and 1923. The publication of
the Balfour note in August 1922, however, made the French reluctant to suspend indemnities while their Anglo-American cred-
itors were demanding repayment of the French war debts. At a
reparation conference in London, French Premier Raymond Poincaré refused to consider the moratorium unless Germany provided
"productive pledges" that could be used as security against private
loans. Specifically, he wanted Allied control of German customs
receipts, formation of a customs barrier between occupied and
unoccupied territory, new taxes on the occupied area, Allied control of certain state mines and forests, and distribution among the
Allied governments of shares in leading German industries within
the occupied zone. In October the British retorted with a new
scheme that would grant the Germans a four-year moratorium in
return for rigorous efforts to balance their budget and stabilize the
mark. Again the French refused to consider the proposal without
"productive pledges" and, by the end of 1922, the reparation controversy had reached an apparently hopeless deadlock.[2]

Yet clearly the deterioration of Anglo-French relations was

1. The Anglo-French controversies over reparations can be followed in
Documents on British Foreign Policy, Series 1, especially vols. 7, 10, 15, and 16
(London, 1958, 1960, 1967, 1968). Quotations are from *Documents on
British Foreign Policy*, Series 1, vol. 10, note 6, p. 203, and vol. 15, p. 62.

2. Foreign Office, "Memorandum Respecting the Reparation Situation,"
14 June 1922, F.O. file: C8534/99/62; and Foreign Office, "Memorandum on
the Attitude of the French, Belgian and Italian Governments to the latest De-

matched by the emerging Anglo-American consensus on the reparation issue. Indeed, at the meeting of Allied Prime Ministers in
Paris in January 1923, the British delegation presented a new
reparation plan remarkably similar to the American formula. At
that time the Allies concluded that Germany was in default on its
reparation payments, and, subsequently, French and Belgian
troops occupied the Ruhr. But the British delegates at the Paris
meeting refused to sanction the invasion of the Ruhr and suggested
instead a revised indemnity plan based on a reduction in payments,
a four-year moratorium, and an experts' committee composed of
private Allied and American leaders to draft a scheme for reor-
ganizing Germany's finances and stabilizing the mark. "All this,"
according to a Foreign Office memorandum, "was very much on
the lines of Mr. Hughes' [New Haven] proposal."[3]

The merging of British and American thinking on the reparation
imbroglio and the new creditor entente made possible by the British funding agreement also spawned a common strategy that linked
reparations and war debts in a manner that afforded the Atlantic
partners new leverage to foster Allied cooperation on the German
problem. Following the policy announced in the Balfour note, the
British government promised to limit its own debt and indemnity
claims to an amount equal to its recently funded American obligation, provided the Allies accepted the Anglo-American formula
and negotiated similar reductions in the structure of Continental
indebtedness, including reparations. At one point, the Foreign Office and the British Treasury even considered using their claims on
France more aggressively, by threatening to demand prompt and
full repayment unless the French government became more cooperative on the reparation problem.[4] Secretary of State Hughes
employed a similar tactic, suggesting that only an adjustment of

---

velopments in the Reparation Negotiations," 5 December 1922, F.O. file:
C16640/99/18.

3. Harold G. Moulton and Leo Pasvolsky, *War Debts and World Pros-
perity*, pp. 155–56; *Parliamentary Papers*, 1923, Cmd. 1812, "Inter-Allied
Conferences on Reparations and Inter-Allied Debts, London and Paris, De-
cember 1922 and January 1923"; and Foreign Office minute, "Note on the
Question Raised by Mr. Lloyd George . . . ," 18 January 1924, F.O. file:
C945/70/18.

4. "Treasury Memorandum on Reparations and Inter-Allied Debts," 4
August 1923, F.O. file: C13584/1/18; Foreign Office to the Treasury, 14
November 1923, Treasury to the Foreign Office, 4 January 1924, and Foreign
Office memorandum, 28 January 1924, F.O. file: C19472/1/18.

the reparation schedule, together with responsible European fiscal policies, would "dispose" the American people "to deal generously with the debts in the light of the actual conditions of the debtors."[5]

II

The consensus on war debts and reparations between the governments in London and Washington was paralleled by cooperation between British and American bankers in advancing the private approach to European recovery. The leading institutions in this cooperation were the House of Morgan, its London affiliate, Morgan, Grenfell & Co., the New York Federal Reserve Bank, and the Bank of England. Morgan & Co. had enjoyed historically close connections with the major British and Continental banks. It had acted as the United States purchasing agent for the British and French governments during the war and, in 1919, had become the fiscal agent for the British Treasury in the United States. This fortified Morgan's support for cooperation with its Continental counterparts in stabilizing Europe through private financial channels. For their part, central bankers Benjamin Strong and Montagu Norman appreciated the connection between continental recovery and prosperity in Great Britain and the United States. And both were firm believers that the quasi-governmental central banks should remain above "political" considerations and cooperate in promoting world stability on a purely economic basis.[6]

Accordingly, private and central bank cooperation characterized the negotiations leading up to the Austrian reconstruction plan in 1923. The background for this dated back to the war period, when the Bank of England assumed liability for the commercial bills accepted by the Anglo-Austrian Bank of Vienna. Reorganized as a British institution after the war, this bank helped to restore London's financial position on the Continent and stimulated British interest in Central European reconstruction. Already in 1919, British officials were discussing private and governmental assistance for Austria, with one scheme calling for a commercial syndicate to

5. Charles Evans Hughes to Henry Fletcher, American Ambassador, Belgium, 17 August 1923, and Hughes to the British Chargé, 15 October 1923, in *Foreign Relations, 1923*, 2 vols., vol. 2, pp. 67, 70–73.
6. Carl P. Parrini, *Heir to Empire: United States Economic Diplomacy, 1916–1923*, pp. 55–57; Strong to Norman, 22 November 1918 and 21 March 1921, and Norman to Strong, 11 December 1918, Benjamin Strong-Montagu Norman Correspondence.

aid Austria in return for a mortgage on real and personal property and control of the Austrian railways. British assistance, it was hoped, would stymie Bolshevik expansion, discourage a union between Austria and Germany, and, most important, secure for Great Britain a significant commercial and financial influence in Central Europe. "By this means," as one British official explained, "we should control the key to the East." But unstable conditions in Austria discouraged private investors, and, at the same time, Great Britain's weakened financial position made it difficult for the British Treasury to assume new liabilities on behalf of the Austrian government.[7]

These factors fostered British interest in a financial scheme that would stabilize Austria's credit and encourage participation by American banks in the private financing of Austrian recovery. This interest became particularly pronounced in 1921, leading to a plan composed by the League of Nations for reconstructing Austria. In January, the British presented the Austrian case at an Allied conference in Paris. They wanted a stabilization scheme devised by private experts and founded on business principles. As they saw it, this would clear the way for private investment in Austrian recovery. Initially at least, the French demanded government credits and a plan devised and controlled by the Allies through the Reparation Commission. In March, however, Allied financial delegates meeting in London accepted the British proposal, agreed to release the liens on Austrian assets awarded the Allied governments under the Treaty of St. Germain, and urged the financial section of the League of Nations to implement a scheme for Austrian stabilization.[8]

As suggested at the London meeting, the League plan called for

7. Colonel Cuninghame (Vienna) to Arthur Balfour, 17 July 1919, Foreign Office memorandum by Howard Smith, 15 August 1919, C. K. Butler (Vienna) to Lord Charles Hardinge, 13 October 1919, and Hardinge to Butler, 25 October 1919, in *Documents on British Foreign Policy*, Series 1, vol. 6 (London, 1956), pp. 84–85; 153–56; 287–88, 307–8; and Henry Clay, *Lord Norman*, p. 179.

8. Clay, *Lord Norman*, pp. 180–84; "Proceedings of the Second Conference of Paris, January 1921," and "Proceedings of the Third Conference of London, March 1921," in *Documents on British Foreign Policy*, Series 1, vol. 15, pp. 20–28, 411–30, 444–47; Foreign Office memorandum, 14 March 1921, Foreign Office minute by Sidney Waterlow, Central Department, 8 March 1921, and "Statement Read to the Austrian Minister Respecting Relief of Austria," 22 March 1921, all in F.O. file: C5371/C5374/C5567/75/3; "Parliamentary Question: Government Response to a Question by Lord Parnoor

suspending the Allied liens on Austrian assets, pledging these assets as security against private foreign credits, and appointing a neutral agent to supervise Austrian loans and budgetary reforms. But this plan was scrapped because the Italians now refused to release their Austrian liens, objected to a genuinely independent supervisory agency, and insisted on an Allied control commission under Italian leadership and with complete authority over the Austrian economy.[9] The Italians could not "afford to run Austria themselves," complained Harold Nicolson of the Foreign Office, so they wanted the "other Powers to run her but under Italian direction." Their proposal, he warned, was a dangerous proposition; it would "arouse the apprehensions of the little entente," threaten central European stability, and deliver an "undeserved and gratuitous slight to the League of Nations."[10] For officials in the British Treasury and the Bank of England, it would also discourage private bankers, especially in the United States and the former neutral countries, from underwriting the Austrian stabilization scheme. The Americans, noted Basil Blackett of the British Treasury, would "look askance at any Commission appointed by or representing the Entente Powers being entrusted with the task of supervising Austrian finances."[11] It was much better, the British Cabinet decided, to have the scheme directed by "some international body" or neutral power if "substantial financial assistance" from private bankers was to be forthcoming.[12]

The next stage was a plan initiated by Norman for a central bank concert to devise a formula for eastern European reconstruction.

---

by the Earl of Crawford, First Commissioner of Works," 4 November 1921, F.O. file: C21113/75/3; and Foreign Office, "Memorandum on the Austrian Situation," 9 August 1922, F.O. file: C11425/74/3.

9. Lord Hardinge to the Foreign Office, 1 July 1921, Italian Ambassador to the Foreign Office, 19 June 1922, Foreign Office minute by Basil Barber, Second Assistant Secretary of State, 26 June 1922, and Milne Cheetham to the Foreign Office, 24, 28 June 1922, F.O. file: C13607/C8832/C9075/C9289/74/3.

10. Foreign Office minute by Harold Nicolson, 26 June 1922, F.O. file: C8832/74/3.

11. Basil Blackett of the British Treasury to A. M. Cadogan of the Foreign Office, 21 June 1921, F.O. file: C12842/75/3. See also Blackett to the Foreign Office, 10 July 1922, and memorandum by Blackett, n.d., F.O. file: C9866/C13045/74/3; Norman to Strong, 14, 23 May and 9 June 1921, and Strong to Norman, 2, 13 June 1921, Strong-Norman Correspondence.

12. Extract of minutes of the Cabinet, 30 June 1921, F.O. file: C13651/75/3.

The proposed coalition was to be led by the Bank of England and the New York Federal Reserve Bank. Accordingly, Strong sent an agent to investigate conditions in Vienna while the Austrian Minister of Finance journeyed to London and Paris to mobilize support for the proposal.[13] In November 1921, however, when Hughes vetoed the Hoover-Strong proposal for a central bank conference, Norman's plan folded. "Between the lines," Strong wrote Norman, "I read that there would in fact be no objection if the matter were undertaken privately and without governmental support or responsibility." But as Norman admitted, the scheme did not meet this standard; it was intended by the French and Italians "to rely upon political support from the Entente" with "ultimate power" in their hands.[14]

The following December, the idea of an Anglo-American partnership reappeared, to be organized now at the private level. The British government approached the House of Morgan about a private loan to the Austrian government. The loan was to be floated on the London and New York markets using the famous Gobelin tapestries as security. Morgan & Co. expressed interest but was hesitant to act without an official request from the Allied and United States governments. Although the British quickly complied, Secretary of State Hughes worried that such a governmental initiative might exert undue influence in what "must necessarily be a private banking matter." Instead, a promise not to oppose the loan was as far as he would go.[15] This apparently satisfied Morgan because in May negotiations began in London between representatives of the Austrian Ministry of Finance, the Anglo-Austrian Bank, directors of the Bank of England, Lamont of Morgan & Co., and representatives of Morgan, Grenfell. Subsequently, Lamont approached the leading London investment houses concerning their participation in an Austrian loan to be floated on the New York and London markets. Prior to making a decision, however, the Anglo-American group sent G. M. Young, a British subject and

13. Strong to Hughes, 24 September 1921, enclosing Piere Jay to Strong, n.d., RG 59, file, 863.51/366.

14. Strong to Norman, 1 November 1921, and Norman to Strong, 14 November 1921, Strong-Norman Correspondence.

15. State Department memorandum to the British Embassy, 13 December 1921, Geddes to Hughes, 15 December 1921, Geddes to Morgan & Co., 15 December 1921, Morgan & Co. to Geddes, 20 December 1921, and State Department to the British Embassy, 22 December 1921, all enclosed in Geddes to the Foreign Office, 22 December 1921, F.O. file: C74/74/3.

a director of the Anglo-Austrian Bank, to investigate conditions in
Austria. And when his report proved discouraging, plans for the
loan were abandoned.[16]

The Austrian government then appealed for a reconsideration
of the League scheme at a meeting of Allied representatives in
August 1922. The Allies again referred the matter back to the
League of Nations, and, in September, the League's financial committee offered a formula similar to its earlier proposal, including
reform of the Austrian budget and currency, creation of an independent bank of issue, and provision of adequate collateral for an
external loan. The plan also stipulated that its signatories must "respect the political independence and territorial integrity and
sovereignty of Austria" and "seek no special or exclusive or financial
advantage which would compromise that independence." In order
to insure fulfillment of this stipulation, the scheme was to be ad-
ministered by a politically independent commissioner.[17] In effect,
these provisions would override Italian political considerations and
would place Austrian reconstruction on a business basis as favored
by the British and Americans.

Many of the reforms proposed in the League plan had been implemented by early 1923. Its ultimate success, however, depended
upon cooperative efforts by the bankers in arranging a large private
credit to underwrite the Austrian government. In January, therefore, another meeting of private bankers convened at the Bank of

16. Norman to Strong, 6 March 1922, Strong-Norman Correspondence;
Thomas Lamont to Morgan & Co., 12 May 1922, Lamont to Herman Harjes
of Morgan, Harjes and Co. of Paris, 17 May 1922, and Morgan, Grenfell &
Co. to Baron Frankenstein, Austrian Finance Minister, 22 May 1922, Thomas
Lamont Papers, Series 2, file, 82–17, Austria; H. F. Arthur Schoenfeld, first
secretary of the American Legation, Austria, to Hughes, 24 May 1922 (two
telegrams), J. P. Morgan to Hughes, 5, 8 July 1922, Lamont to Hughes, 3
October 1922, and memorandum "A" enclosed in Lamont to Hughes, 26 January 1923, all in RG 59, file, 863.51/341, 360, 380, 404, 437, 492. A copy
of G. M. Young's final report is enclosed in Morgan & Co. to Hughes, 17 July
1922, RG 59, file, 863.51/387.

17. Aretas Akers-Douglas, British Minister, Vienna, to the Foreign Office,
4 August 1922, "British Secretary's Notes of an Allied Conference at 10 Down-
ing Street," 14 August 1922, Italian Ambassador to Lord Curzon, 16 September 1922, and Owen Phillpotts of the Foreign Office to Akers-Douglas,
20 September 1922, F.O. file: C9866/C11705/C13115/C13399/74/3; Norman to Strong, 15 July and 31 October 1922, and Strong to Norman, 15 November 1922, Strong-Norman Correspondence; Arthur Bliss Lane, secretary
of the American Legation, Berne, Switzerland, to Hughes, 29 August 1922,
James Logan to Hughes, 30 September 1922, and memorandum "A" enclosed
in Lamont to Hughes, 26 January 1923, RG 59, file, 863.51/417, 445, 492.

England to discuss the necessary loan. The plan devised called for a $130 million loan to Austria, guaranteed severally by the governments of Great Britain, Italy, Belgium, and other Continental powers and secured by the customs receipts and tobacco monopoly revenue of Austria.[18] The British already had announced their decision to guarantee 20 percent of the issue. Support from France, Belgium, and the neutral countries was also forthcoming. And while unhappy with the League program, the Italians finally gave in as well, agreeing to cover up to 16 percent of the loan.[19]

Successful floatation of a large bond issue, it was recognized, would also require access to the New York market, and it was hoped that those features of the League scheme neutralizing Austrian reconstruction had now cleared the way for American participation. Accordingly, the House of Morgan quickly solicited opinion on the loan from the leading New York banks, only to discover that they wanted guarantees beyond those offered by the Continental governments and Austria. On January 26, therefore, Lamont proposed to Hughes that the United States accept a further guarantee. But again he found that official sympathy did not extend this far. At the end of February, Hughes notified Lamont that it was impossible for the government to participate.[20] Subsequent efforts by Lamont to win government assistance were also defeated.[21] And when Morgan & Co., following the usual loan control procedures, asked for approval of the loan as a political proposition, it was simply informed that the State Department offered no objection.[22]

Nevertheless, the Austrian loan was a great success for British

18. Norman to Strong, 27 November 1922, Strong-Norman Correspondence; Morgan, Grenfell & Co. to Morgan & Co., 16 January 1923, Joseph Grew, American Minister, Berne, to Hughes, 6 February 1923, and Lamont to Hughes, 8 February 1923, RG 59, file, 863.51/387, 489, 602.

19. Chancellor of the Exchequer to Arthur Balfour, British representative to the League of Nations, 25 September 1922, Ronald Graham, British Ambassador, Rome, to the Foreign Office, 30 September 1922, Phillpotts to Akers-Douglas, 4 October 1922, and Maurice Hankey, Cabinet Secretary, "Cabinet Memorandum," 13 October 1922, all in F.O. file: C13460/C13684/C13928/C14206/74/3.

20. Norman to Strong, 9 April 1922, Strong-Norman Correspondence; Lamont to Hughes, 26 January 1923, and Hughes to Lamont, 26 February 1923, RG 59, file, 863.51/492, 515b. See also Leland Harrison to Hughes, 5 February 1923, Lamont to Hughes, 8 February 1923, and Arthur N. Young to Harrison, 3 March 1923, RG 59, file, 863.51/496, 602, 493.

21. Lamont to Hughes, 24 April 1923, and Hughes to Lamont, 26 April 1923, Lamont Papers, Series 2, file, 82–18, Austria.

22. Morgan & Co. to Hughes, 9 June 1923, and Harrison to Hughes, 9 June 1923, RG 59, file, 863.51/583, 605.

and American bankers. Morgan & Co. organized a financial syndicate of the major American banks to accept that portion of the loan offered in the United States. Its affiliate, Morgan, Grenfell, led a similar syndicate in London. In the United States the books were opened on the loan on 11 June 1923. And by 10:15 that morning they were filled with subscriptions totaling $125 million, nearly enough to carry the entire Austrian credit and a sum five times larger than that portion of the loan for which American banks were committed.[23]

III

Application of the private approach in Austria was an important victory for the policy of cooperation among multinational, especially Anglo-American, bankers. More important, together with the British debt settlement and the new Anglo-American consensus on reparations, it created the broad base of Anglo-American cooperation upon which a final resolution of the German issue was to be built. Thereafter, British and American officials joined forces and demanded Allied compliance in a revised reparation scheme.

Following the Paris meeting in January 1923, the British worked to mediate the Franco-German dispute, reiterating their opposition to the Ruhr occupation and urging the Germans to abandon passive resistance, reform their fiscal policies, and declare their readiness to meet a revised schedule of payments to be drawn up by private financial authorities. In June, under British guidance, the Germans finally submitted a proposal based on this approach. The Foreign Office submitted the German plan to the Allied governments and, in August, issued a similar proposal of its own, one calling for evacuation of the Ruhr and an "impartial inquiry" into Germany's capacity to pay reparations. Taking a cue from a presidential press statement reviewing United States policy, the British government also notified the State Department that it was ready to cooperate in implementing the proposal for an experts' investigation outlined by Hughes in New Haven the preceding December. In effect, then, the British were acting as agents for Anglo-American policy on the reparation problem. And Hughes's warning that

23. Henry G. Chilton, British Chargé, Washington, to the Foreign Office, 15 June 1923, F.O. file: C10996/16/3; Harrison to Hughes, 11 June 1923, RG 59, file, 863.51/606. "It is Jack Morgan *personally*," Norman wrote Strong, "whom we have to thank for the fact that Austria got money in N. Y." See Norman to Strong, 8 October 1923, Strong-Norman Correspondence.

London's initiative should not convey the impression of "a British-American understanding" only served to underline the new consensus on European reconstruction between the two countries.[24]

At the end of October, Belgium and Italy formally accepted the Anglo-American formula, leaving France isolated. Unhappy with the proposal, the French were also reluctant to accept responsibility for its defeat. In addition, their position was weakened by the general failure of the Ruhr occupation. The cost involved, together with the German program of passive resistance, had touched off a precipitous decline in the value of the franc and increased the French need for foreign credits to bolster their declining currency. Already in 1922, however, Lamont of Morgan & Co., a major American source of credit for the French government, had warned that only a modified French attitude toward the reparation question could win assistance for the flagging franc.[25]

This financial pressure and Germany's decision to abandon passive resistance led the French to suggest a compromise. Under it, the experts' inquiry would be limited either to Germany's immediate capacity to pay or to its capacity over a six-year period. Such a compromise was more apparent than real, however, since the restrictions involved were similar to those confining the examination of the previously unsuccessful bankers' committee led by J. P. Morgan. Accordingly, both the British and United States governments rejected the limitations, whereupon the French accepted but expanded the Anglo-American formula. Convinced that Germany

24. Foreign Office memorandum, "Summary of the Policy of His Majesty's Government from the Paris Conference of January 1923 . . . ," 9 January 1924, F.O. file: C702/C900/70/18; Curzon to the French, Italian, Belgian, and Japanese Ambassadors, 11 August 1923, in *Parliamentary Papers*, 1923, Cmd. 1943, "Correspondence with the Allied Governments Respecting Reparation Payments by Germany," pp. 48–61; and British Chargé to the Secretary of State, 13, 19 October 1923, in *Foreign Relations, 1923*, vol. 2, pp. 68–70. For Hughes's remark see Hughes to George Harvey, 16 October 1923, in *Foreign Relations*, 1923, vol. 2, pp. 73–74.

25. *Foreign Relations, 1923*, vol. 2, pp. 85, 87; Frank C. Costigliola, "The Politics of Financial Stabilization: American Reconstruction Policy in Europe, 1924–1930," pp. 90, 94, 100–101; Melvyn Leffler, "The Struggle for Stability: American Policy Toward France, 1921–1933" (Ph.D. dissertation), p. 102. The British were watching the French financial situation very closely. See Foreign Office, "Memorandum Respecting the French Budgetary Situation," 4 April 1922, F.O. file: C8206/99/18. Already in mid-1922, R. F. Wigram of the Foreign Office had declared that if "the French really want any money, it begins to look as if they had better make their *'beau geste'* fairly soon." See Foreign Office minute by Wigram, 14 June 1922, F.O. file: C8534/99/62.

was failing to tap its available foreign assets to meet reparation payments, they proposed two committees. One was to consider methods for stabilizing Germany, including an adjustment of reparations. Another was to devise means for tabulating the capital that had "escaped from Germany and forcing this capital to return." On December 11, Hughes communicated his acceptance to the French.[26]

Over the next ten months, the first German reconstruction scheme was devised and implemented. In January, a committee of private experts convened under the auspices of the Reparation Commission. Charles G. Dawes, president of the Central Trust Company of Illinois, Owen D. Young, chairman of the board of the General Electric Company of New York, and Henry M. Robinson, president of the First National Bank of Los Angeles, were the American members. By mid-April, an experts' report had been recommended to the Allied governments. It included a new reparation scheme that adjusted payments to accord with the state of Germany's economy. A Transfer Committee chaired by an agent general was to accept reparation payments and transfer them to the Allied governments in a fashion that would not undermine German financial stability. And the members of this committee, while formally appointed by the Reparation Commission, were to be independent financial experts rather than political agents.[27]

In addition to these provisions, a group of British and American banks, led by Morgan & Co., wanted immediate evacuation of the Ruhr and guarantees against unilateral reoccupation by the French in the event of a future German default. These and other conditions, the bankers argued, were necessary to solicit assistance from private investors in underwriting the German economy. At meetings in London in the summer and fall of 1924, British and American officials joined the bankers in urging the French to accept this program. And for their part, the French seemed ready to make the necessary concessions. In June, the more conciliatory Edouard Herriot had succeeded Poincaré as head of the French government. Morgan & Co. also eased French approval with a six-month credit of $100 million to stabilize the franc. And Lamont was now insisting that renewal of the credit together with additional long-

    26. *Foreign Relations, 1923*, vol. 2, pp. 90–107; "The Dawes Plan," [Beeritz Memorandum], Charles Evans Hughes Papers, box 172; and Foreign Office memorandum, 9 January 1924, F.O. file: C702/70/18.
    27. Harold G. Moulton, *The Reparation Plan*, pp. 149–92.

term assistance required French concessions. "I said that sovereignty was dear to the heart of the French people," explained Lamont, "but the Franc was much dearer, as Herriot would find out—too late—to his cost." As a result, a settlement was worked out, which all parties could accept, including a French pledge to evacuate the Ruhr within one year, and provisions making it impossible for the French to act independently in the event of another German default. With support from their governments, then, British and American bankers had their way at the London Conference. For Lamont and Norman, the only disappointment was their subsequent failure to win approval of Dwight Morrow, a Morgan partner, as agent general for reparations, a choice that would have enhanced Morgan's control over the reparations program and would have symbolized the new Anglo-American partnership. But President Coolidge, worried that such an overt link between Wall Street and the reparations program might jeopardize support for the Dawes Plan in Germany and the United States, nominated Owen Young as temporary agent general and former Undersecretary of the Treasury S. Parker Gilbert as his successor.[28]

Despite the favorable arrangements, a dispute over placing Germany's currency on the gold standard nearly destroyed the chances for cooperative action by multinational, especially British and American, bankers in floating a large German reconstruction loan. American experts on the Dawes Commission believed that a gold basis would help to stabilize Germany's currency. It would also promote economic reconstruction by acting as a powerful inducement for other European countries to reform their monetary and fiscal policies and to return to the gold standard. For the Europeans, however, a German gold bank would be a blow to their prestige.

28. Costigliola, "The Politics of Financial Stabilization," pp. 126–37; Stephen V. O. Clarke, *Central Bank Cooperation, 1924–1931*, pp. 45–57; Charles G. Dawes, *A Journal of Reparations*, pp. 159–60; Leffler, "The Struggle for Stability," pp. 111–19; memoranda (2) by Chester Lloyd Jones, American commercial attaché, Paris, 10 January 1924, Owen D. Young Papers, box R–1, file, 13–2–Dawes Plan; Morgan & Co. to Young, 14 April 1924, Young Papers, box R–13–Dawes Plan; and Lamont to Dwight Morrow, 28 July [1924], Lamont Papers, Series 4–C, file, 176–20, Germany and Reparations. The bankers' demands and the close cooperation between British and American bankers, especially Lamont and Norman, during the London negotiations can be traced in the Lamont Papers, Series 4–C, file, 176–8 through 176–24. The bankers' major demands are summarized in Lamont to Prime Minister Theunis of Belgium, 9 August 1924, Lamont Papers, Series 4–C, file, 176–23.

Worse, it might drain gold reserves from European banks still on a paper basis. The British were especially apprehensive about establishing a powerful German rival on the Continent and instead, hoped to gain by having the new German currency put on a sterling-exchange basis. As a result, a great part of Germany's gold reserves would be sent to London, thereby promoting German exchange operations in the London market, raising the value of the pound, and increasing British trade with Germany. On the other hand, since the United States was the only major country on the gold standard, placing German currency on a gold basis would divert the lion's share of German reserves to New York, deflect the commissions on German financing and exchange operations from London to New York, and pressure the British to return pound sterling to the gold standard. Accordingly, when the Americans demanded that German currency be placed on the gold standard, the British experts intimated that the important London banks would not participate in the proposed loan to underwrite the German economy.[29]

In the final days of the debate, however, a compromise was reached. Looking for direction, Young canvassed the opinion of American bankers who indicated a willingness to make concessions in order to avoid a rift that might jeopardize British support for the Dawes loan. As a result, the Dawes report left the issue unresolved, and it was not until later that the directors of the new German bank of issue settled the matter in a fashion largely acceptable to the American experts. By this time, however, the British, with support and assistance from the United States, were laying plans to return sterling to the gold standard. And this move, as Strong had predicted earlier, helped to "solve" the debate over the "supremacy of dollars or sterling" in Germany.[30]

This compromise made cooperation possible at the private level. The House of Morgan again organized an American syndicate to accept the German loan. Yet, despite the success of the Austrian

29. Logan to Hughes, 14 March and 14 April 1924, Young to Hughes, 22 February and 14 April 1924, and Young, "The Question of the Gold Standard in Germany and the Experts' Report," 9 June 1923, RG 59, file, 462.OOR296/213, 223, 268, 285½, 348; Alan Goldsmith, chief, Western European Division, BFDC, to Hoover, 23 April 1924, HHP, Commerce, Official File, box 136; Norman to Strong, 7, 30 January and 16 June 1924, and Strong to Norman, 3 June and 9 July 1924, Strong-Norman Correspondence.

30. In addition to the citations in the preceding note see Clarke, *Central Bank Cooperation*, pp. 60–66; and Strong to Young, 16 July 1924, Young Papers, box R–14.

credit, American bankers worried about the new venture. Writing Hughes in September 1924, Morrow, partner in J. P. Morgan & Co., wondered whether the European economy would collapse if failure to extend the loan undermined the Dawes Plan. He remained especially apprehensive about Germany's willingness to live with the restrictions imposed by the plan. Hughes replied that any failure to execute the proposal would be "disastrous." It would produce "widespread economic distress" from which those "who have substantial interests in this country would not wholly escape." Germany, he assured Morrow, would accept the burden of reconstruction peacefully. But in conformity with the principle of private management, he refused to pledge the government to securing the loan. American bankers, he hoped, would "undertake the participation which the world expects and which is believed to be essential to the success of the plan."[31]

Three weeks later, Morgan & Co., on behalf of the American syndicate and following the usual loan control procedure, applied for the State Department's consent for making the loan. The following day Assistant Secretary Leland Harrison gave a perfunctory two-sentence reply: the Department, he said, "offers no objection" to the transaction.[32] Accordingly on October 15, the Dawes loan was issued. The New York market subscribed to over half of the total credit of $200 million, while London took three-fourths of the balance.[33]

IV

The Dawes Plan and the bankers' loan to Germany were further realizations of the American plan to organize cooperation in European recovery through private programs, arranged by financial experts, and proceeding through normal investment channels. And appropriately enough, they were followed by Anglo-American cooperation in returning sterling to the gold standard. This conformed with Strong's desire to collaborate in schemes designed to

31. Morrow to Hughes, 18 September 1924, and Hughes to Morrow, 19 September 1924, RG 59, file, 462.OOR296/604, 611. President Coolidge, Secretary Andrew Mellon, and Frank Kellogg, the American Ambassador in London, also urged the bankers to make the loan. See Lamont to Morgan & Co., 19 August 1924, and Kellogg to Lamont, 19, 20 August 1924, Lamont Papers, Series 4–C, file, 177–2, Germany and Reparations.

32. J. P. Morgan & Co. to Hughes, 10 October 1924, and Harrison to Morgan & Co., 10 October 1924, RG 59, file, 462.OOR296/653.

33. Clarke, *Central Bank Cooperation*, pp. 67–69.

stabilize key currencies. Such collaboration, as he saw it, would help facilitate European recovery and make New York an international center for long-term lending. If achieved, sterling convertibility would also reverse the flow of gold reserves into the United States and reduce the threat of domestic inflation. Like Norman, moreover, he believed that it would force other countries to return to the gold standard, stabilize international exchanges, and stimulate world trade.

To expedite England's return to gold, therefore, both Strong and Norman had long been talking of a plan based on the manipulation of British and American interest rates. They agreed that interest rates in London should be higher than in New York. This would attract international balances to London, relieve the burden on Britain's balance of payments, and assist England's return to gold. It would also encourage liberal lending by New York and this, in turn, would help to finance European recovery and alleviate the imbalance in international exchange by bringing the dollar into line with other currencies. Because of the conflict between domestic and international demands, however, it was not until 1924 that the Federal Reserve System felt able to adopt a rate policy favorable to both spheres. At that time, signs of impending recession in the United States merged with a new sense of confidence engendered by the Anglo-American debt settlement and the Dawes Plan, making low rates in the American market appropriate for both domestic and international reasons. And by the end of 1924, this policy, along with stabilization efforts in England, had adjusted British and American price levels sufficiently to encourage both Strong and Norman.[34]

Accordingly, during a visit to the United States in January 1925, Norman discussed the possibility of placing sterling on gold with Strong, Morgan, and Secretary of the Treasury Andrew Mellon. All agreed that Britain's failure to convert threatened dangerous consequences. It would be an admission of fundamental monetary disequilibrium that could result in violent exchange fluctuations, a further deterioration of foreign currencies in relation to the dollar, and a rapid movement of the world's gold reserves

---

34. Strong to Norman, 21 February, 3 June, 9 July, and 4 November 1924, and Norman to Strong, 16 June and 16 October 1924, Strong-Norman Correspondence; Lester V. Chandler, *Benjamin Strong, Central Banker*, pp. 297–307; Clay, *Lord Norman*, pp. 140–49; and Clarke, *Central Bank Cooperation*, pp. 72–73, 75–77.

into the United States. This latter would cause credit expansion and price inflation in the United States, and, while the resulting "monetary crisis" might produce a return to the gold standard eventually, stabilization by this route would involve "a period of hardship and suffering and possibly some social and political disorder."[35]

To facilitate England's return to gold they agreed on a general plan for Anglo-American cooperation at both the private and central bank level. Although unable to make binding commitments, Strong and Norman agreed to encourage a proper balance between New York and London interest rates. They also agreed that the New York Federal Reserve Bank would open a $200 million credit in favor of the Bank of England, to be used, if needed, to offset pressure for specie payment in London. The House of Morgan matched this with a $100 million revolving fund established for the Bank of England to meet similar exigencies. Secretary Mellon fully approved of these arrangements, agreeing with Strong that resumption of specie payments by Great Britain was "almost as greatly in the interest of this country as it was in Europe."[36]

The British, or so it seemed at the time, also stood to gain from immediate action. In January 1925, Chancellor of the Exchequer Winston Churchill wrote a long memorandum on the politics of the gold standard for his colleagues in the British Treasury and the Bank of England. Given the "gold glut" in the United States, he pointed out, Americans had an obvious interest in Great Britain's return to the gold standard. At the same time, they were anxious to make their gold holdings "play as powerful and dominant a part as possible" in world affairs. The question, he noted, "is whether our interest is the same." Once England had established a free gold market, he warned, new pressure on sterling might increase bank rates with resulting ill effects on industry and employment. Higher rates could also curb the market for long-term loans and cause a further erosion of London's position as an international financial center. Under these circumstances, he won-

35. Chandler, *Benjamin Strong*, p. 311.
36. Norman to Deputy Governor of the Bank of England Cecil Lubbock, 6 January 1925, Treasury Papers, T172/1500A; Clay, *Lord Norman*, p. 152; Chandler, *Benjamin Strong*, pp. 308–16; Morgan, Grenfell (for J. P. Morgan & Co.) to Chancellor of the Exchequer Winston Churchill, 28 April 1925, Lamont Papers, Series 2, file, 96–13, Great Britain. Negotiations for the credits from Morgan & Co. and the Federal Reserve Bank of New York can be followed in Treasury Papers, file, T172/1500A.

dered if returning to the gold standard truly could be called a "British achievement." Might it not be better, he asked, to continue the "managed finance" that had worked well enough over the previous three years? At the same time, the British government could dump two-thirds of its gold reserve on the American market in payment for war debts, goods, and services. This would exacerbate the gold glut in the United States and compel Americans to accelerate their foreign-loan and investment activities. And this, in turn, would depreciate the dollar and increase the value of the pound.[37]

Churchill had not intended his memorandum as a personal attack on plans to restore sterling convertibility but as an "exercise" designed to elicit a defense of these plans from his associates. This defense was quickly forthcoming in a torrent of long rejoinders by Norman, Bradbury, Controller of Finance Otto Niemeyer, and R. G. Hawtrey of the British Treasury. According to them, Great Britain, as well as the United States, had a deep interest in sterling's return to gold. Continuing the present "managed finance," Bradbury warned, would produce an "appreciable setback in the exchange value of the pound" and a severe, but necessary, credit restriction. Still worse, Niemeyer asserted, it would be a great "setback to financial reconstruction," one accompanied by a "world wide opinion that Great Britain did not really mean to return to gold," and the probability that it "would not for a generation be *able* to return to gold." To be sure, higher rates might be necessary to maintain parity. But in the long run, they contended, sterling convertibility would be advantageous to British industry and commerce. It would eliminate fluctuating exchanges that hampered British exporters and reestablish London as an international center for short-term financing. For them, moreover, any decline in London's status as a center for long-term lending would not be the product "of a golden 1925" but of a war that had left Great Britain "relatively poor." Even should higher rates in London than in New York cause a further decline in this status, Norman still maintained that the "interest" of the United States in such a policy was "identical with that of Great Britain and the world." At any rate, Niemeyer explained, the results would be the same if Great Britain did not establish a free gold market. British bankers, he argued, were "*over-lending*" anyway, and the gold standard would help to cor-

37. Churchill, "Exercise," 29 January 1925, Treasury Papers, T172/1499B.

rect this. In addition, both Norman and Niemeyer were sanguine about London's chances of recouping its former prestige. Sterling's convertibility, they believed, together with the long experience of British banking, would eventually restore London's weakened position. And in the meantime, Niemeyer did not "fear that we shall not get quite as many foreign (and Dominion) loans as we wish: and nothing could be more desirable than that [the] United States take some" as well.

Nor did these officials feel that Americans were pursuing a purely selfish policy either at home or abroad. Like themselves, they argued, American leaders were convinced that restoration of the gold standard, in England and in Europe, would facilitate financial reconstruction. Norman reminded Churchill that British experts had insisted on currency stabilization in the Austrian, Hungarian, and German reconstruction schemes. So could they now complain "if the U. S. approves in our case the very same course which we had required in other cases?" Far from being selfish, he stressed that the Federal Reserve Board had followed an "astute" policy that prevented undesirable inflation in the United States, "permitted general stability," and "given time for reconstruction to begin." Any other policy, he argued, "would have reduced most of Europe to medievalism." Accordingly, neither he nor Niemeyer favored an attack on the Federal Reserve Board's financial position by heavy shipments of England's metallic reserves to the United States. Such a maneuver would only discredit the pound at home, further destabilize the exchange, and shift the world's financial center "permanently and completely from London to New York."[38]

For these officials, then, British and American interests largely coincided. And for them, the gold standard diplomacy of both countries served the best interest of the world as well. Only Niemeyer's complaint about the superfluous nature and harsh terms of the dollar credits arranged by Morgan and Strong for the Bank of England disturbed the harmony of their views.[39] Indeed, their detailed expositions even overwhelmed the irascible Chancellor of

38. Niemeyer, commentary on Churchill's "Exercise," n.d., Norman, commentary on Churchill's "Exercise," 2 February 1925, R. G. Hawtrey, "The Gold Standard," 2 February 1925, Bradbury, commentary on Churchill's "Exercise," 5 February 1925, and Niemeyer, "The Gold Standard and the Balance of Payments," n.d., all in Treasury Papers, T172/1499B.

39. On this dispute see Niemeyer to Deputy Governor Cecil Lubbock, 9 January 1925, Niemeyer to Norman, 8 December 1924 and 16 March 1925, Treasury Papers, T172/1500A.

the Exchequer. Early in February 1925, Churchill wrote Niemeyer that "your papers and the report" of a special British Treasury committee urging restoration of gold parity had "marshalled for the first time . . . arguments for the policy you advocate" and provided "a solid foundation both of argument and authority justifying the action proposed."[40] Later, when John Maynard Keynes warned that gold parity might produce higher interest rates and exacerbate England's unemployment problem, Niemeyer quickly circulated a private rebuttal. And while Churchill sympathized with Keynes's fear, he again admitted that Niemeyer's arguments were persuasive.[41] Accordingly, England returned to the gold standard in the spring of 1925, and, throughout that year at least, Churchill played a central role in defending this action both in Parliament and throughout the country.[42]

V

The Austrian, German, and British stabilization schemes, and the successful cooperative efforts by private and central bankers in achieving them, led to a series of subsequent initiatives to reinstate the gold standard across Europe. The whole process was designed to rationalize and stabilize international finance through cooperative programs, organized and led by financial experts, and supposedly divorced from political considerations. Americans had long advocated this program as the basis for European recovery. And it was this program that they now celebrated. "Many of us have realized from the days of the armistice," Hoover remarked shortly after the Dawes Commission had adjourned, "that there were economic issues born of the war for which no solution was possible until time and bitter experience" allowed a settlement

40. Churchill to Niemeyer, 6 February 1925, Treasury Papers, T172/1499B. Churchill had also solicited the opinion of Austen Chamberlain, head of the special Treasury Committee, who staunchly endorsed a return to the gold standard. See Chamberlain to Churchill, 8 February 1925, Treasury Papers, T172/1499B.

41. See John Maynard Keynes, "The Return Towards Gold," in *The Nation & The Athenaeum*, 21 February 1925, copy in Treasury Papers, file, T172/1499B; commentary by Niemeyer, 21 February 1925, and Churchill to Niemeyer, 22 February 1925, Treasury Papers, T172/1499B.

42. See for example Churchill's presentation in the House of Commons, 5 August 1925; *The Sheffield Telegraph*, 4 November 1925; and "Mr. Churchill in Edinburgh," *The Times*, 14 November 1925, all in Treasury Papers, T172/1520.

"founded solely upon economic ground" rather than "political considerations." The United States government's great contribution to "disinterested statesmanship," he continued, was in launching this movement for "economic peace." And the "unofficial mission of disinterested private citizens" in the Dawes Commission, "giving as it did a setting free" from "political relations," further "strengthened these forces." It was, he concluded, "a peace mission without parallel in international history."[43]

An emerging Anglo-American economic entente had made it possible to implement the American program. This entente was reflected in central and private bank cooperation, and in a common British and American approach to the important issues of war debts and reparations. The new entente first appeared in January 1923 with the opening of negotiations leading to an Anglo-American debt settlement, with the initiation of private banker discussions on the Austrian loan, and with the British presentation of a revised reparation scheme to the meeting of the Allied Premiers in Paris. Through cooperation and compromise, then, the United States and Great Britain had submerged originally conflicting goals in a new pattern of rapprochement.

43. Address of Secretary Herbert Hoover at a dinner given to Owen Young by the businessmen of New York City, 1 December 1924, HHP, Commerce, Personal File, box 75.

CHAPTER 5

Private Management and
the Problem of Foreign Loan Supervision

The business approach to foreign investment that was implemented in Europe was also applied in other areas of the world where American and multinational bankers were cooperating to stimulate the constructive development favored by the United States. Under this approach, banking officials became the agents for regulating capital exports without excessive government interference. Instead, the system of banker supervision was to be paralleled by voluntary business-government collaboration to insure the reproductive use of scarce capital resources. At both the national and international levels, it was hoped, such cooperation would limit the need for politically dangerous and economically wasteful government intervention, increase the sum of capital available for investment, foster economic growth, and guarantee world peace.

In applying this program internationally, however, it proved difficult to reconcile conflicting tendencies towards nationalism and internationalism, state management and business self-regulation. American bankers were ready to collaborate with their foreign, especially British, counterparts in developing cooperative structures for managing international finance and investment. But they soon resented even the mild form of government supervision implied in the domestic loan control program. Instead of enlightened self-regulation and government-banker cooperation, they often reverted to undisciplined and competitive activity. At the same time, other factions demanded more vigorous government regulation in order to guarantee quality investment abroad, expand American commerce, and avoid military entanglements. The loan control program thus demonstrates the mixture of public and private cooperation that characterized American efforts to regulate the international economy, a mixture in this case largely unacceptable to the parties involved and one that eventually proved unworkable.

I

Americans were anxious to use their surplus capital to stimulate world development and to promote the export trade. In particular, they wanted to forge the kind of foreign investment system used by the British to foster the export of British technology. Prior to the war, British bankers had over two thousand branch banks scattered throughout the world, cooperating with British merchants and investment houses in developing and financing foreign trade. In addition, the London bill discount market was generally used to finance day-to-day commercial transactions across the globe, making London the "financial center" of the world's trade. As American exporters saw it, by creating similar mechanisms the United States could challenge London's centripetal pull on international commerce, extend American trade and investment, and foster world development.[1]

Accordingly, exporters had long campaigned for a banking system that could be used to promote foreign trade and investment. And in 1913, they had won an important victory when Congress passed the Federal Reserve Act. It had allowed national banks, with the approval of the Federal Reserve Board, to establish foreign branches. And it had provided for a bill discount market in the United States that was essential for financing short-term import and export transactions.[2]

After the war, however, this system was inadequate to meet the heavy demands on American capital. European nations now turned to the United States for financial assistance in reconstruction while underdeveloped countries looked largely to American banks for the money needed to stimulate internal improvement. These demands, as the bankers saw it, could not be met entirely through individual initiatives. The risks involved in foreign lending, the large

1. Carl P. Parrini, *Heir to Empire: United States Economic Diplomacy, 1916–1923*, p. 43; and Federal Trade Commission, *Report on Cooperation in the American Export Trade*, pp. 29–30.

2. Clyde William Phelps, *The Foreign Expansion of American Banks*, pp. 131–66; and Cleona Lewis, *America's Stake in International Investments*, pp. 191–98.

amounts of capital required to underwrite many foreign-trade transactions, and the need to commit this capital over long periods of time all called for cooperative financing. This was especially important in financing the export of capital goods needed in Europe. For this, importers required credit terms of five years or more. Yet, neither the Federal Reserve Act, nor an amendment to the act in 1916, had permitted American banks to engage in international finance as well as banking.[3]

Congress rectified the bankers' problem with new legislation after the war. In 1919, it amended the Federal Reserve Act to allow foreign subsidiaries of national banks to engage in international finance. Later that year, it also passed the Edge Act, which authorized federal charters for short-term and long-term debenture issuing foreign investment corporations. By permitting American bankers and manufacturers to combine in these investment cooperatives, the Edge Act allowed them to increase the capital available for investment while spreading the risk involved. Under its provisions, for example, these combines were required to have a minimum capital stock of $2 million but could lend up to ten times the capital and surplus borrowed from investors who purchased their debentures in the American market.[4]

If the heavy demands on American capital required cooperative action, the large stakes involved in satisfying these important obligations seemed to require that distribution of financial resources not be left to untrammeled market forces. For some officials in the Wilson and Harding-Coolidge administrations, the state itself should play an aggressive role in guiding these resources into paths that would maximize development and increase trade. In 1918, for example, the State Department promoted a plan for government management of capital invested in Latin American development. It would permit the United States to accept Latin-American bonds held by the Allied governments as payment for their war debts, would bind the Treasury Department to guarantee new Latin-American issues by United States banks, and would require the Latin-American governments involved to institute sound monetary reforms as a condition for additional assistance from the United States.[5] The scheme, its advocates claimed, would eliminate "for-

3. Burton I. Kaufman, "The Organizational Dimension of United States Economic Foreign Policy, 1900–1920," pp. 42–43.

4. Ibid.; Lewis, *America's Stake in International Investments*, p. 195; and Parrini, *Heir to Empire*, pp. 80–81.

5. Jeremiah Jenks (financial adviser to the State Department), "Financial

eign influences" from the hemisphere, stabilize Latin-American currencies, and encourage private investment and the expansion of United States trade in the region.[6] Later, Secretary of Commerce William Redfield proposed government control and rationing of capital that was needed for European reconstruction. This control he insisted, would be necessary to insure that capital resources be equitably distributed and contributed alike to world recovery and United States expansion.[7] And in 1921, the State Department considered another scheme based on a government guarantee for private capital invested in Central America. Designed to eliminate "European influence in the government finances of the Central American Republics," it also sought to encourage investors in the United States and to "effect through the medium of American loans urgently needed financial reforms and public improvements."[8]

The loan control procedure finally adopted, however, rejected state management and preference in favor of business self-regulation and informal business-government cooperation. Under it, the State, Commerce, and Treasury departments were to evaluate the political merits of loan propositions, leaving the bankers responsible for their business virtues. The government's function, moreover, was to be completely advisory, and the bankers were to act as the ultimate regulators of capital exports for both public and private purposes.

A group of leading bankers accepted such an arrangement after two White House meetings in May and June 1921.[9] Confusion

Assistance to Certain Latin American Countries," 1918, RG 59, file, 811.51/2058; and Joseph Tulchin, *The Aftermath of War: World War I and U.S. Policy Toward Latin America*, pp. 156–57.

6. Jenks, "Financial Assistance," 1918; Glenn Stewart, Latin American Division, memorandum, 4 March 1918; Frank Polk, Assistant Secretary of State, to the Secretary of the Treasury, 3 April and 8 August 1918, and Albert Strauss, Assistant Secretary of the Treasury, to Assistant Secretary of the Treasury Russell Leffingwell, 21 August 1918, enclosed in Leffingwell to Polk, 24 August 1918, all in RG 59, file, 811.51/2058, 267, 417a, 616a, 2063.

7. William Redfield to President Woodrow Wilson, 11 November 1918, RG 40, file, 77977.

8. Morton D. Carrel, Latin American Division, to Sumner Welles of the Latin American Division, 29 September 1921, RG 59, file, 811.51/2981; and Dana G. Munro, Latin American Division, to Welles, 9 November 1921, RG 59, file, 813.51/5.

9. J. P. Morgan of Morgan & Co. to President Warren G. Harding, 6 June 1921, and Mortimer Schiff of Kuhn, Loeb & Co. to Harding, 6 June 1921, RG 59, file, 811.51/2981. See also the list of invitations and replies in the Herbert Hoover Papers, HHPL, Commerce, Official File, box 129.

quickly arose, however, over the method for giving effect to the White House understanding. Officials in the Treasury Department were ready to let banker-government contact center on the State Department. But Secretary of Commerce Herbert Hoover envisioned a central role for his agency. He had already established a Finance and Investment Division in the Bureau of Foreign and Domestic Commerce, and he was especially anxious for the new division to consider the relationship between private loans and American foreign trade. The resulting conflict left the bankers confused about which department to consult, and by late 1921 they had begun to ignore their original promise to seek government consent for proposed transactions.[10]

In December, therefore, Secretary of State Charles Evans Hughes sent Hoover and Secretary of the Treasury Andrew Mellon a proposed press release designed to clarify the procedure for banker-government cooperation.[11] The announcement disavowed government responsibility for the financial merits of particular ventures, reaffirmed the voluntary character of the White House understanding, and made the State Department the primary agency for banker-government consultation. Mellon endorsed the statement, especially the stipulation against government responsibility for loan transactions as business propositions.[12] And while Hoover objected to the press release, he too favored private rather than state management of American loans. For him, however, a public announcement of the loan control procedure would force bankers to advise borrowers and subscribers that the government had passed upon the merits of the loan. To the investing public, he feared, this would imply a measure of official responsibility and control over the transaction as a business proposition. To avoid this dilemma and make his agency the main vehicle for banker-government contact, he proposed securing the bankers' cooperation through private negotiations conducted by the Commerce Department. Acting independently, he already had established an informal liaison with the banking community through the American Bankers Association. And in December 1921, he met with a group

10. Memorandum by Foreign Trade Adviser W. W. Cumberland, 6 September 1921, RG 59, file, 811.51/2981; S. Parker Gilbert, Assistant Secretary of the Treasury, to Governor Benjamin Strong, 21 May 1921, RG 56, box 83, file, Foreign Trade; and Tulchin, *Aftermath of War,* pp. 177–78.

11. Charles Evans Hughes to Andrew Mellon and Hughes to Herbert Hoover, 7 December 1921, RG 59, file, 811.51/2981.

12. Mellon to Hughes, 9 December 1921, RG 59, file, 811.51/3045.

of New York bankers to mobilize their support for this informal arrangement.[13]

Yet officials in the State Department remained adamant. The bankers were concluding transactions without official sanction, they pointed out, and the proposed announcement would revitalize the White House understanding. It would also clarify the department's role, and this was especially desirable since the government might later be called upon to protect the bankers' investments. In their opinion, moreover, the wide press coverage given to Hoover's meeting with the bankers had undermined the credibility of his argument for keeping consultation on a private basis. Accordingly, Hughes was determined to issue the press statement but at the same time tried to satisfy Hoover's objections. The announcement, he insisted again, would not only eliminate existing confusion concerning the procedure for government-banker cooperation, it would also make clear that administration approval did not imply government responsibility for any transaction.[14]

When the press statement was finally released in March 1922, it rested firmly on this division of public and private responsibility and the policy of business self-regulation. The State Department, it acknowledged, lacked the legal authority to require reports on foreign transactions, and the bankers were requested to volunteer the necessary information. The government would then determine if a loan violated public policy. But as the bankers were reminded, this did not entail a judgment concerning the business virtues of the loan. Nor did it imply government responsibility for the transaction, and bankers were cautioned against conveying this impression to borrowers and subscribers.[15]

United States loan policy, then, rejected both rigorous state management and thoroughgoing business individualism. Instead, American officials favored cooperative action by bankers along with business-government consultation in directing capital into the kinds of constructive enterprises that would "promote our ex-

13. Hoover to Hughes, 14, 30 December 1921, RG 59, file, 811.51/3044.

14. Assistant Secretary of State Leland Harrison to Hughes, 23 January 1922, RG 59, file, 800.51/306; Harrison to Hughes and Under Secretary of State Henry Fletcher, 16 January 1922, Economic Adviser Arthur N. Young, "Attitude of the Department Toward Foreign Loans: Proposed Public Statement," 1 February 1922, and Hughes to Hoover, 24 December 1921, RG 59, file, 811.51/3107, 3108, 3044.

15. A copy of the statement is printed in *Foreign Relations, 1922*, vol. 1, pp. 556–58.

ports, increase the productivity of foreign lands, increase their standard of living, and increase their buying power."[16] For the men involved, moreover, there could be a similar approach in the international sphere. Multinational financial arrangements could be devised that would prevent wasteful lending, channel capital resources into reproductive undertakings, and avoid the political complications involved in aggressive and state-managed foreign investment programs. In both China and Europe, however, this approach would founder on the inability of American bankers and exporters to submerge their divergent interests in cooperative programs. The bankers often were reluctant to undertake the kind of responsible investment programs that government officials considered essential to achieve peace and stability. And as for the exporters, they were unwilling to subsume short-term national gains within the larger vision of peaceful growth and prosperity for all.

II

Developments in China revealed the American plan for constructive cooperation among multinational bankers rather than excessive competition or politically dangerous government intervention. For both American and British policymakers, financial cooperation at the private level, together with informal political collaboration between the governments in Washington and London, could eliminate destabilizing economic conflict, safeguard American and British interests, and, most important, control aggressive Japanese imperialism. The second China financial consortium, organized during the Wilson administration, institutionalized the private approach to loan regulation in the Far East. And under the Republicans, the Washington Conference treaties provided additional abutments for this private structure of cooperation.

The background for this dated back to 1913, when President Woodrow Wilson withdrew support from the American bankers in the first financial consortium in order to prevent American capital from becoming involved in the division of China into special spheres of influence. Subsequently, Wilson had attempted to main-

16. Herbert Hoover, *The Memoirs of Herbert Hoover*, vol. 2, p. 89. See also Robert E. Olds, Assistant Secretary of State, "Foreign Loans," 12 October 1925, RG 59, file, 800.51/561.

tain an Open Door for American commerce and to defend China's economic and territorial integrity against rising Japanese ambitions. By late 1917, however, this competitive posture seemed increasingly untenable. The United States and Japan were now allies and, as Secretary of State Robert Lansing saw it, a new rapprochement would help to solidify Japan's commitment to the wartime coalition and protect America's weakened diplomatic position in the East. Accordingly, he urged a reluctant Wilson to accept Japan's claim to a special position in China in return for Japanese recognition of the Open Door.[17]

If Lansing's pleas suggested a paradox similar to Theodore Roosevelt's readiness, apparent in the Root-Takahira Agreement, to rely on Japanese beneficence for protection of the Open Door, then his second proposal recalled President William Howard Taft's attempt to contain Russian and Japanese imperialism through the pooling arrangements of the first financial consortium. Lansing wanted to create a new international consortium; a cooperative financial structure, in other words, that could regulate Japanese expansion by providing a multinational system for supervising loan transactions. This was especially desirable since Germany, the United States, and Russia were now out of the original consortium, the capital resources of France and Great Britain were committed to the war and, as a result, Japan had been left with a monopoly over loans to China. Beyond this, officials like Colonel House envisaged a cooperative effort by Japan, the United States, and the Entente to rationalize competition in the Orient and regulate development of the China market on an equitable basis.[18]

These plans peaked in the last year of the war. Under the Lansing-Ishii Agreement of November 1917, the United States accepted Japan's special interest in northern China and Manchuria in exchange for Japanese recognition of the Open Door and the territorial integrity of China.[19] Subsequently, Wilson invited

17. Robert Lansing's views had crystallized as early as the Twenty-one Demands crisis of 1915 and were presented again at the outset of the Lansing-Ishii discussions in 1917. See Burton F. Beers, *Vain Endeavor: Robert Lansing's Attempts to End the American-Japanese Rivalry*, pp. 36–51, 102–3, 108–9.

18. Beers, *Vain Endeavor*, pp. 141–42; N. Gordon Levin, Jr., *Woodrow Wilson and World Politics: America's Response to War and Revolution*, pp. 113–14; and Charles Seymour, ed., *The Intimate Papers of Colonel House*, vol. 3, p. 25.

19. See Beers, *Vain Endeavor*, pp. 109–19 for negotiation of the Lansing-Ishii Agreement. See also Levin, *Wilson and World Politics*, p. 114; and Roy

American bankers to reenter a revitalized international financial consortium. The new consortium, it was hoped, would neutralize China for development.[20] Under it, American banks would subsidize British and French participation, and, in turn, the Allies would "withdraw their claims to spheres of influence," giving the United States a three-to-one vote against Japan in favor of the Open Door.[21] Moreover, all loans to China were to be pooled and placed under joint management by the national groups, with each group submitting proposed transactions to its government. In theory, this system of multinational banker regulation and banker-government consultation would allow the United States to prevent a division of China into separate economic spheres and to insure reproductive rather than political investment. These results, in turn, would enhance China's potential as a market and contribute to its political and economic stability. Cooperation on this basis, so it seemed to Americans, would preserve and develop China as a market for American exporters while avoiding the antagonism and conflict that resulted from independent political and economic action.[22]

At a meeting in Paris in mid-May 1919, private American, British, Japanese, and French bankers organized a new consortium

Watson Curry, *Woodrow Wilson and Far Eastern Policy, 1913–1921*, pp. 177–85.

20. The State Department's negotiations with the American bankers can be followed in *Foreign Relations, 1918*, pp. 169–73. See also Alfred Whitney Griswold, *The Far Eastern Policy of the United States*, pp. 208–13; Levin, *Wilson and World Politics*, p. 115; Beers, *Vain Endeavor*, pp. 142–46; and Curry, *Wilson and Far Eastern Policy*, pp. 188–98.

21. Lansing to Wilson, 20 June 1918, in *Foreign Relations, 1918*, pp. 169–71. See also Breckenridge Long, Third Assistant Secretary of State, to Lansing, 12 February 1919, RG 59, file, 893.51/1894.

22. American Group to Secretary of State Lansing, 8 July 1918, Lansing to the American Group, 9 July 1918, Lansing to Walter Hines Page, American Ambassador to Great Britain, 11 July 1918, J. V. A. MacMurray, Far Eastern Division, to Lansing, 6 August 1918, Polk to MacMurray, 10 August 1918, and Lansing to the French Ambassador, 8 October 1918, in *Foreign Relations, 1918*, pp. 172–77, 186–87, 188, 193–95; unsigned memorandum, 20 March 1917, Long, "Memorandum of a Conversation with American Bankers," 26 June 1918, Wilson to Lansing, 22 August 1918, enclosing "Memorandum on Chinese Finance" by Paul Reinsch, American Minister to China, 24 August 1918, Lansing to Colville Barclay, British Embassy, 8 October 1918, and Long, "Memorandum of a Conversation with Frank Vanderlip," 19 December 1918, all in RG 59, file, 893.51/2008, 1916½, 1979, 2039a, 2086.

that embodied the American program. The bankers agreed to pool all existing and future options on public loan issues except those for industrial projects already under construction. In addition, the American and Japanese bankers agreed to carry the European share during the period of financial stringency following the war. The British and French governments endorsed this arrangement, provided the bankers modified a provision concerning the degree of diplomatic support promised by each government to its group within the consortium. The original proposal had called for exclusive support, a provision the British Foreign Office, in particular, refused to accept so long as its group did not represent all British bankers interested in loans to China. A compromise formula was soon worked out—one the Europeans agreed to endorse, even though it deviated little from the original provision. Under it, the governments promised "collective support" for the consortium in the event of competition from outside interests.[23]

At this point, however, the Japanese government refused to support the consortium agreement unless it incorporated that provision in the Lansing-Ishii Agreement recognizing Japan's special interest in China. Specifically, the Japanese wanted to exclude South Manchuria and eastern Inner Mongolia from the pooling arrangements. They argued that this provision was necessary in order to protect Japan's vital economic and security interests. For the other governments, however, such exclusions would represent a reversion to the old policy of special spheres of influence. Instead of opening China to the "combined activities of an international group," explained Max Muller of the British Foreign Office, the Japanese plan would "stir up the very difficulties which the consortium is designed to obviate."[24]

Given this Japanese intransigence, a number of American policymakers urged a more competitive program. Worried that protracted discussions might force the Chinese government to negotiate a

23. *Parliamentary Papers 1921*, Cmd. 1214, "Correspondence Respecting the New Financial Consortium in China," pp. 7–35 (hereafter cited as *Parliamentary Papers*, Cmd. 1214); and *Foreign Relations, 1919*, vol. 1, (Washington, D.C., 1934), pp. 435–45, 461–62, 466–70.

24. For Japan's position see *Foreign Relations, 1919*, vol. 1, pp. 451–53, 480; and *Parliamentary Papers*, Cmd. 1214, pp. 29–30. For the American and European response, see *Foreign Relations, 1919*, vol. 1, pp. 453–55, 471–73; *Parliamentary Papers*, Cmd. 1214, pp. 37–38; and *Documents on British Foreign Policy, 1919–1939*, Series 1, vol. 6, pp. 608–9, 629–32, 650.

separate loan with Japanese bankers, they now were ready to form a tripartite consortium that excluded Japan.[25] And if the British and French rejected this approach, one group of officials favored independent action by American bankers.[26] The British agreed that close Anglo-American cooperation was desirable and of "very much greater importance to us than any arrangement with Japan." But they opposed independent action that might endanger the chances for future Japanese collaboration.[27] This attitude, together with the collapse of tentative plans for a separate American loan to China, prevented independent action by the United States, reinvigorated the Anglo-American consensus on the consortium, and made possible a united front against the Japanese.[28] They were ready, both governments now insisted, to exempt from the pooling arrangements all Japanese contracts on which substantial progress had been made. But they would not consent to the geographical exclusion of South Manchuria and eastern Inner Mongolia.[29]

Negotiations remained deadlocked until early 1920, when Thomas Lamont of Morgan & Co., the spokesman for the American Group in the proposed consortium, worked out a compromise that

25. *Foreign Relations, 1919,* vol. 1, pp. 486–87, 493–96; and *Documents on British Foreign Policy,* Series 1, vol. 6, pp. 624–32, 697, 737.

26. For recommendations on independent American action, see Reinsch to Lansing, 18 August 1919, Paul Whitham, Commercial Attaché, China, to Secretary of Commerce Redfield, 20 August 1919, Hugh Marshall, Far Eastern Division, to Lansing, 21 August 1919, and Malcolm Simpson, Secretary of the American Group, to Long, 27 June 1919, all in RG 59, file, 893.51/2372, 2374, 2377, 2288.

27. Sir John Alston to Sir John Tilley, 7 October 1919, British Foreign Secretary Earl Curzon to Sir John Jordan, British Ambassador to Peking, 4 October 1919, Curzon to Edward Grey, 24 October 1919, in *Documents on British Foreign Policy,* Series 1, vol. 6, pp. 755–56, 761–65, 797–99; and *Foreign Relations, 1919,* vol. 1, pp. 491–92, 499.

28. President Wilson originally favored an independent loan to China by the Chicago Continental and Commercial Trust and Savings Bank, but the plan folded when the bank's negotiations with the Chinese government collapsed. See *Foreign Relations, 1919,* vol. 1, pp. 525–32; and *Documents on British Foreign Policy,* Series 1, vol. 6, pp. 799–801, 816–17.

29. Jordon to Curzon, 13 November 1919, Grey to Curzon, 13 November 1919, Curzon to Alston, 20 November 1919, in *Documents on British Foreign Policy,* Series 1, vol. 6, pp. 827–28, 839–43; *Parliamentary Papers,* Cmd. 1214, pp. 37–38; and *Foreign Relations, 1919,* vol. 1, pp. 502–4. The State Department agreed to withhold support from independent American loans to China in favor of a British proposal for a small loan to the Chinese government by British, American, Japanese, and French bankers. The loan was to be made without prejudice to the negotiations regarding a new consortium. See *Documents on British Foreign Policy,* Series 1, vol. 6, pp. 799–801, 816–17; and *Foreign Relations, 1919,* vol. 1, pp. 500–501.

the Japanese agreed to accept. Under the Lamont-Kajiwara accord, Japan decided to pool its China interests with the exception of certain partially developed railway projects in South Manchuria and Mongolia. In return, the British and United States governments assured Japan that action by the new consortium would not compromise its "economic life and national defense," a guarantee later endorsed by the French government as well.[30]

Although the new consortium went a long way toward institutionalizing the Anglo-American program in China, British and American leaders wanted to fortify it with a new cooperative political arrangement for the Pacific. In the spring of 1920, J. Butler Wright, the American chargé in London, discussed with British officials the possibility of closer Anglo-American cooperation along lines "already indicated in the consortium." Shortly thereafter, policymakers in the Foreign Office began a serious reevaluation of the Anglo-Japanese alliance. In June, Victor Wellesley, British Assistant Secretary of State for Far Eastern Affairs, outlined the new developments affecting British policy. As he saw it, Japanese economic penetration in China was "more ruthless, more brutal and more insidious than that employed by Germany" before the war. Unless controlled, this new "Prussian imperialism" would mark a "sad ending to the high-falutin phrases about China's integrity and equal opportunity." He felt that the organization of the consortium had shown how close Anglo-American cooperation could work to restrain Japan and protect the Open Door. And he now wanted to underwrite this system of collaboration at the private level with a new political understanding between the two governments, one based on the principles underlying "our mutual alliance with America" and giving "expression to the similarity of British and American aims in the Far East."[31]

Other important policymakers in both the Foreign Office and

30. The close collaboration and united front maintained by the British and U. S. governments during the negotiations leading up to the Lamont-Kajiwara accord and the final establishment of the consortium in October 1920 can be followed in *Foreign Relations, 1920*, vol. 1, pp. 497–585; *Parliamentary Papers*, Cmd. 1214, pp. 40–47, 49–56; and *Documents on British Foreign Policy*, Series 1, vol. 6, pp. 1045, 1057, 1072–73, and *Documents on British Foreign Policy*, Series 1, vol. 14 (London, 1966), p. 1. For the Lamont-Kajiwara accord see *Foreign Relations, 1920*, vol. 1, pp. 555–57.

31. See Victor Wellesley, memorandum, 1 June 1920, in *Documents on British Foreign Policy*, Series 1, vol. 14, pp. 32–36. For the information on J. Butler Wright's discussions with British officials see *Documents . . .*, Series 1, vol. 14, note 2, p. 32 and note 7, p. 36.

the State Department shared this assessment. For example, during a dinner party at the British Embassy in Washington, Secretary of State Bainbridge Colby, Assistant Secretary Norman Davis, British Ambassador Auckland Geddes, and others all agreed that an Anglo-American understanding in Asia would reinforce the consortium, guarantee Anglo-American naval superiority in the Pacific, and deter Japanese imperialism.[32] The British, however, wanted to include Japan in this understanding. Several alternatives were considered. Wellesley favored renewing the Anglo-Japanese alliance (without a military clause), negotiating a parallel agreement with the United States, and then consolidating the two bilateral treaties into a new multilateral agreement. Charles Eliot wanted to renew the alliance, bring it into harmony with the League of Nations covenant, and rely on a vigorous financial consortium to protect the Open Door. And in Washington, Ambassador Geddes was advocating renewal of the alliance and a parallel executive agreement between the United States and Great Britain affirming the Open Door and pledging Anglo-American naval cooperation in the Pacific.[33]

In January 1921, a special Foreign Office committee studying the Anglo-Japanese alliance provided a more definitive statement of British strategy. According to the committee, the alliance encouraged Japanese actions at variance with British interests, made it difficult to "cultivate the closest relations with the United States," and hampered Anglo-American collaboration in maintaining peace throughout Asia and around the world. The consortium already embodied such collaboration in controlling Japan's economic penetration and fostering a "constructive policy for the rehabilitation of China." And the committee wanted to bolster this private structure by replacing the Anglo-Japanese alliance with a

32. The American Ambassador to Japan and the British Ambassador to China were also present at the dinner meeting. See Sir John Alston, "Memorandum Respecting Conversations at Washington, July 26–27," 1 August 1920, in ibid., pp. 77–80. See also Alston, "Memorandum Respecting Suggestions for an Anglo-Saxon Policy for the Far East," 1 August 1920, in ibid., pp. 81–86.

33. "Memorandum by Wellesley Respecting the Anglo-Japanese Alliance," 1 September 1920, Auckland Geddes to Curzon, 5 November and 3 December 1920, and Eliot to Curzon, 12 December 1920, in ibid., pp. 106–11, 177–78, 187–89, 194–96. For a further elaboration of British attitudes toward the Anglo-Japanese alliance see M. G. Fry, "The North Atlantic Triangle and the Abrogation of the Anglo-Japanese Alliance," pp. 47–49.

new tripartite pact between the United States, Great Britain, and Japan. This pact would reaffirm Anglo-American principles and rely on close Anglo-American cooperation for their support and protection. More important, Anglo-American cooperation in the Pacific could affect the whole range of "world politics, which are dominated by our relations with the United States as constituting the prime factor in the maintenance of order and peace throughout the world."[34]

By 1921, then, British officials were hoping to replace the Anglo-Japanese alliance with a wider system of political cooperation, one founded on close Anglo-American relations and designed to restrain Japan. American officials had similar hopes. For Secretary of State Hughes, as for his predecessors in the Wilson administration, the old alliance encouraged Japanese aggressiveness and threatened the Open Door. And since the United States and Great Britain shared similar beliefs and interests, he expected Great Britain to support American policy. In particular, he counted on "cooperation between Great Britain and the United States" to protect the Open Door and the territorial integrity of China.[35]

This informal understanding set the stage for the Washington Conference of 1921 and 1922, where British and American officials worked successfully to bolster the Open Door basis for cooperation institutionalized in the consortium. Before the conference adjourned, Japan had agreed to return Shantung to China and had signed the Nine Power Treaty recognizing the Open Door. The Five Power Treaty had guaranteed Anglo-American naval supremacy in the Pacific. And Hughes had worked closely with the British to replace the Anglo-Japanese alliance with the Four Power Treaty,

34. Report on the Anglo-Japanese alliance signed by Wellesley, William Tyrrell, Assistant Secretary of State for Foreign Affairs, Jordan, British Ambassador to China, and Conyngham Green, British Ambassador to Japan, 21 January 1921, in *Documents on British Foreign Policy*, Series 1, vol. 14, pp. 221–27. In addition to this internal discussion within the Foreign Office, it should be noted that the British dominions led by Canada were also urging the British government to modify the Anglo-Japanese alliance in favor of Anglo-American cooperation in the Pacific. For somewhat different accounts of opinion in the British dominions and the Imperial Conference of 1921 see Fry, "The North Atlantic Triangle," pp. 46–64; and John Chalmers Vinson, "The Imperial Conference of 1921 and the Anglo-Japanese Alliance," pp. 257–67.

35. "Memorandum of a Conversation Between the Secretary of State and the British Ambassador," 23 June 1921, in *Foreign Relations, 1921*, vol. 2 (Washington, D.C., 1936), pp. 314–16.

a new cooperative political arrangement shorn of all military provisions and balanced by French participation.[36] The "most striking
result of the Conference," as Ambassador Geddes ebulliently reported to London, was "its effect on Anglo-American relations."
The American people, he concluded, had "witnessed the spectacle
of America apparently finding a greater and more sustained support
of her policies from Great Britain than from any other Power."[37]

Despite this success, it proved difficult to bring American exporters into the cooperative framework. They viewed the financial
consortium as a poor vehicle for extending American commerce in
China. In particular, they argued that American bankers connected with the consortium were indifferent to their need for
markets and financing and would not accept the responsibilities
assumed by their counterparts in Great Britain, where investors
worked closely with manufacturers to insure that British loans promoted British exports.[38]

In 1921, for example, the consortium refused to back a scheme
by the Federal Telegraph Company of California to build a system
of wireless stations across China. Officials in the Commerce Department considered the project of paramount importance to the
"furtherance of American trade and prestige" in the Orient. Failure
to implement it, they warned, would "irreparably" injure American
influence.[39] The difficulty lay in financing the undertaking. In ac-
cordance with the consortium agreement, the Federal Company

36. Thomas H. Buckley, *The United States and the Washington Conference, 1921–1922*, see especially pp. 75–103 and 127–66. Buckley's work
gives the best account of the Washington Conference negotiations.

37. Geddes to Curzon, 13 January 1922, in *Documents on British Foreign
Policy*, Series 1, vol. 14, pp. 601–6.

38. On British activity in China and the failure of American bankers to
cooperate with American exporters see Julian Arnold, American Commercial
Attaché, China, to Julius Klein, Director of the Bureau of Foreign and Do-
mestic Commerce, 29 March 1921, RG 59, file, 893.77/1894; F. R. Eldridge,
Jr., Chief of the Far Eastern Division, BFDC, "Memorandum for Secretary
Hoover," 2 May 1921, enclosed in Hoover to Hughes, 5 May 1921, HHP,
Commerce, Official File, box 280; Paul Whitham, American Commercial
Attaché, China, to Frederick Stevens, representative of the American Group,
19 May 1921, and Whitham to James Farrell, Chairman of the Foreign Trade
Council, 23 May 1921, both attached to Whitham to Hoover, 24 May 1921,
and Eldridge, memorandum, 24 June 1921, HHP, Commerce, Official File,
box 55.

39. Eldridge to Arnold, 21 February 1921, Arnold to the BFDC, 9 April
and 21 September 1921, and C. C. Batchelder, Far Eastern Division, BFDC,
to Christian Herter, secretary to Hoover, 9 December 1921, RG 151, file, 544,
Radio-China.

applied to the American Group for assistance in marketing the Chinese bonds needed to underwrite the enterprise. But with other Japanese and British interests claiming prior rights over the development of China's external communications, their spokesmen in the consortium turned down the proposal with the consent of the American Group. Taken as a lack of confidence in the project, this veto, along with China's default on payments due under a previous foreign loan, discouraged other banks from underwriting the venture.[40] And the result nearly scuttled the company's enterprise.[41]

For supporters of the Federal Telegraph Company in the Commerce Department, the incident represented a failure by the bankers to appreciate that "strategic investments" in "wireless and cable [communications], shipping and overseas terminals may become decisive factors in the big game of the Pacific and Asia." Real trade promotion, they believed, required the formation of American banking facilities in China, through which financial interests in the United States could direct their investments to forward American commerce "along broad constructive lines." They wanted "cooperation by manufacturers and bankers" in creating an aggressive and competitive commercial banking apparatus that could promote the independent interests of American trade. And one such scheme called for a separate industrial banking group to compete with the consortium in financing commercial enterprises.[42]

But since the international consortium was the instrument chosen by the United States for the cooperative development of China, the State Department held firmly to it as the main avenue for American investment. Already in 1918, when the American Minister in China had attempted to organize a joint Chinese-American industrial bank, the State Department had reprimanded him for pushing an exclusive American program while delicate

40. Arnold to BFDC, 5 May 1921, R. P. Schwerin, president of the Federal Telegraph Company, to Batchelder, 30 November 1921, RG 151, file, 544, Radio-China; J. P. Morgan & Co. to Hughes, 28 March 1921, in *Foreign Relations, 1921*, vol. 1, p. 420; Joan Hoff Wilson, *American Business & Foreign Policy, 1920–1933*, pp. 204–7; and Harry W. Kirwin, "The Federal Telegraph Company: A Testing of the Open Door," pp. 271–86.

41. For more information on the Federal Telegraph's enterprise see Chapter 7.

42. Whitham to Stevens, 19 May 1921, enclosed in Whitham to Hoover, 24 May 1921, and Eldridge, "Memorandum for the Secretary of Commerce," 24 June 1921, HHP, Commerce, Official File, box 55; Batchelder to Klein, 6 December 1921, and Batchelder to Herter, 9 December 1921, RG 151, file, 544, Radio-China.

negotiations were underway with the Japanese for a cooperative enterprise.[43] And under the Republicans, the later proposal for a commercial banking group outside the consortium met with a similar fate. Although briefly considered by the Commerce Department, the project was never implemented.[44]

For policymakers and bankers in the United States and Great Britain, even the indifference of the consortium had its value. It prevented reckless lending to "irresponsible Chinese officials" while encouraging native Chinese bankers to consolidate their control over the chaotic political and economic affairs of China.[45] As an institution, they argued, it would preserve a pathway for eventual commercial expansion when political and economic conditions stabilized. By preventing unsound loans, it would hopefully encourage reform and stabilization in China, thereby making it easier for the Japanese to satisfy their economic needs without resorting to military intervention or preferential policies. And this, in turn, would facilitate eventual expansion without risking political and military entanglements. Our "financial interests," explained Miles Lampson of the Foreign Office, "have the wisdom to see they will benefit by the formation of a gigantic international Cooperative Society for the development of China." The consortium, echoed Morgan & Co., "was largely in the nature of a public service designed to substitute the principle of international cooperation [for] competition on the mainland of Asia." It was founded on the "conviction that, in the interest of the future economic development of our own country," Americans must be assured equality of opportunity in the development of China. Any "break-up of the Consortium" would undermine this goal, "lead to a reversion of conditions in the Far East gravely detrimental to the welfare of China," cause the "re-establishment of baneful spheres of influence," and undo the gains made at the Washington Conference.[46]

43. Reinsch to Lansing, 10 December 1918, and Polk to Reinsch, 18 December 1918, RG 59, file, 893.51/2079.

44. Batchelder to Arnold, 10 January 1922, RG 151, file, 620, China-Investments; and Wilson, *American Business & Foreign Policy*, pp. 206–7.

45. Eldridge, memorandum for Secretary Hoover, 24 June 1921, HHP, Commerce, Official File, box 55; Klein to Arnold, 23 August and 10 October 1921; RG 151, file, 620, Consortium; Foreign Office, "Memorandum on the China Consortium," 23 November 1920, F.O. file: F2753/2/19; and Wilson, *American Business & Foreign Policy*, pp. 204–5.

46. Foreign Office minute by Lampson, 13 November 1920, F.O. file: F2786/2/10; J. P. Morgan & Co. to Hughes, 24 April 1922, enclosing Morgan & Co. to the American Group, 24 April 1922, Hughes to Thomas Lamont,

Committed to the consortium, bankers and government officials were also determined to collaborate in regulating the flow of capital to China, primarily to guarantee that American loans did not underwrite preferential Japanese programs. In 1923, for instance, the State Department and the National City Company agreed to withhold a large loan from the Oriental Development Company, a Japanese firm interested in development projects in China, largely because they feared that the loan would facilitate Japanese efforts to shut American interests out of Manchuria. Only when assured that the proceeds would be expended in Japan, not China, did the State Department agree to the loan.[47] For similar reasons, it later discouraged loans by the National City Company and the House of Morgan to the Japanese-controlled South Manchurian Railway Company.[48]

Through banker-government collaboration in regulating capital exports, then, American officials sought to neutralize China for development. In addition, they worked with their British associates to organize a multinational system of economic control, institutionalized at the private level through the financial consortium, founded on close Anglo-American relations, and buttressed by the treaty structure of the Washington Conference. For American officials, the long-range benefits of multinational collaboration for both China and the United States outweighed the immediate gains to be won from independent action. The consortium, in particular, could be used to guarantee reproductive investment, encourage constructive development, prevent independent efforts to divide China into separate preferential spheres, and protect the economic stake of the United States without risking dangerous governmental conflicts. Supposedly intended to safeguard the Open Door,

13 April 1922, and Morgan & Co. to Hughes, 12 June 1922, enclosing "Report of the Council of the Consortium," in *Foreign Relations, 1922*, vol. 1, pp. 764–67, 773–79. See also the report on a speech by Sir Charles Addis, head of the Hong Kong and Shanghai Banking Corporation, the leader of the British Group, in *Times*, 9 November 1920, extract in F.O. file F2899/2/10.

47. Arthur N. Young, memorandum, 16 December 1922, Milton E. Ailes, president of the Riggs National Bank, to Young, 17 February 1923, enclosing Victor Schoepperle of the National City Company to Ailes, 16 February 1923, and Harrison to Ailes, 23 February 1923, in *Foreign Relations, 1923*, vol. 1, pp. 503–7; Joseph Brandes, *Herbert Hoover and Economic Diplomacy: Department of Commerce Policy, 1921–1928*, p. 203; and Herbert Feis, *The Diplomacy of the Dollar: First Era, 1919–1932*, pp. 34–35.

48. Ailes to Harrison, 7 June 1923, and Harrison to Ailes, 15 June 1923, in *Foreign Relations, 1923*, vol. 1, pp. 508–9; Brandes, *Hoover and Economic Diplomacy*, p. 204; and Feis, *Diplomacy of the Dollar*, p. 35.

therefore, the consortium was actually designed to eliminate the economic and political conflict that could result from the kind of wide-open competition inherent in that concept. In effect, the collective diplomatic support promised by the governments gave the consortium a multinational monopoly over loans to China. Even competitive American investment, as in the proposed commercial banking combine, was discouraged in favor of this new system of cooperative multinationalism and managerial regulation.

III

The bankers applied a similar approach toward Europe. As we have seen, American bankers engaged in wide-ranging cooperation with their continental counterparts in financing European reconstruction. The role played by the leading New York banks and by the New York Federal Reserve Bank in launching the Austrian and German reconstruction loans and in facilitating England's return to the gold standard pointed up their readiness to collaborate in economic schemes designed to rationalize financial activity and foster constructive recovery. The government, too, sanctioned this policy as allowing cooperation in reconstruction through private and businesslike programs without entangling the United States in political complications on the Continent.[49]

Yet, policymakers had hoped to parallel this multinational structure of loan supervision with a system of domestic banker-manufacturer cooperation designed to funnel American capital into reproductive enterprises. This had been an important feature of the Lamont-Davis memorandum of May 1919.[50] And in December, the passage of the Edge Act had created a framework for banker-manufacturer cooperation in arranging long-term investment credits for Europe. In this case, Hoover had taken the lead in organizing an Edge company, the Foreign Trade Financing Corporation (FTFC), for the cooperative management of capital

49. See Chapter 4. This notion of cooperation also involved a greater interrelationship between American and European, especially British, money markets. A "better spirit of cooperation will be promoted between your country and ours," argued Strong in a statement that Norman could accept, "by a larger common financial interest by American investors in your markets and by your investors in our markets." Strong cited the example of British investment in Paul Warburg's newly created International Acceptance Bank. See Strong to Montagu Norman, 18 February 1922, and Norman to Strong, 20 March 1922, Benjamin Strong-Montagu Norman Correspondence.

50. See Chapter 2.

exports "with proper checks against speculative, wasteful and bad loans."[51]

The FTFC was the largest of the long-term investment corporations organized under the Edge Act. With an authorized capital of $100 million, it could lend up to a billion dollars in financing American exports. Originally conceived by the Commerce and Marine Division of the American Bankers Association, the plan for this investment combine had been approved by groups represented at the Chicago Foreign Trade Financing Conference in December 1920. These included a wide sampling of important banking and commercial interests, among them the American Bankers Association, the National Foreign Trade Council, the Chamber of Commerce of the United States, and the American Manufacturers Export Association.[52]

But subsequent policy disagreements among bankers and exporters prevented the FTFC from ever soliciting the requisite capital to begin operations. By the end of 1920, American bankers had extended approximately $4 billion in short-term credits to European importers. Importers, however, lacked sufficient capital to liquidate this debt and were forced instead to renew their short-term bills, in effect transforming them into long-term credits in short-term form. Anxious to liquidate these frozen credits, the bankers wanted the FTFC to absorb them as the price for their cooperation in arranging long-term financing for the export of capital goods, a policy that American manufacturers found unacceptable. At the same time, the bankers were apprehensive about committing new capital to long-term investment projects in Europe. So long as unstable conditions persisted, they preferred to keep their assets liquid by selective investment in secure, short-term commercial bills used largely to finance raw-material exports. Indeed, with bankers and manufacturers unable to cooperate in a long-term investment scheme, the FTFC itself was transformed eventually into a short-term acceptance bank.[53]

Bitter about the lack of banker cooperation in financing the export of capital goods, manufacturers further complained that bank

51. Hoover, *Memoirs*, vol. 2, p. 13.

52. Parrini, *Heir to Empire*, pp. 91–96; Robert H. Van Meter, Jr., "The United States and European Recovery, 1918–1923: A Study of Public Policy and Private Finance," pp. 208–11.

53. Parrini, *Heir to Empire*, pp. 96–98; Van Meter, "The United States and European Recovery," pp. 212–17. See also Strong to Norman, 21 March 1921, Strong-Norman Correspondence.

loans to Europe were used to "purchase from our competitors" commodities that were also available in the United States.[54] On 11 May 1922, O. K. Davis of the National Foreign Trade Council discussed this matter with the State Department's Economic Adviser Arthur Young. Using figures made available by the Commerce Department, he argued that over half of the proceeds from the bankers' loans were not returned to the United States in the form of purchases. It was this, he claimed, that accounted for sluggishness and unemployment in the industrial sector. To correct this situation, American exporters had begun working through the U.S. Chamber of Commerce and the National Foreign Trade Council to secure arrangements that would force bankers to tie foreign loans to the purchase of American goods. And they now sought the State Department's assistance in imposing this procedure on the bankers.[55]

The issue badly divided government officials. In response to the exporters' attack, Governor Strong of the New York Federal Reserve Bank defended the bankers. He argued that the proceeds from any dollar loan would eventually return to the American market through debt payments or new purchases. Restrictions on foreign lending, therefore, would exacerbate the debt problem, reduce the level of borrowing in the United States, drive potential borrowers to England, and contract the overall market for American exports. Unrestricted lending, on the other hand, would aid American exporters by eliminating the premium on dollar exchange, making their products cheaper in international markets, and helping to stimulate the reconstruction of America's European export markets.[56]

For his part, Secretary Hoover wanted to use the informal loan controls to force the kind of responsible private action that would

54. O. K. Davis, secretary of the National Foreign Trade Council, to Charles Gwynne, Secretary of the Chamber of Commerce of the United States, 10 March 1922, RG 59, file, 800.51/319.

55. Arthur N. Young, "Memorandum of Conversation with Mr. O. K. Davis of the National Foreign Trade Council," 11 May 1922, Davis to Gwynne, 10 March 1922, and Young to Fred Morris Dearing, Assistant Secretary of State, 21 December 1922, RG 59, file, 800.51/481, 319, 298, 482.

56. For Strong's views see Strong to Gilbert, 23 May 1921, RG 56, box 83, file, Foreign Trade, 1920–1923; Strong to Gilbert, 2 June 1921, RG 56, box 70, file, Federal Reserve Board, 1921; and Strong to Hughes, 14 April 1922, RG 59, file, 800.51/312. The memorandum attached to Strong's letter to Hughes of 14 April can be found attached to Hoover to Hughes, 29 April 1922, RG 59, file, 800.51/316.

benefit both the domestic and international economies. Bankers, he insisted, had certain responsibilities to the American producer, consumer, and government. Like their counterparts in Great Britain, they should work to expand the trading system, and, while it might be bad economics to tie loans, American bankers should cooperate with domestic producers by giving them an equal chance to compete for contracts resulting from the expenditure of loan proceeds.[57] Bankers should also refuse loans to foreign-export monopolies that exacted unfair prices from American consumers, led to inefficient production, and generated international friction. In addition, they should "cooperate with the government" in promoting the American plan for European recovery, especially since nothing would insure a reasonable settlement of the indemnity issue more expeditiously "than to have it clearly understood that the government and individual American bankers were pursuing the same policy." And nothing could better stimulate Continental recovery than a decision by the bankers to decline loans for unreproductive purposes, particularly loans that would underwrite European arms spending. For Hoover, reduced military expenditures would help to stabilize European currencies, promote sound fiscal policies, and, more important, alleviate the political tensions that formed the "primary obstruction to reconstruction and recuperation" on the Continent. Unless loans were "applied for reproductive purposes," he told President Warren Harding, "surplus capital available in America will be wasted," and world resources "will be exhausted."[58]

Although loans for unreproductive expenditure might provide bankers with immediate rewards, Hoover considered the long-run results of such investment detrimental to international prosperity, world peace, and the private management of American investment. Such "destructive use of capital," he warned, was merely "piling

57. Hoover to Hughes, 29 April 1922, RG 59, file, 800.51/316. Hoover's complaint reflected the desire of officials in the Commerce Department that American bankers and exporters emulate the coordinated approach to foreign trade used by the British. They were especially envious of the way British loans were supposedly planned to help promote British commerce. See for example Walter Rastall, Industrial Machinery Division, BFDC, to the American Commercial Attaché, London, 24 January 1922, RG 151, file, 640, General.

58. Christian Herter, "Memorandum of a Conversation between Hoover and Hughes," 22 April 1922, HHP, Commerce, Personal File, box 29; Hoover to Harding, 11 May 1921, HHP, Commerce, Official File, box 235; Hoover to Harding, 12 January 1922, HHP, Commerce, Official File, box 375; Hoover, *Memoirs*, vol. 2, p. 90; and Brandes, *Hoover and Economic Diplomacy*, p. 77.

up dangers for the future of the world." And if it led to defaults, there was always the possibility of dangerous government embroilment in diplomatic controversies. The best policy was to insure quality investment abroad, thereby avoiding defaults and promoting an "increased standard of living, increased demand for further goods and increased social stability." And the best way to insure quality was through public-private cooperation in regulating the flow of American capital. It was to avoid a precedent for a formal system of government regulation that he had originally opposed publicizing the loan control arrangements. And he now wanted the government to use the informal loan control procedures to encourage an enlightened investment program that would avoid the need for thoroughgoing government regulation.[59]

For Strong and the bankers, however, Hoover's proposal was going too far. Strong contended that cooperation among British bankers and manufacturers was the natural product of years of foreign trade experience. While the result functioned largely to promote British interests, it was achieved, he insisted, without government intervention. Once intervention began, he warned, there was "no limit" to the "responsibility" that the government might "ultimately be called upon to assume." And this could involve the United States in the very "disputes and dissentions" that the Secretary hoped to avoid. Strong did agree that loans for unreproductive expenditure should be discouraged, but for him the business aspects of any proposition must remain within the area of business self-regulation. Lamont offered similar advice, warning ominously that Hoover's "doctrine" would put the government in a "bureaucratic position heretofore not assumed by any capital country that we know anything about."[60]

Lacking consensus on the loan program, the moderate procedures in force came under increasing attack from all sides. During congressional hearings in 1925, critics accused the administration of

59. Hoover to Hughes, 29 April 1922, RG 59, file, 800.51/316. Hoover's letter is based upon three memoranda by Grosvenor Jones of the Finance and Investment Division of the BFDC. See Jones to Hoover, 1 and 5 April 1922, and Grosvenor Jones, "Comments on Mr. Hoover's Suggestions in Connection with Foreign Loans," n.d., attached to Hoover, "Suggestions in Connection with Foreign Loans," 6 April 1922, all in HHP, Commerce, Official File, box 375.

60. Strong memorandum, 14 April 1922, attached to Hoover to Hughes, 29 April 1922, and Strong to Hughes, 9 June 1922, RG 59, file, 800.51/316, 506; and Lamont to Hughes, 31 March 1922, Lamont Papers, Series 2, file, 94–18, Foreign Credits.

collaborating with bankers to extend American financial control abroad, particularly in South America. But for the administration officials involved, the government was merely working with the bankers to insure the constructive use of scarce financial resources. They denied charges that banker-government cooperation entailed guarantees on the security of American loans or that American investment policy was narrowly exploitive. By distributing useful information and statistical data to the bankers, they argued instead that government experts in agencies like the Commerce Department's Finance and Investment Division were helping to promote the kind of reproductive investment that contributed alike to United States and South American prosperity.[61]

Dissatisfaction with government loan policy mounted on other fronts as well. Senatorial opponents charged that it lacked congressional sanction. They also wanted guarantees that government efforts to protect private investments abroad would not lead to military intervention. Exporters continued to push for provisions tying bank loans to American commercial expansion. And Hoover still pressed for more rigorous federal supervision, warning now that payments on loans being negotiated with German states and municipalities might interfere with Germany's efforts to meet its reparation obligations. The bankers, however, ignored these criticisms. They continued to oppose tying clauses in loan transactions, refused to comply voluntarily with the high investment standards sought by Hoover, and, instead, followed a policy that came closer to laissez-faire prescriptions than enlightened self-regulation.[62]

For their part, State Department officials lacked both the will and the power to force the bankers into line. To be sure, they did maintain a rigorous ban on loans to governments that had not negotiated war debt settlements with the World War Foreign Debt Commis-

---

61. See Senate, Subcommittee of the Committee on Foreign Relations, *Hearings on S. C. R. 22: Relative to Engaging the Responsibility of the Government in Financial Arrangements Between Its Citizens and Sovereign Foreign Governments*, 25–26 February 1925, and Samuel Guy Inman, "Imperialistic America," pp. 107–16, for criticism of American loan policy in South America. For a rebuttal from the State Department see Sumner Welles, "Is America Imperialistic?" pp. 412–23. See also Robert N. Seidel, "Progressive Pan Americanism: Development and United States Policy Toward South America, 1906–1931" (Ph.D. dissertation), pp. 500–579, for a discussion of American investment policy in South America.

62. Hoover, *Memoirs*, vol. 2, p. 90; Brandes, *Hoover and Economic Diplomacy*, pp. 183–84; and Wilson, *American Business & Foreign Policy*, pp. 117, 119.

sion. With less certain results, they also tried to discourage loans to foreign raw-material monopolies or to finance arms expenditures. But they would not act forcefully to guarantee that loans promoted American commercial expansion. While favoring the expenditure of loan proceeds in the American market, they would only incorporate in statements approving of proposed transactions after 1926 a provision announcing the Department's hope that American manufacturers would be treated equitably in competition for contracts generated by American loans.[63] Nor would they intervene directly to insure quality investment abroad. The "relation of the Government to such financing is a limited one," explained Arthur Young, and the Department had "no warrant in law for interfering with loan transactions even should it clearly appear that they tend to be economically injurious."[64]

More important, despite repeated reports that American bankers were not following a responsible investment program on the Continent, the State Department would not act to guarantee that loans fostered German stabilization and European recovery. In 1925, for example, warnings of a possible conflict between the bankers and the government, conflict that might result from the inability of foreign governments to repay both war debts and private loans, did not diminish the emphasis on business self-regulation. When the bankers were admonished for their wasteful loans to German states and municipalities, the Department still refused to comment directly on the business virtues of particular transactions. It merely added to its cautionary comments in approving loan ventures and counted on the bankers to regulate their own affairs in an enlightened fashion. For their part, however, the bankers continued their unrestricted lending. Even appeals for caution by the older investment houses could not deter the younger, more aggressive firms from abandoning enlightened self-regulation in favor of unrestrained and competitive action.[65]

63. Feis, *Diplomacy of the Dollar*, pp. 20–25, 30–32; Young and Harrison to Hughes, 29 March 1922, Hoover to the State Department, 17 May 1926, enclosing draft letter dated 17 May 1926, Mellon to Secretary of State Frank Kellogg, 3 July 1926, Young to Harrison, 17 July 1926, unsigned draft of a letter to Hoover, 22 July 1926, and Young to Harrison, 20 November 1926, RG 59, file, 800.51/482, 536, 538, 557.

64. Young to Kellogg, 11 March 1925, RG 59, file, 800.51/503.

65. Gerrard Winston to Kellogg, 26 August 1925, and Kellogg to Mellon, 23 October 1925, RG 59, file, 800.51/518; unsigned "Memorandum of a Conversation Between S. Parker Gilbert, Agent General, and Mr. Castle on Monday, January 4, 1926," 5 January 1926, William R. Castle Papers, box 5,

A 1925 review of the loan control arrangements did not alter government policy. Officers in the State Department admitted that the heavy European demand for American capital affected the public interest. They were equally certain, therefore, that the "usual economic forces" could not be permitted to "operate uncontrolled." Still, they decided against seeking formal congressional authority to control private loans and continued to rely on business self-regulation tempered by informal and voluntary banker-government cooperation. The result, as one official noted, was a "sort of twilight zone" between complete government responsibility and the total absence of control. The informal and "extralegal control" outlined in the 1922 press statement did give the State Department a "veto power" over certain loans, especially loans to governments that had not funded their war debts to the United States. But in most cases, ultimate regulation lay in private hands.[66]

During the rest of the decade, moreover, this policy remained intact despite additional warnings that it was not working. New reports of unreproductive lending to Germany did not produce a retreat from the 1922 formula. Nor did hints that Wall Street considered the loan control procedure tantamount to government approval of private transactions. Instead, in its letters to bankers after 1929, the State Department simply replaced the usual "no objection" with the new "not interested," removing any suggestion that the government, rather than the bankers, was responsible for the business merits of particular ventures.[67]

IV

In effect, the ban on state management left the responsibility for large areas of public policy in private hands. The State Department refused to interfere with private investment managers when coop-

---

folder: Germany; *Foreign Relations, 1925*, vol. 2, pp. 172–87; Feis, *Diplomacy of the Dollar*, p. 44; and Wilson, *American Business & Foreign Policy*, p. 121.

66. Harrison to the Secretary of State, 10 April 1925, enclosing Arthur N. Young, "The Department of State and Foreign Loans," 3 April 1925, and Arthur N. Young, "The Department of State and the Flotation of Foreign Loans," 2 April 1925, Leland Harrison Papers, General Correspondence, box 17; Winston to the Secretary of State, 26 August 1925, R. E. Olds, "Foreign Loans," 12 October 1925, RG 59, file, 800.51/518, 561.

67. Harrison to Kellogg, 28 January 1927, Western European Division Memorandum, 21 June 1927, RG 59, file, 800.51/558, 566; *Foreign Relations, 1927*, vol. 2, pp. 728–30; and Feis, *Diplomacy of the Dollar*, pp. 13–14.

eration between them and the manufacturers broke down and when Hoover insisted that foreign loans should help to construct a more efficient American trading system. After 1925, moreover, it held firmly to the policy of private management despite the deteriorating quality of loans to Europe, reports of unrestrained activity by the bankers, and repeated warnings by Hoover and others that without more rigorous controls the whole program of voluntarism and cooperative action might collapse, and with it the vision of permanent peace, prosperity, and progress.

At middecade, however, the reliance on self-regulation and cooperation among private multinational bankers seemed in many ways to be fulfilling public goals. The American Group and the State Department were contemplating the long-range benefits of Anglo-American collaboration, especially at the private level, in regulating the flow of capital to China. And in Europe, the Dawes Plan and the cooperative financing of reconstruction by private, particularly British and American bankers, was engendering confidence in a new era of prosperity. At the same time, moreover, the cooperative approach was being extended to other areas of the international economy. In these areas, early attempts to build independent and competitive systems were being abandoned, and despite warnings that the new cooperative arrangements violated traditional policies, notably the Open Door, they often won support from the United States government. For in these areas too, these private programs seemed to be extending American interests, regulating business enterprise on a stable and efficient basis, and stimulating global development. And alternative policies, or so it seemed, would involve the kind of government action deemed incompatible with contemporary economic realities, world peace, and the private character of the American political economy.

CHAPTER 6

The Private Structure
of Cooperation in Communications

Cable Policy in the Postwar Decade

Although few areas of postwar diplomatic and business history have been so largely ignored, the development of international communications formed an important arena in which the United States and Great Britain worked out their New Era understanding. Existing accounts, moreover, do not deal effectively with the factors involved in government-business relations, especially the American belief that government operation was not the best method of extending international communications. Nor do they fully appreciate how an initial tendency toward independent action in both British and American policy gave way to cooperative programs at the private level.[1] Cooperative action, it was argued, would avoid unprofitable competition, allow maximum extension of cable lines at the lowest possible costs, provide adequate facilities without unnecessary duplication, and encourage trade and the growth of international understanding.

In cable policy, the State Department withdrew its original demand for an all-American cable system, acquiesced in the cooperative arrangements that private officials had worked out with the British, and, concomitantly, softened the competitive overtones of its Open Door policy. For its part, the Foreign Office also shifted to a cooperative approach as the best way to protect the British

1. The existing literature includes F. J. Brown, *The Cable and Wireless Communications of the World*; Keith Clark, *International Communications: The American Attitude*; Linwood S. Howeth, *History of Communications-Electronics in the United States Navy*; Leslie B. Tribolet, *The International Aspects of Electrical Communications in the Pacific Area*; Brady A. Hughes, "Owen D. Young and American Foreign Policy, 1919–1929" (Ph.D. dissertation). Henry W. Kirwin's "The Federal Telegraph Company: A Testing of the Open Door" covers radio communications with China, and Joseph Tulchin's *The Aftermath of War: World War I and U.S. Policy Toward Latin America* devotes a chapter to U.S. cable policy in South America. The works by Hughes and Tulchin are especially useful.

stake in international cable communications and as a realistic alternative to reckless and unprofitable competition. Thus, the policies pursued by both governments, in South America and the north Atlantic, met the private sector's need for order, stability, and security, absorbed British and American cable conflict into a pattern of cooperation institutionalized at the private level, and widened the area of informal Anglo-American understanding.

I

For American officials, expanding United States cable lines became an important postwar policy objective. An extensive and dependable cable network, they believed, was "as important as ships and foreign banks to successful foreign trade." Yet, clearly the existing network was neither as extensive nor as dependable as they desired. Cable lines had been disrupted during the war, resulting in traffic congestion and long delays.[2] "Many organizations feel that if the present situation continues," reported the Bureau of Foreign and Domestic Commerce regarding congestion in the Pacific cable service, "it will render futile the efforts of the Shipping Board, the Federal Reserve Bank, the Bureau of Foreign and Domestic Commerce, [the] banking houses which are establishing branches in foreign countries, the corporations formed under the Webb-Pomerene law, and many other agencies, to promote American commerce in the Far East."[3]

Still worse, British interests dominated cable communications. Cables of the so-called Eastern group of companies, headed by Sir

2. Hurley to the Commissioners of the United States Shipping Board, 21 June 1919, and Henry Robinson of the Shipping Board to Hurley, 26 June 1919, RG 32, "Shipping Board General File," 580–697; unsigned "Memorandum for the Third Assistant Secretary of State: How American Interests are Prejudiced by Present Status of Ex-German Cables," 12 October 1920, "International Cable Communications: Commerce of the World Dependent on Adequate Cable Facilities," *Commerce Monthly,* vol. 2, no. 7, and Walter S. Rogers, "Memorandum on Pacific Intercommunications," 23 May 1921, all in Record Group 43, "General Records of the United States Participation in International Conferences, Commissions, and Expositions," "Records of the Preliminary International Conference on Electrical Communications, 1920," box 97 and box 103 (hereafter cited as RG 43, Communications Conference).

3. F. R. Eldridge, Jr., Far Eastern Division, BFDC, to J. V. A. MacMurray, Chief of the Far Eastern Division, State Department, 6 September 1919, with enclosed "Report on Pacific Communications," 15 August 1919, RG 59, file, 811.73/144.

John Denison-Pender, belted the globe, while the government-owned "All-Red" system connected London with every outpost of the British Empire. In addition, the British monopolized gutta-percha, the vital raw material used as cable insulation, and owned the only cable manufacturing plant in the world, the Telegraph Construction and Maintenance Company of the Eastern group.[4] Such control over world cable lines, so Americans felt anyway, enabled the British to censor business messages, scoop American companies in foreign trade transactions, and dominate world commerce.[5] As one cable company official explained, London's efforts to control cable development went hand in hand with its drive for "commercial supremacy."[6] Worried that British censorship might be used to discover its maritime secrets, the Shipping Board even devised its own cable code rather than rely on one of the usual commercial codes that could be easily deciphered.[7]

Given this British domination, the idea of a government-sponsored and independent cable system centering on the United States gained momentum during and after the war. The Department of Commerce began researching the development of a cable manufacturing capacity in the United States.[8] The Post Office Department, long an advocate of thoroughgoing government ownership of all United States telegraph and telephone systems, now considered the consolidation of private cable companies into a single system to be managed by private officials but supervised and

4. See American Consul General, London, to Charles Evans Hughes, 25 April 1921, enclosing an extract from *Lloyd's List*, 23 April 1921, RG 59, file, 800.73/54; memorandum on submarine cables enclosed in Hurley to Shipping Board Commissioners, 21 June 1919, RG 32, Shipping Board General File, 580–697; Earnest E. Powers, "General Report on the International Cable Situation," 15 January 1919, Norman H. Davis Papers, box 30; William Redfield to Mark Prentiss, 19 May 1919, RG 40, file, 78332.

5. Regarding Britain's alleged use of cables to discriminate against American trade, see British Ambassador to the Secretary of State, 2 November and 10 March 1921, and Alvey Adee to the British Ambassador, 21 December 1920, in *Foreign Relations, 1920*, vol. 2, pp. 699–704. The memorandum mentioned in Adee's letter, which is not printed, provides specific illustrations of alleged cable censorship by the British and can be found in RG 43, "Communications Conference," box 97.

6. John Merrill of All America Cable Co. to William Phillips, 5 February 1918, and Merrill, "Memorandum for the State Department," 12 February 1918, RG 59, file, 811.74/147, 146.

7. See "Official Minutes of the Proceedings of the United States Shipping Board," 3 December 1920, RG 32, "Official Minutes."

8. Information on this story is contained in RG 40, file, 78332.

subsidized by the government.[9] And in 1919, important officials in the Commerce and State departments urged that the government construct and operate a new cable line across the Pacific.[10]

As in other spheres, however, most officials regarded excessive government intervention as detrimental to world peace and harmful to business efficiency. In 1918, Secretary of State Robert Lansing worried about the diplomatic complications that might arise from any attempt by the government to control cable landings on foreign soil.[11] Complaints by businessmen regarding the inefficiency of cable lines operated by the Post Office during the war prompted the return of these lines to private management in the spring of 1919.[12] And later, President Harding refused permission to expend government revenues for construction of a new Pacific cable, a decision that was approved by both Secretary of State Hughes and Secretary of Commerce Hoover. For them, the project was a responsibility squarely in the private sector.[13]

Moreover, most American officials did not support rigorous intergovernmental control over cable communications under the International Telegraph Convention. Such control, its supporters argued, would bring American cable lines into harmony with the

9. W. H. Lamar, former solicitor for the Post Office Department, "Memorandum for the Postmaster General," 25 September 1922, enclosing Theodore N. Vail of American Telephone and Telegraph Company to Postmaster General Albert Burleson, 22 October 1918, RG 59, file, 811.73/697. On official Post Office support for government ownership, see Post Office Department, *Annual Reports of the Postmaster General, 1916–1920.*

10. Frank Rutter, Statistical Adviser, BFDC, to Roy MacElwee of the BFDC, 15 May 1919, RG 40, file, 78332; Eldridge to MacMurray, 6 September 1919, with enclosed "Report on Pacific Communications," 15 August 1919, RG 59, file 811.73/114; Walter S. Rogers, State Department's Communication's Expert, "Memorandum on Bill for the Construction of a Pacific Cable," n.d., RG 59, file, 811.7394C73/2; and Senate, Subcommittee of the Committee on Commerce, *Hearings on S. 1651, A Bill Providing for the Construction of a Pacific Cable and for Other Purposes,* 22, 26 September and 14 November 1919, p. 11.

11. Robert Lansing's fears were in connection with the proposed government seizure of cables for wartime operation. See Lansing to Wilson, 15 July and 6 November 1918, Woodrow Wilson Papers, Series 4, case file, 350K, box 217.

12. Hundreds of complaints of the long delays caused by government manipulation of cables for political purposes, particularly censorship, were presented to the Commerce Department. See RG 40, file, 78267.

13. Hoover to Sen. Wesley Jones, 27 April 1921, Warren G. Harding to Charles Evans Hughes, 12 July 1921, and Hughes to Harding, 19 July 1921, RG 59, file, 811.7394C73/3, 6.

"largely government owned and operated" cables abroad, thus making for a more orderly, efficient, and integrated world network.[14] But as spokesmen for the cable companies saw it, the United States would be outnumbered by other signatories to the convention, and this would mean domination of American communication policy by foreign governments. Still worse, they complained, government control would involve a rigid bureaucratic inertia that was detrimental to efficient business operations and harmful to the rapid development of communication technology.[15]

This preference for private management did not mean that policymakers and company officials would rely entirely on individual incentive to expand American cable facilities. Instead, they envisioned some form of government-business partnership. The cable companies would organize on a cooperative basis, eliminating wasteful and inefficient competition and alleviating pressure for thoroughgoing state management. Private industry then would be "assisted by the Government" in overcoming the artificial British restrictions that were blocking the flow of news and information and contributing to the growth of international misunderstanding.[16] An Open Door for communications, so these progressives believed, would foster an informed world opinion, thus preventing ignorance from breeding suspicion, leading to enlightened governmental policies, and helping to preserve world peace. At the same time, it would help to guarantee equal access to world

14. Rogers was the major exponent of this view. See, "Conference Between the American Delegates and the Representatives of the Cable and Telegraph Companies," 4 November 1920, and Rogers to RCA, 13 November 1920; RG 43, "Communications Conference," box 98; "Unsigned Notes of a Meeting of the American Delegates to the Preliminary Communications Conference," 3 November 1920, RG 43, "Communications Conference," box 126; Rogers to Henry Fletcher, 8 June 1921, and Rogers to Hughes, 10 March 1922, RG 59, file, 574.D1/511, 512.

15. Clarence Mackay, President of the Mackay Companies, to Rogers, 30 September 1920, Newcomb Carlton, president of Western Union Company, to Rogers, 4 October 1920, "Conference Between the American Delegates and the Representatives of the Cable and Telegraph Companies," 4 November 1920, RG 43, "Communications Conference," box 98; Merrill to Rogers, 15 June 1921, RG 43, "Communications Conference," box 100; and Commercial Cable Company to Norman Davis, 15 November 1920, RG 59, file, 574.D1/287½.

16. See for example the remarks by Davis in, "Meeting of the American Delegates for the International Conference on Electrical Communications and the Representatives of the United States Cable and Radio Companies," 21 September 1920, RG 43, "Communications Conference," box 126.

markets and remove still another source of international conflict.[17]

Yet, in practice this attack on "artificial" restrictions frequently meant reciprocal bargaining between American and British interests, especially after early efforts to ban monopolies had failed. These efforts had been made particularly at a communications conference convened at Washington in 1920 to allocate captured German cables and to draw up general principles to guide the development of world communications. At the conference, American proposals for banning exclusive cable privileges and for requiring reciprocity in the awarding of cable permits had been ignored.[18] Only the British and Italian experts had temporarily supported the reciprocity idea.[19] Following the conference, however, American negotiators had moved to hammer out an informal Anglo-American understanding. Using the so-called Kellogg Act (which empowered the President to prohibit cable landings on American territory by companies having preferential privileges) as leverage, they were able to move the British toward a more cooperative attitude.[20] And when this move was combined with the desires of private businessmen for cooperation and the growing willingness of American statesmen to renounce hopes for an independent cable system, the result was a series of compromise arrangements that added a new dimension to the spreading pattern of Anglo-American harmony.

17. Rogers, "Memorandum on Pacific Intercommunications," 31 May 1921, RG 43, "Communications Conference," box 103; Norman H. Davis, "Speech Opening the Preliminary Communications Conference," 8 October 1920, Norman H. Davis Papers, box 9; Rogers to Wilson, 12 February 1919, in Ray Stannard Baker, *Wilson and World Settlement*, vol. 3, pp. 428–42; Senate, Subcommittee of the Committee on Interstate Commerce, *Hearings on S. 4301: A Bill to Prevent the Unauthorized Landing of Submarine Cables*, 15 December 1920, pp. 50–51, 126–28; and Hughes to Ambassador George Harvey, London, 3 February 1923, in *Foreign Relations, 1923*, vol. 2, pp. 271–79.

18. For a discussion of the former German cables at the Communications Conference of 1920 see "Minutes of the Proceedings of the Subcommittee on German Cables," Davis Papers, box 30. On American efforts to ban monopolies and gain recognition of the reciprocity doctrine, see "Minutes of Subcommittee #4 on International Cable and Radio Law and Cable Landing Rights of the Conference on Electrical Communications," RG 43, "Communications Conference," box 43, especially meetings 2, 3, 4, 6, and 7.

19. *Foreign Relations, 1922*, vol. 1, pp. 538–42.

20. According to Sen. Frank Kellogg, the bill was designed to enable "the President to insist on equal rights" for American companies overseas. See Kellogg to Hughes, 16 June 1922, RG 59, file, 811.7353b/92.

II

In South America, British and American interests had long dominated cable communications. All America Cables Incorporated, a United States corporation, controlled most of the Pacific coast traffic through its subsidiaries, the Mexican Telegraph Company and the Central and South American Telegraph Company. The cables of this system extended from Galveston, Texas, to Valparaiso, Chile, and thence across the Andes to Buenos Aires. The British Western Telegraph Company, a member of Pender's Eastern group, controlled the commercially more lucrative Atlantic coast traffic. Its cables stretched from the Azores in the north Atlantic to the principal coastal cities of Brazil, ran southward to Uruguay and Buenos Aires, crossed the Andes to Santiago and Valparaiso, and then ran up the Pacific coast to Callao, Peru. Its two Brazilian monopolies, moreover, assured British Western of most of the Atlantic coast business with both the United States and Europe. The first, a sixty-year concession granted in 1873, entailed a monopoly of cable connections between points on the Brazilian coast and prevented other companies from landing at more than one port of entry. The second, acquired in 1893 for a twenty year period, gave the company exclusive control over cable communications between Brazil and Argentina and Brazil and Uruguay. These concessions prevented All America from extending its lines up the Atlantic coast from Argentina, made a direct United States connection with Brazil impractical, and left the British in control of American cable traffic with the Atlantic coast.[21]

Even before the outbreak of war in Europe, the State Department had hoped to foster a direct connection between the United States and the Atlantic coast of South America.[22] This became particularly important after 1914 because of fears that the British Western cable might be disrupted by the Central Powers. Ac-

21. "Confidential Memorandum for the State Department from the Central and South American Company," 14 June 1919, RG 59, file, 811.73/139; "Monopolies of Cable Landing Rights," enclosed in Rogers to William Benson, chairman of the U. S. Shipping Board, 21 September 1920, and "Memorandum on the British Cable Monopoly in Brazil," enclosed in Elihu Root, Jr., attorney for All America Cables, to Benson, 1 October 1920, RG 32, "Shipping Board General File," 580–697.
22. The Department's efforts in this direction began as early as 1910 and can be followed in RG 59, file, 832.73/-., 38, 52, 68.

cordingly, with State Department encouragement, All America managed to block British Western's attempt to renew its 1893 concession. It then applied for permission to land cables between Buenos Aires and Rio de Janeiro and Buenos Aires and Santos, separate lines being necessary to circumvent British Western's continuing interport monopoly.[23] In 1917, it also joined the Western Union Telegraph Company in applying for permission to land cables connecting the United States directly with Brazil.[24]

The British Western resisted these initiatives since, if achieved, the American companies would encircle South America with a completely independent cable network, one that would deprive British Western of its control over traffic between the United States and the Atlantic coast and offer an alternate route for Europe-South America business via the United States. To protect its privileged position, British Western at first contended that separate lines from Buenos Aires to Rio and Santos violated its 1873 interport monopoly. The result was a legal battle in the Brazilian courts that was not resolved in All America's favor until 1917. Thereafter, British Western continued to delay the concession's confirmation by the Brazilian Ministry of Communications, despite protests by the State Department at both Rio de Janeiro and London. Indeed, it was not until 1920 that All America's lines to Santos and Rio finally opened.[25]

While stalling any extension of All America's lines up the Atlantic coast, British Western also proposed a cooperative settlement of the South American cable controversy on a business basis. Specifically, it suggested consolidating British and American cable systems and dividing all South American business on terms that would protect its domination of Europe-South America traffic. Under its proposal, the British company would confirm All America's

23. American Embassy, Brazil, to the Secretary of State, 12 and 24 August 1914, Latin American Division Memorandum, 2 September 1914, and the Secretary of State to the American Embassy, Brazil, 10 November 1914, RG 59, file, 832.73/77, 75, 78, 81.

24. Carlton to Lansing, 13 July 1917, Polk to the American Embassy, Brazil, 3 August 1917, American Embassy, Brazil, to Lansing, 12 December 1917 and 14 March 1918, Merrill to Lansing, 16 April 1918, and Lansing to the American Embassy, Brazil, 19 April 1918, RG 59, file, 832.73/106, 109, 129, 139, 144, 143a.

25. This story can be followed in RG 59, file, 832.73/84, 93, 97, 110, 111, 170a, 173, 174a. See also "Confidential Memorandum for the Honorable Lester Woolsey, Solicitor of the Department of State," 11 December 1919, in Root to Lansing, 15 December 1919, RG 59, file, 811.73/169.

monopoly of the Pacific coast by withdrawing from Chile and Peru. In turn, All America would surrender the more profitable Atlantic coast business to British Western, which then would join Western Union in constructing a new through line from Brazil to Miami via Barbados. This joint line would handle traffic between the Atlantic coast and the United States, while British Western would manage all business between South America and Europe over its Atlantic lines via Ascension, St. Vincent, and the Azores. Should All America reject the proposition, Western Union and the British company would then divide all South American business, extending their system to the Pacific coast in competition with All America and monopolizing all South American messages received by Western Union's extensive land lines in the United States.[26]

The State Department wanted a united front among American companies against the British monopoly. But despite warnings that any compromise with the British would hamper efforts to lay an independent line to Brazil, Western Union's president, Newcomb Carlton, accepted British Western's proposal as a realistic business proposition. For him, "divergent policies" and interests made it "impossible for the various cable companies of the United States to present a united front." Moreover, British Western already had permission from the Brazilian government for a cable from Brazil to Barbados and thence to Canada or the United States. And as Carlton saw it, the cost involved in constructing a duplicate line made it wiser to utilize "available means and have better connections with foreign cables." These factors, along with British Western's continuing interport monopoly, the need to renew the British landing permits for several of Western Union's transatlantic cables, and reliance on the British-owned Telegraph Construction and Maintenance Company for cable, led him to conclude a cooperative working arrangement with the British along lines favored by British Western.[27]

26. In addition to the last citation in the previous note see Merrill to Lansing, 9 April 1919, John Bassett Moore to Assistant Secretary Phillips, 4 July 1919, J. H. Murray, memorandum of a conference between Carlton and W. H. Taff of Western Union and Leo S. Rowe and Murray of the Latin American Division, 1 May 1920, W. H. Lamar, memorandum for the Postmaster General, with attachments, 25 September 1922, RG 59, file, 811.73/134, 136, 254, 697; and Assistant Secretary Leland Harrison, "Summary of the Western Union's Memorandum," 5 October 1921, and "Summary of the All America's Memorandum," 5 October 1921, RG 59, file, 811.73W52/137, 125.

27. For Carlton's views see Winston, memorandum to Lay, 11 July 1919, W. W. E. Atkins of Western Union to Redfield, 29 January 1920, Murray,

But at this point at least, the State Department was determined to gain control over all cable traffic between the United States and South America. It supported All America's rejection of the British Western proposal and attempted to force British concessions to American cable expansion on the Atlantic coast. It refused to permit Western Union to land the Miami end of the proposed Anglo-American line until its British associate had surrendered all exclusive privileges in Brazil. And when Western Union tried to land the Miami cable before Congress had affirmed the President's power to regulate cable landings, naval vessels were dispatched to interdict the cable ship off the Florida coast.[28] Even William Gibbs McAdoo, whose law firm represented Western Union, failed to shake the State Department's determination. And President Wilson turned down all appeals by his former Secretary of the Treasury, pending a resolution of the Brazilian conflict.[29]

At the same time, however, the Wilson administration did suggest a compromise for dividing South American traffic. Under it, existing monopolies were to be left intact, but American and British companies would be prohibited from acquiring new preferential concessions. It would also permit construction of an Anglo-American cable from Miami to Brazil but would require Western Union to purchase or lease the entire line, as well as one of the

memorandum of a conference, 1 May 1920, Latin American Division, "Memorandum of a Conference on the All America Cable Situation," 12 May 1920, RG 59, file, 811.73/134, 164, 254, 378; "Memorandum of a Conference between Representatives of the State Department and Carlton on April 24, 1920," dated 4 May 1920, RG 59, file, 832.73/201; and Carlton to Lamar, 4 June 1920, RG 43, "Communications Conference," box 62. See also "Agreement Between the Western Union Telegraph Company and the Western Telegraph Company Ltd., July 15, 1919," RG 43, "Communications Conference," box 104.

28. W. R. Vallance, memorandum, 28 April 1920, "Minutes of a Conference with All America Cable Officials," 21 May 1920, Colby to the British Ambassador, 30 July 1920, Rear Admiral Decker to the Navy Department, 2 August 1920, and Vallance, memorandum, 10 August 1920, RG 59, file, 811.73/193, 378, 235a, 232, 508; Colby to Wilson, 17 July and 19 November 1920, Wilson Papers, Series 2, boxes 197 and 199; and Davis, "Memorandum of a Conversation with Mr. Peterson of the British Embassy," 10 August 1920, Davis Papers, box 9.

29. McAdoo, Cotton, and Franklin, representing Western Union, to Colby, 25 August 1920, RG 59, file, 811.73/306; McAdoo to Colby, 20 August 1920, in McAdoo to Davis, 20 August 1920, Davis Papers, box 40; McAdoo to Wilson, 11 and 17 October 1920, and Wilson to McAdoo, 12 October 1920, Wilson Papers, Series 2, box 198.

British Western's several port-to-port cables along the Brazilian coast. All America would be allowed to lay a second Brazil-United States cable to compete with Western Union for South American business, but neither could offer their lines for South America-Europe traffic.[30] In effect, this proposal sought to reconcile a limited degree of multinational collaboration with the goal of a competitive and independent all-American cable system. It would permit the combination of British and American capital but divide Atlantic coast traffic, with American companies handling those messages to and from the United States and the British Western transmitting all cablegrams to and from Europe and England.

Neither Denison-Pender nor officials at the Foreign Office were ready to accept this plan. F. J. Brown of the General Post Office wanted an agreement whereby both All America and British Western would allow their South American monopolies to lapse. This, he hoped, would remove American objections to the Western Union-British Western cable and give that combine an opportunity to extend its system up the Pacific coast of South America in competition with All America's lines. His recommendation, however, was not relayed to the State Department. Instead, following a meeting at the Foreign Office, the British simply notified the American Ambassador in London that any proposals for a settlement of the Brazil dispute should be referred directly to the British Western.[31]

Subsequently, the Harding administration improved on the American offer. In a memorandum of August 1921, Assistant Secretary of State Leland Harrison suggested three possible solutions to the South American stalemate. The first two combined various versions of a ban on monopolies with the proposal that Western Union should control the entire Miami-Brazil line. The third, however, would permit Western Union and British Western to operate jointly a South American cable system that would share in United States traffic and compete with an independent system to be organized by the All America. Both systems would be assured equal

30. Carlton to Davis, 9 February 1921, Davis to Carlton, 28 February 1921, and Davis to F. J. Brown, British Post Office, 19 and 21 February 1921, RG 59, file, 811.73/560.

31. Brown to Rowland Sperling, Foreign Office, 21 February 1921, Foreign Office minute by Sperling, 23 February 1921, and Sperling to Ambassador Davis, 25 February 1921, all in F.O. file: A1240/26/45. See also J. Butler Wright, counselor, American Embassy, London, to Davis, 9 March 1921, RG 59, file, 811.73/600.

opportunity by provisions prohibiting the renewal of existing monopolies and guaranteeing equitable arrangements for the exchange of traffic.[32]

This last proposal outlined the general policy of the State Department in resolving the South American cable controversy. After Congress had passed the Kellogg Cable Landing Act in 1921, which confirmed the President's authority to regulate cable landings, the Department prepared a draft license prohibiting cable landings by any company that held privileges denied to American interests. This prohibition formalized Wilson's earlier refusal to permit the landing of Western Union's cable at Miami, and it was aimed, in particular, at forcing All America and the Western Union-British Western combine to surrender their monopoly rights so far as other British and American companies were concerned.[33]

Both All America and British Western were amenable to this arrangement. For the British, it resembled Brown's earlier recommendation. Once more, as they understood, the State Department's refusal to grant a landing permit at Miami for the newly laid Western Union-British Western line had "manoeuvered the Western Co. into a position where they would either have to surrender their monopoly or lose a great part of the [$3,000,000] spent in laying the Brazil-Barbados section of the cable." And as a British representative at the Washington Naval Conference reported to the Foreign Office, any effort to get better terms from the State Department "would be doubtful of success."[34] Accordingly, both companies agreed to the American plan, and, subsequently, the State Department abandoned its earlier demand that Western Union control

32. Harrison, memorandum, 1 August 1921, RG 59, file, 811.73/670.

33. Undersecretary Fletcher, "Memorandum of a Conversation Between McLaren of All America, Ames of Western Union and Fletcher," 4 August 1921, RG 59, file, 811.73/720; Hughes to Harding, 24 May 1921, "Brief of the Hearing Before the Undersecretary of State on September 22, Upon the Application of the Western Union for a Landing License for the Miami-Barbados Cable," 6 October 1921, "Summary of the Hearing on September 14, 1921, Upon the Application of the Western Union for a Landing License for the Miami-Barbados Cables, 8 October 1921, Harrison to Fletcher, 8 November 1921, Carlton to Harding, 5 December 1921, "Memorandum with Regard to the Application of Western Union for Permission to Land its Miami Cable," 7 December 1921, and unsigned memorandum for Fletcher, 21 December 1921, RG 59, file, 811.73W52/31a, 120, 124, 136, 47, and FW811. 73W52/-.

34. Foreign Office minute by Sperling, 12 May 1921, F.O. file: A3314/1442/45; minute by Sperling, 25 May 1921, F.O. file: A3622/1442/45; and Balfour to the Foreign Office, 7 January 1922, F.O. file: A202/202/25.

the entire Miami-Brazil cable. As a result, in August 1922, after a delay caused by the need to gain confirmation of the British Western's waiver from the South American governments concerned, it formally issued the license for Western Union's Miami landing.[35]

In South America, then, the State Department followed the cooperative thrust of private policy and combined a reciprocal abandonment of monopolies with a readiness to accept Anglo-American cooperation in handling United States-South America traffic. For Western Union, this cooperation conformed with business realities, making it possible to provide increased facilities without duplicating British lines. Compromise on this dispute, moreover, probably helped to facilitate a successful settlement of the north Atlantic cable controversy. Here, business considerations also led American companies to favor cooperative arrangements with the British, both to avoid destructive competition and to regulate cable traffic on a business basis. And here again, the State Department withdrew its early demand for a completely independent system in favor of compromise arrangements that undercut the competitive implications of the Open Door principle and widened the private structure of Anglo-American cooperation.

III

As Americans saw it, the British effectively controlled transatlantic cable traffic. Although American companies owned or operated thirteen of seventeen transatlantic cables, twelve of these terminated in Ireland or England under landing grants issued by the British Post Office and permitting the British Board of Trade to censor American traffic. In addition, the Commercial Cable Company's line from New York to Havre proceeded via the Portu-

35. Post Wheeler, American Embassy, London, to Sperling, 31 August 1922, F.O. file: A5495/202/45; Clarence Wilson of Western Union to Fletcher, 20 December 1921, Wilson to Hughes, 23 and 29 December 1921, Harrison to Fletcher, 28 December 1921, Rush Taggart of Western Union to Hughes, 10 January 1922, Harrison to Paul Lesh, 11 January 1922, "Memorandum with Regard to the Application of Western Union Company for Permission to Land its Miami Cable," 7 December 1921, Hughes to Carlton, 10 April 1922, RG 59, file, 811.73W52/49, 48, 50, 136, 135, –, 47, 61; Sheldon Crosby, American chargé, Rio de Janeiro, to Hughes, 24 June 1922, RG 59, file, 832.73/231; Root to Hughes, 8 October 1923, RG 59, file, 832.73A1/5; unsigned memorandum for Fletcher, 21 December 1921, RG 59, file, FW811. 73W52/–.; Phillips to Harding, 24 August 1922, and "Copy of the License granted to Western Union, 24 August 1922," RG 59, file, 811.73W52.

guese Azores, where the Europe and Azores Telegraph Company, a member of Pender's Eastern group, controlled all landing concessions. Even the Commercial Company's 1898 concession for its Azores relay ran indirectly through the British company. Consequently, after the wartime seizure and diversion of two German cables from Emden to New York, the United States did not have a direct continental connection free of possible British manipulation.[36]

Accordingly, the State Department encouraged American cable companies to lay new lines after the war. In 1919, the Commercial Company responded by applying to the Portuguese government for a direct cable connection at the Azores.[37] Together with Western Union, it also opened negotiations with the German Ministry of Posts for new lines to Emden.[38] The Germans wanted to own the proposed cables from Emden to the Azores, where they would meet with the American lines from New York. Their proposal was likely to receive State Department approval, and in late 1921 Western Union concluded an agreement along these lines with a German cable company.[39] Shortly thereafter, Commercial signed a similar agreement with another German firm.[40]

36. Paul Edwards to Assistant Secretary of State Van S. Merle-Smith, 13 October 1920, RG 43, "Communications Conference," box 97; P. E. D. Nagle, communications expert, BFDC, to Alan Goldsmith, chief of the Western European Division, BFDC, 11 November 1922, Harrison Papers, General Correspondence, box 3; Solicitor's memorandum, "Western Union Cables Having Transatlantic Connections," 24 November 1920, RG 59, file, 811.73/28; and E. S. Gregg, BFDC, to Hoover, 20 June 1922, HHP, Commerce, Official File, box 288.

37. Mackay to Lansing, 17 November 1919, Phillips to Lansing, 13 December 1919, and Phillips to Frederic Coudert of the Commercial Company, 18 December 1919, RG 59, file, 811.7353b/10, 10a.

38. Military Intelligence Division memorandum, 6 October 1920, Davis Papers, box 29; Ellis Loring Dresel, American chargé, Berlin, to Hughes, 5, 25 August and 30 September 1921, Fletcher to Dresel, 25 October 1921, Dresel to Hughes, 26 October 1921, and Richard Pennoyer, American chargé, Berlin, to Hughes, 29 December 1921, RG 59, file, 811.7362W52/-., 2, 3, 4.

39. Pennoyer to Hughes, 2 January 1922, and Carlton to Hughes, 25 January 1922, RG 59, file, 811.7362W52/6, 7; "Notes on a Conversation Between Fletcher and Messrs. Carlton, Atkins, and Wilson of Western Union," 17 January 1922, and J. A. Metzger, Solicitor's Office, "Memorandum for the Solicitor," 29 April 1922, RG 59, file, 811.7353bW52/213, 8½; and Dresel to Hughes, 14 September 1920, RG 59, file, 574.D1/136.

40. Dresel to Hughes, 27 February 1922, and Solicitor's Office memorandum, 18 October 1924, RG 59, file, 811.7362C73/1, 8; and Mackay to Hughes, 7 February 1922, RG 59, file, 811.73b/32.

Concurrent with its German negotiations, Western Union was also negotiating with a newly formed Italian syndicate for a line from the United States to Italy. The Italians wanted a joint venture, with separate Italian and American cables meeting at the Azores, and with American assistance in financing the Italy-Azores end. They also favored joint ownership of one of the ex-German transatlantic cables then controlled by Great Britain and France for the Allied and Associated powers.[41] But when the Allies could not agree on a formula for distributing the captured German lines, the negotiations shifted toward a private arrangement with Western Union.

After long and complicated discussions, the Western Union concluded a contract with the Italian group providing for separate cables meeting at the Azores. Western Union would help finance and would supervise the production, laying, and repair of the Italy-Azores section. All construction would conform to specifications for the newly discovered "loaded" cable, which allowed simultaneous transmission over four channels. As a result, the United States-Azores line would provide Western Union with two channels each for its Italian and German connections, and the Azores-Italy end would transmit United States-Italy and Italy-South America traffic. The latter eventually would be transferred at the Azores to a second Italian cable laid to Brazil, but until completion of this second line it would pass over the Western Union's cable to New York and then go by land down the Atlantic coast to Miami for transmission over the new Anglo-American through line to Brazil.[42] Again, the State Department tentatively approved the proposed combine with the usual stipulation regarding equal opportunity for other American interests.[43]

41. Merle-Smith, "Conference(s) with the Italian Delegation," 20, 27 September 1920, and unsigned memorandum of a conference with the Italian delegates on 7 October 1920, RG 43, "Communications Conferences," box 97.

42. The negotiations can be followed in F. M. Gunther, American chargé, Berlin, to Hughes, 22 April, 8 May, 27 November, and 11 December 1922, Ambassador Child to Hughes, 14 October and 3 November 1922, Gunther to Hughes, 23 January and 6 February 1923, Francis Stark of Western Union to Hughes, 24 July 1923, all in RG 59, file, 811.7365W52/5, 6, 13, 14, 11, 12, 18, 20, 31; Child to Dearing, 5 June 1923, RG 59, file, 811.7353b/194; and Harrison to Hughes, 10 May 1923, Harrison Papers, General Correspondence, box 11.

43. Fletcher to Carlton, 5 October 1921, Hughes to Child, 26 October 1921, Fletcher, "Memorandum of a Conversation with Carlton, McKisick, and Taff of Western Union," 30 January 1922, RG 59, file, 811.7365W52/-., 47.

Implementation of these plans, however, required access to the Azores. And in securing this, the American companies were opposed by the Pender group. Pender was willing to permit American companies to connect directly with the Continent, but he opposed any attempt to diminish his control over traffic between Europe and South America. Such traffic usually moved over lines of the Eastern group between Europe and the Azores, and then over the British Western's cable from the Azores to Brazil. Now the Commercial Company's arrangement with its German partner was to offer an alternate service, one that would route traffic from Emden to New York, across the United States over land lines operated by the Postal Telegraph Company, an affiliate of the Commercial Company, and then over the All America's lines to Central and South America.[44] Pender reacted by pressuring the Portuguese government to block the Commercial Company's concession. He was supported by the Foreign Office, the General Post Office, and the British Admiralty, all of which hoped to protect Pender's interests and, equally important, prevent an independent Europe-South America connection that would make British censorship of this traffic impossible in the event of a new war. Yielding to this public and private pressure, the Portuguese government rejected Commercial Company's bid for an independent landing permit at the Azores.[45]

For similar reasons, Pender managed to delay implementation of Western Union's plans. He insisted that its agreements to allow Europe-South America traffic to proceed via New York and Miami to Brazil would violate British Western's 1919 contract with Western Union providing for the construction of the Miami-Brazil through line.[46] As a result of his objections, a provisional concession

44. This was possible under a traffic agreement between the Commercial Company, the Postal Telegraph Company, and All America dated 5 September 1922. See RG 59, file, 811.7353bP84/19.

45. Sperling, "Memorandum of a Conversation with Sir John Denison-Pender," 18 July 1921, Foreign Office to Sir Lancelot Carnegie, British Minister, Lisbon, 26 July 1921, F.O. file: A5214/1442/45; H. A. Grant-Watson, British Embassy, Lisbon, to the Foreign Office, 29 July 1921, F.O. file: A5798/1442/45; British Admiralty to the Foreign Office, 27 August 1921, F.O. file: A5798/1442/45; Admiralty to the Foreign Office, 29 November 1921, F.O. file: A8869/1442/45; General Post Office to the Foreign Office, 28 December 1921, F.O. file: A116/116/45; and Foreign Office minute by Sperling, 26 May 1922, F.O. file: A3364/116/45. In American records see RG 59, file, 811.7353b/12, 28, 29, 33, 34, 57.

46. Mackay to Harrison, 10 April 1922, Dearing, American Minister, Lis-

secured by Western Union in July 1919 was not ratified by the lower house of the Portuguese parliament until three years later. And as finally confirmed, it contained stipulations that prohibited Western Union from canvassing in Europe for South American business and demanded that the company hand over all unordered South American traffic to the British Western at the Azores. This stipulation pleased neither Western Union nor the Pender group. The American company hoped for untrammeled landing privileges; Pender wanted his company to control both ordered and unordered South American traffic; and agents of both redoubled their efforts as the Portuguese senate began deliberations on the provisional concession.[47]

While these efforts were in progress, the British government stoutly supported Pender against attacks by the State Department. British interests, according to officials in the Foreign Office, were suffering severe financial losses because of competition resulting from the State Department's insistence upon equal opportunity. Therefore, it must be recognized that under certain conditions monopolies were "legitimate inducements" to successful business operations and that this applied in particular to the Pender monopoly of Europe-South America traffic. Besides, the Americans had their way in the Brazilian controversy and should now be willing to accommodate the British in the Azores dispute. Privately, British officials were angered by what they considered to be unjustified American criticism of Britain's wartime control of world cable communications, especially British censorship. Of course, their public defense of Pender's position at the Azores did not mention their desire to prevent a new American line from making such censorship impossible in the future. "This is not a consideration we could use openly," explained Rowland Sperling of the

---

bon, to Hughes, 26 May 1922, Mackay to Hughes, 22 June 1922, Carlton to Western Union's Washington Office, 10 August 1922, Dearing to Herbert Gould of Western Union, 15 May 1923, RG 59, file, 811.7353b/59, 72, 85, 106, 181; Metzger to Harrison, 1 November 1922, Stark to Hughes, 29 December 1922, RG 59, file, 811.7353bW52/44, 53; Dearing memorandum enclosed in Dearing to Harrison, 25 July 1922, Harrison to Dearing, 20 November 1923, Harrison Papers, General Correspondence, box 4.

47. Grant-Watson to the Foreign Office, 5 August 1922, F.O. file: A5018/116/45; Dearing to Hughes, 18 February 1922, Harrison to Fletcher, 23 February 1922, Norval Richardson, American chargé, Lisbon, to Hughes, 22 March and 24 April 1922, Dearing to Hughes, 26 May 1922, RG 59, file, 811.7353b/41, 35, 45, 61, 72.

Foreign Office, "least of all to the [United States Government] who may complain that we are hampering a legitimate form of U.S. enterprise."[48]

For American policymakers, however, "an American cable operated by the courtesy of a British company" could not be considered "an independent American route." Secretary Hughes already had instructed the American Minister at Lisbon to support requests by Western Union and Commercial Company for landing permits free of British manipulation.[49] And later, he rejected efforts by the Foreign Office to link the Brazil and Azores issues together. While not disputing the British defense of monopoly as necessary in some instances to promote business, he did deny that such conditions existed either at the Azores or in Brazil. Instead, he claimed that by placing American companies in an inequitable position and by rendering all cables "extending from the Azores to the Continent mere feeders" of the British Western, Pender's demand for control of all South American traffic retarded the development of modern communication services at the cheapest rates possible.[50]

Moreover, American policymakers accused the British of using financial pressure to maintain their cable privileges. In September 1922, in fact, the British Minister in Lisbon did urge Pender to negotiate a loan to the Portuguese government in order to protect his position at the Azores.[51] And for many American officials, this was also the time for Washington to exert some financial pressure of its own. Dana Richardson of the State Department's Western European Division wanted to use American dollars to displace

48. The official British position can be followed in, *Foreign Relations, 1922,* vol. 2, pp. 373–77, 381–83. See Foreign Office minute by Sperling, 26 May 1922, F.O. file: A3364/116/45.

49. Rogers, memorandum for Leland Harrison, 5 October 1921, Fletcher to the American Minister, Lisbon, 1 November 1921, and Hughes to the American Minister, Lisbon, 3 November 1921, RG 59, file, 811.7353b/17, 2, 18.

50. See *Foreign Relations, 1922,* vol. 2, pp. 367, 383–91; and *Foreign Relations, 1923,* vol. 2, pp. 271–79.

51. Dana Richardson, memorandum for Harrison, 11 August 1922, RG 59, file, 811.7353b/222; Carnegie to the Foreign Office, 30 September 1922, F.O. file: A6268/116/45. In a minute on this document, Sperling wrote, "It is quite legitimate for the company to lend the Portuguese Govt. money on any conditions they like to make, but I think the less we know about such a transaction, officially, the better." In a follow-up, Sperling noted that he had discussed the question of a loan with Pender, who said his banking connections might be induced to undertake the project. The records, however, contain no subsequent information. See Sperling minutes of 9 and 10 October 1922, F.O. file: A6268/116/45.

British influence and to offer loans that would entice the Portuguese government into making cable and fuel bunkering concessions to American interests.[52] Officials of the Commercial Cable Company suggested tying favorable funding arrangements for the British debt to the elimination of British obstructionism at the Azores, a trade-off that Ambassador George Harvey did discuss with British officials in London.[53] And Fred Morris Dearing, the American Minister in Lisbon, informed Portuguese officials that cable rights in the Azores were likely to be a condition when American financial assistance was needed.[54] In addition, Western Union and the Commercial Company were trying their best, through favors to Portuguese officials, to buy their way into the Azores.[55]

These initiatives, however, failed to move either Pender or the Portuguese government. And given this threat of indefinite delay, the Commercial Company abandoned its original plans for an unrestricted Azores concession. Ignoring pleas to maintain a united front against British opposition, it asked for renewal of a cancelled 1913 concession, which was issued indirectly through the Europe and Azores Telegraph Company, and, at the same time, the company agreed to transfer to the British Western all South American traffic proceeding over the Emden-Azores line of its German affiliate. Under the circumstances, the company preferred to settle for strategic arrangements with Pender rather than to continue the conflict or to agree to arrangements that would be competitive with Western Union's superior loaded cable. Already it had worked out preferential arrangements with the Eastern group for handling

52. Richardson, memorandum, 22 January 1921, and Richardson, memorandum for Harrison, 11 August 1922, RG 59, file, 811.7353b/225, 220; and Richardson to Dearing, 9 June 1921, RG 59, file, 853.51/116½.

53. Mackay to Hughes, 2 February 1923, John Goldhammer to Dearing, 2 February 1923, Hughes to Mackay, 8 February 1923, and Mackay to Hughes, 10 February 1923, RG 59, file, 811.7353b/149, 160, 152; and Ambassador Harvey to Hughes, 20 February 1923, in *Foreign Relations, 1923*, vol. 2, pp. 280–81.

54. See for example Dearing memorandum, 15 August 1922, in Dearing to Hughes, 18 August 1922, RG 59, file, 811.7353b/124; Dearing to Harrison, 12 December 1922, Harrison Papers, General Correspondence, box 4; and Dearing memorandum, 21 March 1923, in Dearing to Hughes, 24 March 1923, RG 59, file, 811.7353bW52/83.

55. Both companies, however, refused to extend loans sought by the Portuguese government. See Mackay to Harrison, 25 September 1922, Dearing memorandum, 11 December 1922, in Dearing to Hughes, 15 December 1922, Dearing to Harrison, 12 February 1923, in Dearing to Hughes, 17 March 1923, and Dearing to Harrison, 13 March 1923, RG 59, file, 811.7353b/222, 134, 160, 165.

unordered United States traffic collected by the latter in England and Europe, and apparently it was now willing to build on this relationship.[56]

Shortly thereafter, Western Union also resumed private negotiations with the Pender group. In this case, Western Union's application for an independent line was still pending in the Portuguese parliament, and the British thought it stood a good chance of eventual ratification. In April 1923, the Portuguese senate overturned the previous ruling of the lower house, which required Western Union to route unordered South American traffic via the British Western's cable. All that remained was for the two houses to negotiate the final terms for a license. At the same time, Western Union and the Italian company were threatening to bypass the Azores and construct an independent line to South America via the Canary Islands, one in other words that would compete directly with the British Western. These developments pressured Pender to salvage what he could through a cooperative arrangement with the American company. Specifically, it seemed desirable to accept a compromise that would give way on the point of ordered traffic. This idea had been broached first by F. J. Brown of the General Post Office and, by mid-1923, it had found support in the Foreign Office as well.[57]

Accordingly, a compromise was eventually worked out during a series of meetings, especially one between Pender and Carlton at the Foreign Office in November 1923. Pender abandoned his previous demand for a monopoly over all Europe-South America business and, pending completion of a direct Italy-South America line, the Western Union and its Italian affiliate agreed to hand all

56. Pender to the Foreign Office, 23 May 1923, F.O. file: A3082/319/45; and Brown to Pender, 15 June 1923, F.O. file: A3697/319/45; Harrison, "Conversation with Goldhammer and Burden of Commercial Company," 22 November 1923, RG 59, file, 811.7353bW52/175½; Goldhammer to Dearing, 3 March 1923, Dearing memorandum, 12 March 1923, in Dearing to Hughes, 17 March 1923, Goldhammer to Dearing, 31 March 1923, in Dearing to Hughes, 7 April 1923, Goldhammer to Dearing, 27 April 1923, in Dearing to Hughes, 5 May 1923, RG 59, file, 811.7353b/163, 165, 169, 178; Dearing to Harrison, 8, 13 March and 10 April 1923, Harrison Papers, General Correspondence, box 8; and undated memorandum by Frank Polk, in Polk to Harrison, 1 December 1922, Harrison Papers, General Correspondence, box 9.

57. Foreign Office minute, 26 October 1922, F.O. file: A6438/116/45; Brown to Pender, 15 June 1923, F.O. file: A3697/319/45; Grant-Wilson to the Foreign Office, 27 April 1923, F.O. file: A2492/319/45; Brown to Sperling, 11 May 1923, and minute by Sperling, 16 May 1923, F.O. file: A2815/319/45.

unordered South American traffic to the British Western at the Azores. In addition, Pender was to have a quarter interest in financing the Italian line to the Azores and, in return, was to withdraw all opposition to the landing permits stalled in the Portuguese parliament. Fearing destabilizing and unprofitable competition, both groups turned to a new cooperative arrangement as the best way to protect their interests.[58]

A similar settlement followed for traffic between northern Europe and South America. This was part of a multinational traffic arrangement between the American, Italian, German, and British companies connecting at the Azores. Under its terms, Western Union admitted the Commercial Company into its connection with the Italian group, while Commercial Company admitted Western Union into its traffic arrangements with the British Eastern. Both American companies also agreed to deal on equal terms with the newly consolidated German cable interests. And Western Union accepted the Commercial Company's agreement with Pender for transferring to the British Western all unordered traffic between northern Europe and South America gathered by the German company.[59]

As a consequence of these agreements, Pender and the Foreign Office withdrew their opposition at Lisbon.[60] And in early 1924, the Portuguese parliament formally approved landing permits for Western Union and the Commercial Company. A year later, Western Union's cable would be in operation, connecting the United States directly with Spain and Italy. And in March 1927, the Com-

58. The negotiations leading up to the agreement can be followed in Pender to Brown, 19 June 1923, enclosing a memorandum on a meeting at Electra House dated 8 June 1923, F.O. file: A3697/319/45; Foreign Office memorandum, 22 June 1923, F.O. file: A3698/319/45; "Unsigned Heads of Agreement Between Pender and Carlton," 19 November 1923, F.O. file: A6859/319/45; Pender to Sperling, 4 December 1923, F.O. file: A7158/319/45; Pender to Sperling, 11 December 1923, F.O. file: 7278/319/45; and Gould to Sperling, 14 December 1923, F.O. file: A7341/319/45. In American records see RG 59, file, 811.7353b/187, 191, 194, 204; RG 59, file, 811.7353bW52/29, 30, 34, 150, 178; and Stark to Harrison, 10 November 1923, Harrison Papers, General Correspondence, box 11.

59. Goldhammer to Hughes, 25 February 1925, RG 59, file, 811.7353bW52/249; Mackay to Kellogg, 3 March 1925, Goldhammer to Kellogg, 5 February 1926, RG 59, file, 811.7365C73/1, 2; Mackay to Kellogg, 16 March 1925, RG 59, file, 811.7353bW/251; Stark to Kellogg, 1 April 1925, RG 59, file, 811.7362W52/24; Mackay to Kellogg, 2 April 1924, and Goldhammer to Kellogg, 7 April 1925, RG 59, file, 811.7362C73/9, 10.

60. Foreign Office to Carnegie, 14 December 1923, F.O. file: A1375/94/45.

mercial Company and Western Union would formally inaugurate their direct German connections with an exchange of felicitous greetings between President Coolidge and President Von Hindenburg.[61]

The State Department approved these agreements on condition that the compromises not prejudice the future opportunities of other American interests. This provision had been written into the cable landing license for Western Union's United States-Azores line and, under prodding from the State Department, had been accepted by its Italian associate.[62] The Commercial Company, too, had agreed to insert it in the 1922 landing license for its German connection and subsequently included Western Union in its previously exclusive arrangement with the German cable company.[63] Both companies had also reaffirmed their commitment to equal opportunity for other American interests before the Department had approved their traffic arrangements with the German company.[64]

But for some policymakers, these agreements involved restrictions that could not be concealed by such halfway concessions to the American principle of equal opportunity. Specifically, they

61. Carnegie to the Foreign Office, 25 and 29 February 1924, F.O. file: A1375/A1425/94/45; Dearing to Hughes, 25 January 1924, Mackay to Hughes, 8 February 1924, RG 59, file, 811.7353b/215, 212. For the exchange of first messages see RG 59, files, 811.7353bW52/246, 811.7365W52/69c, and 811.7362/5.

62. Italian Ambassador to Hughes, 28 May 1923, unsigned "Memorandum of an Interview with the Italian Ambassador," 28 May 1923, Hughes to the Italian Ambassador, 9 June 1923, Italian Ambassador to Hughes, 21 June 1923, and Harrison to Stark, 29 August 1923, RG 59, file, 811.7365W52/26, 27, 31; and Phillips to Stark, 10 September 1923, RG 59, file, 811.7362W52/11.

63. Solicitor's Office memorandum, 17 January 1923, RG 59, file, 811.7365W52/16½; Stark to Harrison, 13 June 1924, Harrison to Stark, 20 June 1924, Stark to Harrison, 10 July and 19 September 1924, solicitor's memorandum, 18 October 1924, Stark to Harrison, 27 October 1924, and Mackay to Hughes, 2 January 1925, RG 59, file, 811.7362C73/5, 20, 21, 8, 22, 6; Burden of Commercial Company to Metzger, 5 November 1924, RG 59, file, 811.7353b/237½.

64. Harrison to Goldhammer, 23 April 1925, Goldhammer to Kellogg, 24 April 1925, Harrison to Goldhammer, 30 April 1925, Goldhammer to Kellogg, 6 May 1925, Mackay to Kellogg, 11 May 1925, Goldhammer to Kellogg, 22 May 1925, Harrison to Goldhammer, 13 June 1925, RG 59, file, 811.7362C73/10, 12, 13, 14, 15; Harrison to Stark, 23 April 1925, Stark to Kellogg, 24 April 1925, Harrison to Stark, 30 April and 19 May 1925, RG 59, file, 811.7362W52/24, 27, 31.

blocked the kind of independent and competitive American cable system that, for Dearing at least, had been the ultimate goal of the Department's Open Door diplomacy. As Dearing saw it, the American companies had abandoned the Department before British obstructionism had been defeated, and the principle of equal opportunity had been established without debilitating concessions to the Pender group. "They are 'pikers,' " he wrote his close friend Leland Harrison, "unmoved by any patriotic considerations."[65]

Given the ban on state management, however, the State Department was ready to soften the competitive aspects of the Open Door in favor of cooperative arrangements worked out at the private level. It would not override private business considerations even to gain its postwar objective of a wholly American cable system. When Commercial Company justified its decision to cooperate with Pender as a practical business proposition, for example, the Department did not block the arrangement but merely refused to assist the company in securing its objective.[66] As Hughes elaborated in commenting upon the Western Union's similar compromise: "If American companies desired to accept less than [the] Department has endeavored to assist them to obtain, they are at liberty to do so and must accept [the] consequences and assume responsibility for their action."[67] In 1927, moreover, the Department was still holding to this position. When Dearing obdurately requested permission to renew his fight for "untrammeled landing licenses in the Azores," he was told that it would not be "expedient" to press the matter. Private arrangements already had been concluded, noted Assistant Secretary of State William Castle, and relations with the British concerning cable communications were satisfactory.[68] The United States government, it appeared, had succumbed

65. For Dearing's views see Dearing to Goldhammer, 6 March and 5 April 1923, Dearing to Harrison, 10 April 1923, RG 59, file, 811.7353b/163, 169, 170; and Dearing to Harrison, 8, 13 March and 15 June 1923, Harrison Papers, General Correspondence, box 4.

66. Memoranda (3) of conversations with Lester Woolsey representing the Commercial Company, 20 April, 2 and 17 May 1923, Harrison Papers, General Correspondence, box 8; Dearing to Harrison, 13 March 1923, Harrison Papers, General Correspondence, box 4; and Hughes to Lansing and Woolsey, 17 May 1923, RG 59, file, 811.7353b/175.

67. Hughes to the American chargé, London, 30 June 1923, in *Foreign Relations, 1923*, vol. 2, p. 298.

68. Dearing to Kellogg, 1 May 1927, William R. Castle to Dearing, 28 June 1927, RG 59, file, 811.7353b/250. See also solicitor's memorandum, 24 May 1927, RG 59, file, 811.7353bW53/–.

to arguments originally advanced by the British and was now unwilling to force private leaders to accept the competitive implications intrinsic in a broad application of the Open Door.

IV

As in South America, privately negotiated compromises with the
British in the north Atlantic had led the State Department to
abandon its original plan for an all-American system and accept
less than a complete recognition of the principle of equal opportunity. The British government, too, fell in with this program. This
permitted Anglo-American cooperation at the private level, allowed American interests to gain direct continental connections,
and avoided the pitfalls of either government intervention or reckless and unprofitable competition. Through a mutual abandonment
of postwar plans for separate, national systems, there had emerged
a multinational communications network that was managed by
private officials and dominated by British and American interests.
This development would become even more apparent, however,
when private officials tried to broaden the new cooperative capitalism by incorporating the long-distance radio business into the private structure of Anglo-American cooperation.

CHAPTER 7

The Private Structure
of Cooperation in Communications

Radio Policy in the Postwar Decade

Patterns found in cable policy were also present in the development of long-distance radio during the postwar period. As wartime concern for a secure system of radio communications in the Western Hemisphere began to evaporate, the emphasis shifted to private as opposed to state management of radio facilities. At the same time, in both the domestic and international arenas, private American officials sought to substitute collaboration and combination for competition in the radio business. Such collaboration, they argued again, would encourage orderly and innovative development, eliminate "destructive" competition, and, concomitantly, avoid a wasteful and unprofitable duplication of services. In theory anyway, it would also alleviate any need for excessive government intervention and stimulate the kind of wide-ranging expansion of radio systems not considered feasible under competitive conditions. In the international sphere, British and American radio companies took the lead in organizing such collaboration on a multinational basis. To be sure, the resulting arrangements often amounted to private monopolies, but ones cloaked in appeals for enlightened business self-regulation, foreign-trade expansion, and increased international understanding. To the extent that private officials gained government sanction for their programs, therefore, they again abridged the traditional definition of the Open Door and added another layer to the private structure of cooperative multinationalism.

I

As in cable communications, the British had dominated prewar radio. The United States Navy Department operated a network of radio stations along both coasts of the United States and in American territories, possessions, and certain foreign countries. These stations handled official government radio business as well as commercial traffic in areas where private radio facilities were inadequate.[1] Commercial interests in the United States also operated a small number of competitive radio enterprises, but of these interests only the United Fruit Company and the Federal Telegraph Company of California had facilities abroad, in South and Central America. Marconi's Wireless Telegraph Company of London, on the other hand, had world-wide holdings. Its subsidiary, the Marconi Company of America, virtually controlled ship-to-shore communications in the United States. Marconi Wireless, moreover, could depend on aggressive diplomatic support from the British government. Indeed, soon after the war it became the key to London's plans for an all-British radio system, which would link together the far-flung corners of the British Empire. According to R. P. Schwerin of the Federal Telegraph Company, the British were "leaving no stone unturned" in their effort to control the world's radio communications. And Marconi Wireless control, he concluded, was "but another name for 'British Government Control.' "[2]

In the United States, lack of adequate radio facilities and the peculiar character of the radio industry became the central factors in discussions concerning a governmental role in developing an American radio system. The early debate revolved around legislation drafted by an interdepartmental committee organized under the Navy Department. As considered by Congress in January 1917, the bill was designed to eliminate Marconi's domination of American radio and erect instead an efficient and all-American system of wireless communication. It would authorize the Navy to purchase all privately owned coastal radio stations, would put the government into competition with commercial radio companies for public business, and would deny radio licenses to companies incorporated abroad or controlled by foreign capital.[3] Such mea-

1. Department of the Navy, *Annual Report of the Director of Communications, United States Navy, 1916*, pp. 143–53.
2. Schwerin to the Secretary of State, 9 April 1919, RG 59, file, 811.74/171. See also D. W. Todd, Navy Communication Service, to Boaz Long of the State Department, 12 April 1918, and George S. Davis of United Fruit Company to Long, 23 April 1918, RG 59, file, 810.74/104, 96. On British plans for an imperial wireless system see Alfred Nutting, clerk in the American consulate, London, "Report on Proposed Wireless Chain," 7 April 1920, Consul General Robert Skinner, London, "British Empire Wireless Communications," 21 January 1921, and Skinner, "British Empire Wireless Communications," 27 October 1921, RG 59, file, 841.74/30, 33, 38.
3. House, Committee on the Merchant Marine and Fisheries, *Hearings on*

sures, so Navy officials argued, were necessary to conserve radio frequencies, prevent "destructive" interference caused by duplication of services, and preserve American control over valuable radio facilities in the United States. If enacted, moreover, the bill would guarantee the government an extensive and dependable communications network during national security emergencies, a factor of increasing importance after the outbreak of war in Europe. But as industry spokesmen saw it, existing legislation was already sufficient to permit emergency seizures. And they claimed that commercial operators would cooperate with the government in meeting any national emergency. Consequently, there was no need for further infringements upon private enterprise, which, in practice, were likely to result in greater inefficiency, more costly service, and less technological innovation.[4]

Although Congress did not act on the 1917 bill, United States entry into the war did place the Navy in temporary control of American radio facilities. More important, the Navy's successful operation of these facilities during the conflict rekindled interest in the benefits of a permanent government monopoly. Under the Navy's regime, transoceanic and ship-to-shore radio communications were maintained throughout the war. A new high-powered station was also erected at Annapolis; radio facilities were consolidated; and combining hitherto exclusive patents, private and government laboratories were able to construct more advanced facilities and encourage innovations. The result was both a successful military radio service and a profitable operation of some commercial business. In the minds of those Navy officials involved, such success seemed to clear "the way for making this service entirely governmental."[5]

H. R. 19350: A Bill to Regulate Radio Communications, 11–26 January 1917; Linwood S. Howeth, *History of Communications-Electronics in the United States Navy*, pp. 314–16; and "The New Radio Legislation," pp. 226–40.

4. *Hearings on H. R. 19350: Radio Communications*, especially the testimony of John Griggs and Edward J. Nally of the Marconi Company of America, S. M. Kintner of the National Electric Signaling Company, and Davis of United Fruit Company, pp. 169–95, 271–92. For more on the Navy's view see also *Annual Report of the Director of Communications, United States Navy, 1916*, pp. 143–53, and *Annual Report of the Secretary of the Navy, 1916*, p. 28. See also "Government Ownership of Wireless," pp. 300–308; and "Dangers of the Proposed New Radio Bill," pp. 374–87.

5. Department of the Navy, *Annual Report of the Secretary of the Navy, 1917*, p. 44; Department of the Navy, *Annual Report of the Secretary of the Navy, 1918*, pp. 22–23; and Howeth, *History of Communications-Electronics*, pp. 208–9, 373–75.

Accordingly, in 1918, Secretary of the Navy Josephus Daniels again urged Congress to establish a single, government-owned radio system, free of both destructive interference and foreign influence. The proposed system, it was now asserted, would protect national security, stimulate commercial expansion, promote American influence abroad, and, by facilitating the flow of news and information, increase world understanding.[6] But industry representatives continued to dissent. According to David Sarnoff of American Marconi, government ownership would "stifle . . . growth and development [in] the radio art" by discouraging the individual initiative needed to foster new inventions and innovations. George Davis of the United Fruit Company also denounced the bill as un-American. It amounted, he said, to creeping Germanism. And with this sentiment, several influential congressmen agreed. "Having just won a fight against autocracy," charged Representative William Greene of Massachusetts, "we would start an autocratic movement by this bill that would wipe out everybody." Despite Navy Department support, therefore, such opposition killed the bill.[7]

Given congressional intransigence, the real emphasis was to be on business self-regulation and business-government cooperation. In other words, through collaboration and combination the industry itself was to eliminate unnecessary services, prevent interference, and encourage growth and innovation in the radio business. With diplomatic support from the government, moreover, it was to look out for American interests in the international arena. Such an approach, according to this argument, would eliminate the waste and rigidity inherent in excessive government regulation, and in theory the public interest would be sufficiently protected by general government supervision and by potential interindustry competition from the mail and cable services. Even Secretary

6. House, Committee on the Merchant Marine and Fisheries, *Hearings on H. R. 13159: A Bill to Further Regulate Radio Communications*, 12–19 December 1918. See also Daniels to Joshua Alexander, chairman of the House Committee on the Merchant Marine and Fisheries, 13 November 1918, Record Group 80, "General Records of the Department of the Navy," "Office of the Secretary of the Navy," file, 12479–1172 (hereafter cited as RG 80 with file number); and Josephus Daniels diary, 12 December 1918, Josephus Daniels Papers, box 3.

7. See David Sarnoff, *Looking Ahead: The Papers of David Sarnoff*, p. 11. For quotes by Davis and William Greene see *Hearings on H. R. 13159: Radio Communications*, pp. 29, 314.

Daniels, it was hoped, might now accept such an approach. He agreed, at any rate, that licensing "one private company" with "exclusive power and ownership" was the next best thing to a government radio monopoly.[8]

Accordingly, soon after Daniel's unsuccessful bid for government ownership, important officials in the Navy Department approached the General Electric Company concerning the formation of a private radio enterprise that could take the lead in organizing an all-American radio system. At the time, Marconi Wireless was concluding negotiations with General Electric to purchase the so-called Alexanderson alternator, a generator of continuous, low-frequency radio waves that had the capability to greatly improve long-distance radio transmission.[9] The Navy was worried that control of the alternator would give Marconi Wireless a practical monopoly over transoceanic radio. And having persuaded GE to terminate its negotiations, Adm. William Bullard and Comdr. S. C. Hooper joined forces with Owen D. Young of GE to urge the formation of a powerful American radio company with sufficient capital and technology to compete abroad.[10]

Under their plan, the Navy Department would operate all ship-

8. See *Hearings on H. R. 19350: Radio Communications*, especially the testimony by Nally, pp. 180–87; *Hearings on H. R. 13159: Radio Communications*; and *Annual Report of Secretary of the Navy, 1919*, p. 96.

9. These negotiations had begun earlier but were terminated by the war. See W. Rupert Maclaurin, *Invention and Innovation in the Radio Industry*, p. 100; Testimony of Owen D. Young in *Hearings on S. 4301: A Bill to Prevent the Unauthorized Landing of Submarine Cables*, pp. 331–32; Federal Trade Commission, *Report on the Radio Industry*, pp. 15–16; and Albert Davis, GE general counsel, to Owen Young, GE vice president, 13 May 1919, Owen D. Young Papers, box 75, file, 11–14–1–Wireless, Government.

10. Davis to Young, 13 May 1919, Young to Adm. William Bullard, 16 June 1919, Young Papers, box 75, file, 11–14–1–Wireless, Government; and Davis to Young, 30 June 1919, Young Papers, box 72, file, 11–14–Marconi Co. Later, the question arose as to whether the Navy officials involved were acting upon presidential authority. In 1921 testimony before the Senate, Owen Young did not explicitly involve President Wilson. But in subsequent accounts he contended that Bullard had claimed to be acting under presidential approval. The matter became of some importance because RCA officials frequently asserted this claim of presidential support in defense of their company's monopoly power. When the matter became a public issue, however, neither Bullard nor Wilson was alive to confirm or refute Young's recollection. In 1929, Adm. Cary Grayson, Wilson's personal physician, did offer testimony that suggested that Bullard had approached GE after confering with the President during a visit to the Paris Peace Conference in

to-shore communications and maintain long-distance stations for official government business. But a private company to be established by GE would be given a virtually complete monopoly over long-distance commercial traffic. The government would act as a silent partner in this enterprise, cross licensing valuable patents with the new company, holding a directorship on its board, and assisting it in gaining concessions abroad. In May 1919, the Navy solicitor drew up a contract outlining this proposal. At the same time, Assistant Secretary of the Navy Franklin Roosevelt recommended it to Secretary Daniels who was then at the Paris Peace Conference. The proposition, Roosevelt declared, had the "endorsement of all vitally concerned." It would guarantee the Navy's interest in strategic communications, create the kind of radio network needed to facilitate American trade, and prevent a foreign monopoly over this important means of communication.[11]

The major opposition to the proposal came from administration officials in Paris who still hoped for complete government ownership. Adm. William S. Benson, for example, agreed that nothing would mean more to American commerce than the development of "a purely American system of world communication." But private interests, in his view, lacked the will and capital to resist British influence and construct such a system. Communications expert Walter Rogers agreed, and in the opinion of Vance McCormick,

---

March 1919. For more information concerning these early negotiations and the views of presidential involvement see Young's testimony, *Hearings on S. 4301: Submarine Cables*, pp. 333–34; Testimony of S. C. Hooper, Young, and Cary Grayson in Senate, Committee on Interstate Commerce, *Hearings on S. 6: A Bill to Provide for the Regulation of the Transmission of Intelligence by Wire or Wireless*, vol. 1, 8 May 1929 to 26 February 1930, pp. 310–11, and vol. 2, pp. 1091, 1101–3, 1110–12; and Owen D. Young, "Freedom of the Air," p. 16.

11. Unsigned "Tentative Agreement . . . ," 7 May 1919, Record Group 38, "Records of the Department of the Navy," "General Correspondence of the Director of Naval Communications," file, 110 (hereafter cited as RG 38 with file number); Davis to Young, 30 June 1919, Young Papers, box 72, file, 11–14–Marconi Co.; Davis to Young, 13 May 1919, Young Papers, box 75, file, 11–14–1–Wireless, General; Roosevelt to Adm. William S. Benson and Daniels, 1 May 1919, Daniels Papers, box 37; Elwood to Assistant Secretary of State Norman Davis, 30 September 1920, RG 59, file, 811.74/206; Young testimony, *Hearings on S. 4301: Submarine Cables*, pp. 333–34; and Howeth, *History of Communications-Electronics*, pp. 356–57. An earlier version of the contract drawn up between the Navy and GE and dated 30 April 1919 can be found in the Young Papers, box 75, file, 11–14–1–Wireless, Government.

chairman of the War Trade Board, British interests were secretly behind the GE scheme.[12]

Apparently impressed with these arguments, Daniels put a damper on the proposal in early May 1919. In a conversation with Young and other GE officials later that month he remained cool toward the scheme, although promising now to take the matter up with other cabinet officials. Yet, when Secretary of Commerce William Redfield, following the State Department's initiative, urged government support for a private corporation capable of "carrying out the ideal of American world-wide wireless communication," Daniels dissented and, instead, appealed for a federal radio monopoly under the Navy Department.[13] This appeal failed to win congressional support, however, and in March 1920 the Wilson administration returned commercial radio facilities to private operation.[14]

With thoroughgoing government ownership ruled out, developments in American radio policy were to parallel what Navy officials like Roosevelt had recommended. They would also resemble the pattern established in Europe, where the British, French, and German governments licensed private companies to handle commercial traffic but maintained separate governmental systems, which connected their overseas possessions and which managed as much official business as possible. Such a procedure, Navy officials believed, could produce an expansive and independent radio system, meet the military requirements of the government, assure adequate dissemination of American news abroad, and facilitate the expansion of American trade. With proper safeguards against unfair

12. Benson to Daniels, 2, 5, and 6 May 1919, Daniels Papers, boxes 37, 36; Vance McCormick Diary, 5 May 1919; and Benson to the Navy Department, 4 May 1919, RG 38, file, 110.

13. Daniels to the Navy Department, 4 May 1919, RG 38, file, 110; Albert G. Davis of GE to Young, 26 May 1919, J. W. Elwood of GE, undated memorandum (probably mid-June 1919), Young to Admiral Bullard, 16 June 1919, Young Papers, box 75, file, 11–14–1–Wireless, Government; Davis to Young, 30 June 1919, Young Papers, box 72, file, 11–14–Marconi Co.; E. David Cronon, ed., *The Cabinet Diaries of Josephus Daniels, 1913–1921,* p. 416, entry for 23 May 1919; B. S. Cutler of the Bureau of Foreign and Domestic Commerce to Secretary Redfield, 26 June 1919, Redfield to Daniels, 26 June 1919, and Daniels to Redfield, 21 July 1919, RG 151, file, 75334/20; Young testimony, *Hearings on S. 4301: Submarine Cables,* pp. 334–35; and Department of the Navy, *Annual Report of the Secretary of the Navy, 1919,* pp. 96–99, 193–202.

14. Department of the Navy, *Annual Report of the Secretary of the Navy, 1920,* pp. 66–67, 407–12.

competition, it could also prevent the kind of private monopoly, which was injurious to technological progress and efficient operation.[15]

At the private level, General Electric took the lead in consolidating commercial radio interests into a unified system. As a first step, Young recommended that a new operating company be organized to acquire the property and patents of American Marconi. Indeed, concurrent with his discussions in Washington for a government-sponsored radio monopoly under GE, Young and E. J. Nally of American Marconi were negotiating for a private program that could win government support. Under their proposal, United States citizens holding stock in American Marconi would be compensated with shares in the new operating company, while GE would purchase the shares held by Marconi Wireless. The latter seemed amenable to this proposition, considering the Navy's well-known antipathy toward foreign interests operating in the United States.[16]

The result, in October 1919, was the formation of the Radio Corporation of America. As organized, RCA would have a cross-licensing agreement with GE, would be prohibited from manufacturing its own radio apparatus, and would become the exclusive United States agent for marketing GE equipment.[17] Its articles of incorporation, moreover, attempted to stymie the Navy's drive for government ownership by guaranteeing the American character of the enterprise and providing for business-government collaboration in expanding American radio facilities. They stipulated that only American citizens could be officers or directors in the corporation, limited foreign-stock subscription to 20 percent, and allowed government participation in policy formulation. Under this last provision, President Wilson appointed Admiral Bullard to the RCA

15. By 1921 the Navy Department had extended its half of this mixed system to include, in addition to ship-to-shore traffic, long-distance service for official business with every major area of the world. See S. W. Bryant, acting director of the Naval Communication Service, "Memorandum for the Secretary of the General Board," 1 June 1922, enclosing memoranda on naval communications policy, RG 38, file, 100.

16. J. W. Elwood, "Notes on a Luncheon Conversation Between Nally and Young, May 14 and June 2, 1919," and unsigned "Memorandum of a Conference with Mr. Nally," 22 May 1919, Young Papers, box 72, file, 11–14–Marconi Co.

17. Elwood to Davis, 30 September 1920, RG 59, file, 811.74/206; Federal Trade Commission, *Report on the Radio Industry*, pp. 18–22, 41–42; Young testimony, *Hearings on S. 4301: Submarine Cables*, p. 335.

board in order to protect the government's interest in radio communications and assure permanent American control of the new company.[18]

Subsequently, Young engineered a series of supplemental agreements, pooling existing and future technology and dividing the radio equipment and transmission business among the major American interests. In effect, these agreements provided for a general cross licensing of all patents and gave the American Telephone and Telegraph Company, the United Fruit Company, and the Westinghouse Company stock participation in RCA. They also established RCA as the principal American radio operating company and divided the radio apparatus market, with RCA agreeing to purchase 60 percent of its radio equipment from General Electric and the remainder from Westinghouse. According to Young, the agreements made possible a degree of stability, organization, and technological progress not known in the chaotic radio industry since the end of government controls.[19]

From this base, moreover, despite the talk of a competitive and wholly American system, cooperation and combination were soon extended to the international arena. In November 1919, RCA and Marconi Wireless concluded the first in a series of multinational agreements that were to regulate the scope of competition among the great radio companies of the world. The agreement divided the world into radio zones, guaranteeing RCA's supremacy in United States territory, protecting Marconi Wireless monopoly within the British Empire (excluding British possessions in the Western Hemisphere), and providing for the cross licensing of all

18. Davis of GE to John Gray, British Thomson-Houston Co., 1 November 1919, Young Papers, box 71, file, 11–14–Marconi Co.; Nally, president of RCA, to President Wilson, 3 January 1920, Acting Secretary of the Navy Thomas Washington to President Wilson, 12 January 1920, RG 80, file, 26509–283:23; Federal Trade Commission, *Report on the Radio Industry*, p. 19; House, Committee on the Merchant Marine and Fisheries, *Hearings on H. R. 15430: A Bill Continuing the Powers of the Federal Radio Commission*, 8 January to 4 February 1929, p. 664; Young testimony, *Hearings on S. 6: A Bill to Provide for the Regulation of the Transmission of Intelligence by Wire or Wireless*, vol. 2, pp. 1176, 1184–85.

19. Young testimony, *Hearings on S. 6: A Bill to Provide for the Regulation of the Transmission of Intelligence by Wire or Wireless*, pp. 115–17, 1217; Young testimony, *Hearings on S. 4301: Submarine Cables*, pp. 336–37; Federal Trade Commission, *Report on the Radio Industry*, pp. 44–48; Howeth, *History of Communications-Electronics*, pp. 360–63; Maclaurin, *Invention and Innovation in the Radio Industry*, pp. 105–7; Elwood to Davis, 30 September 1920, RG 59, file, 811.74/206.

patents for use by each company within its exclusive zone. This latter provision even included patent rights on the valuable Alexanderson alternator that Navy officials had originally hoped to keep exclusively in American hands. The agreement also delineated a "No-Man's Land," where competition would remain unregulated, and a "neutral zone," where both companies would compete but could use each other's patents.[20]

Similar agreements followed with other European radio interests. In this case, negotiations by the major private companies to divide the radio business on a world-wide basis had failed.[21] But these negotiations did lead to a series of important traffic agreements for a division of the European radio market and the exchange of transatlantic traffic. A 1921 contract between RCA and the General Telegraph Company of France designated the American company as the agent for messages originating in the United States, its possessions, territories, and Cuba, and assigned the French company a similar position in France, its colonies, and its dependencies. It bound the parties to deal exclusively with each other in transmitting traffic between their territories and provided for the exchange of equal amounts of unrouted messages received from or destined to outside areas. At the same time, RCA concluded an agreement with the German Ministry of Posts and its operating company. It too provided for the exchange of traffic between Germany and the United States and of equal amounts of unrouted business destined to areas beyond the designated territories.[22]

Moreover, these agreements prohibited the parties involved from marketing radio equipment in each other's territory. They also included provisions for the cross licensing of patents in both exclusive and neutral zones, and they delineated unregulated areas for sales and operations. In practice, however, American radio officials worked to alleviate competition in the unregulated zones as well. For example, General Electric was ready to contribute its patent rights to British, French, and German companies operating in countries like Belgium and Italy if these companies would pur-

20. Davis of GE to Young, 18 August 1919, and Young to Davis, 22 August 1919, Young Papers, box 72, file, 11–14–Marconi Co.; Federal Trade Commission, *Report on the Radio Industry*, pp. 52–53, 229–43; Young testimony, *Hearings on S. 4301: Submarine Cables*, p. 343.

21. Walter Rogers, "Memorandum of a Conversation with Mr. Owen Young," 12 November 1921, RG 38, file, 120.

22. Federal Trade Commission, *Report on the Radio Industry*, pp. 54–56.

chase a specified amount of equipment from one of GE's local manufacturing affiliates.[23]

These traffic arrangements afforded the United States direct radio connections with Europe. More important, they combined the patents of the major companies involved in wireless and bound the signatories to deal exclusively with each other in transmitting messages between their respective territories. This arrangement discouraged the development of new radio companies, leading the Federal Trade Commission to wonder if private operators should be licensed in order to prevent monopolistic practices. The Navy Department, too, had misgivings. But for Young, the restrictions involved were an incidental result of traffic and patent agreements that were needed to develop the radio science, connect the continents of the world, and prevent the waste and interference that accompanied an unnecessary duplication of systems.[24] The State Department apparently agreed since it had convinced the French government to negotiate with RCA for a new circuit over which transatlantic traffic could be exchanged. And for Hoover, it was impossible to force European monopolies to exchange radio traffic with more than one American company. As he saw it, moreover, the restrictions entailed were the inevitable by-product of scientific progress. When the Italian government complained that agreements between the major European and American companies gave them a monopoly over international traffic, Hoover joined P. E. D. Nagle, an expert in communications from the Commerce Department, in defending the benefits involved as the natural result of technological superiority.[25]

23. Ibid., pp. 54–56; "Memoranda of Agreement between RCA and the Telefunken Company, February 21, 1921," Young to Nally, 12 January 1923, Young Papers, box 61, file, 6–16–AEG; "Memoranda of Agreement between RCA and the General Telegraph Company of France, February 26, 1921," Young Papers, box 99, file, 11–14–10–South American Radio Situation; and R. G. Handerson of RCA, memorandum, 18 December 1922, Young Papers, box 100, file, 11–14–10–South American Radio Situation.

24. Federal Trade Commission, *Report on the Radio Industry*, pp. 67–68; Young testimony, *Hearings on S. 6: A Bill to Provide for the Regulation of the Transmission of Intelligence by Wire or Wireless*, pp. 1132–35, 1142–43; Howeth, *History of Communications-Electronics*, p. 363; and Maclaurin, *Invention and Innovation in the Radio Industry*, p. 107.

25. Howeth, *History of Communications-Electronics*, p. 363; Herbert Hoover to Charles Evans Hughes, 20 March 1924, RG 59, file, 810.74/136; William Phillips to Hoover, 31 August 1923, enclosing Aide-Memoire from the Italian Embassy dated 25 July 1923, and Hoover to Hughes, 10 Septem-

In its search for stability, RCA was soon extending the policy of collaboration and combination to South America and China. And despite the early talk of an independent and competitive American radio system, these efforts were unaffected by any government concern for the principle of equal opportunity. Only the Navy Department seemed worried that such collaboration would eliminate competition and prevent the expansion of an independent American system. Officials in the Commerce Department, on the other hand, took the lead in reinforcing private efforts to stabilize the long-distance radio business by forging a system of international regulation that would standardize radio practices under government supervision but without infringing upon private management.

II

Initially, the Wilson administration had supported government ownership of radio facilities throughout the Western Hemisphere. This policy was intended to bolster U.S. trade expansion and develop closer ties between Latin America and the United States. Yet it also involved security considerations, especially the fear that foreign-owned radio facilities in South America might compromise the hemisphere's neutrality by transmitting propaganda during the war.

The first major enunciation of this policy had come in October 1915, when the State Department notified all Central and South American governments that it supported government ownership. At that time, the Department expressed a willingness to accept any agreement that would eliminate foreign participation in the ownership of radio and suggested an exchange of views on the matter at the Pan American Scientific Congress, which was to be held in Washington in January 1916. When the conference convened, Navy officials used the occasion to reemphasize the need for governmental systems to prevent violations of neutrality and to guarantee national safety. The South American delegates to the conference agreed to receive a statement of the Navy's position through normal diplomatic channels for consideration at a later date.[26]

ber 1923, enclosing a memorandum by P. E. D. Nagle dated 7 September 1923, RG 151, file, 544, Radio-General.

26. Secretary Daniels to the Secretary of State, 16 June 1915, the Secretary of State to Daniels, 9 July 1915, Acting Secretary of the Navy Franklin Roosevelt to the Secretary of State, 24 September 1915, circular instructions to the diplomatic officers of the United States accredited to Latin American

Accordingly, in March 1916, the State Department again transmitted the Navy's recommendations for a uniform organization of radio facilities throughout the hemisphere. A government-owned and regionally integrated system, the circular explained, would help to guarantee security and encourage a broader Pan-Americanism. And it would do so with greater economy and efficiency, lower costs, and more rapid operation than was possible by the expansion of separate, private systems. With these advantages in mind, the Navy recommended designating a special inter-American committee to devise the regulations necessary to combine the radio services of all American republics. And as a basis for discussion, it suggested dividing the hemisphere into radio zones with one control station for each zone and one centrally located main station for the entire hemisphere.[27]

While pushing this intergovernmental system, however, the Wilson administration was also encouraging private concessions as an alternate means of keeping foreign influences out of the hemisphere. With State Department support, for example, the Federal Telegraph Company of California secured a concession to build a radio station in Argentina, a station the company hoped would be the first in a radio system connecting all South and Central America, Mexico, the Caribbean area, and the United States. In Brazil, too, the Department supported the wholly American Federal Company in preference to the British-controlled American Marconi.[28] And in 1917, it approved the consolidation of the two companies in the Pan American Telegraph Company on the assumption that complete American control of the combine was assured. As Admiral Benson pointed out, the project permitted United States interests to control the Marconi system in South America pending implementation of the Navy's plan for an integrated radio network under government control.[29]

governments, 13 October 1915, Butler Wright, "Minutes of the Informal Conference on Radio Communications held at the Department of State," 7 January 1916, all in RG 59, file, 810.74/–, 1, 5a, 41.

27. Circular letter to the diplomatic representatives of the United States in Central and South America, 15 March 1916, with enclosed recommendations dated 11 March 1916, RG 59, file, 810.74/58b. See also in this connection Daniels to Robert Lansing, 24 January and 8 February 1919, RG 80, file, 12479–A–249:18.

28. Lansing to Daniels, 16 October 1915, RG 59, file, 810.74/5b. See also Alvey Adee to Daniels, 6 July 1916, RG 80, file, 12479–249:32.

29. Jordon Stabler, Latin American Division, to Lester Woolsey, 26 October 1917, enclosing two memoranda dated 25 October 1917, Sydney Stead-

The South American governments, though, failed to act on the Navy's 1916 proposal. And given this inaction, some officials in both the Navy and State departments began to believe that private enterprise was the best means of controlling South American radio. The construction of an intergovernmental system promised long delays and endless political complications, they argued, and unless the administration acted quickly, foreign interests might completely dominate South American radio. Accordingly, they favored consolidating South American radio under one or two U.S. companies, with the government helping to pay the costs of expanding these private systems. In April 1918, Boaz Long, United States minister to Salvador, drafted such a plan in the form of a letter from Secretary of State Robert Lansing to the President. But Secretary Daniels remained an obstacle; he squelched the plan before Lansing could sign the letter,[30] continued to support an intergovernmental system, and stubbornly prevented a change in policy even after Congress had rejected his request for government ownership.[31]

The result, then, was neither government ownership nor a government-subsidized all-American system. Instead, with both blocked, private officials moved toward collaboration with their foreign counterparts and, as national security considerations became less important, government officials followed suit. The first step occurred when RCA absorbed American Marconi in 1919. Under this deal, RCA acquired Marconi's stock in the Pan American Company and other radio enterprises in Argentina. These hold-

---

man to Lansing, 28 October 1917, Loucks and Alexander, counsel for the Pan American Company, to Lansing, 31 October 1917, Lansing to the Pan American Company, 2 November 1917, all in RG 59, file, 811.74/143, 142, 141a; and Daniels to Lansing, 24 November 1917, RG 59, file, 810.74/94. The Navy subsequently withdrew its support for the consolidation when it discovered that the Federal would control only a quarter interest in the new combine. The remaining shares were divided between the British and American Marconi companies. See Davis of GE to Young, 17 June 1919, Young Papers, box 72, file, 11–14–Marconi Co.

30. Memorandum for the Secretary of the Navy, 12 March 1918, Boaz Long to Stewart Johnson of the Latin American Division, 3 April 1919, Long to Skinner, 27 July 1920, enclosing draft letter for the President dated 25 April 1918, memorandum for the Secretary of State, 20 April 1918, and "Confidential Summary," 22 April 1918, RG 59, file, 810.74/103, 97, 108.

31. Assistant Secretary of the Navy Roosevelt to Leo S. Rowe, Assistant Secretary of the Treasury, 6 December 1919, and Foreign Trade Adviser's memorandum for Wesley Frost, 13 April 1920, RG 59, file, 810.74/99, 105. See also Daniels to Lansing, 16 July 1919, RG 80, file, 12479A–362.

ings were to be consolidated into a new South American radio company organized by RCA for communication with a new Marconi station in England. Because of disputes over the distribution of stocks, however, plans for the new company lagged over the next two years. In the meantime, the major French and German companies also acquired concessions from the Argentine government for the erection of new high-powered stations near Buenos Aires. If constructed, these stations would prejudice Anglo-American interests in Argentina and, more important, preempt radio communications between South America, Europe, and the United States.[32]

Accordingly, the British suggested a plan for multinational collaboration in the development of South American radio, one that would incorporate the French and Germans, provide for joint control of a prewar German station in Argentina, and adopt a similar program for all long-distance South American radio communications. In February 1921, the companies involved accepted this program in principle and, in October, they formed the AEFG Trusteeship. Under this arrangement, each national group assigned its patents and existing concessions in South America to a board of trustees for operation by subsidiary national companies. Each group also agreed to deal exclusively with these national companies when transmitting messages to and from a territory served by its radio system. And each would share equally in the business, profits, and management of the new consortium, appropriately named the International Combined System. To appease the State Department, however, the board of trustees was to be chaired by an American citizen, not a spokesman for the American interests, but appointed by RCA and with the power to veto any proposal. Theoretically, this would guarantee the enterprise's American character, enshrine the Monroe Doctrine, and protect the special interests of the United States in South America.[33]

32. Ronald Macleay, British Minister in Buenos Aires, to the Foreign Office, 21 July 1920, F.O. file: A5830/5830/2; and C. Mallet, British Embassy, Buenos Aires, to the Foreign Office, 6 November 1922, F.O. file: A7471/7471/2.

33. Ibid.; Macleay to the Foreign Office, 22 November 1921, F.O. file: A946/1126/2; Nally to Young, 8 February 1921, unsigned memorandum, "Scope of the South American Agreement," 21 February 1921, Godfrey Isaacs, managing director of Marconi Wireless, to Nally, 12 July 1921, Young to Isaacs, 11 August 1921, and Isaacs to Young, 12 August 1921, Young Papers, box 99, file, 11–14–10–South American Radio Situation; Federal Trade Commission, *Report on the Radio Industry*, pp. 57–59, 60–62, 312–29; P. Page, RCA vice president, to the American Embassy, Buenos Aires, 4 Feb-

In 1923 and 1924, the government finally abandoned its efforts to erect a state-managed and strictly American radio system in the Western Hemisphere. In March 1923, J. G. Harbord, president of RCA, asked the State Department to support the new combine and repeal the 1916 South American circular that had endorsed government ownership. Secretary Hughes forwarded this request to Hoover and Secretary of the Navy Curtis Wilbur. The principal reason behind the 1916 declaration, Hughes noted, had been the advantages of government ownership during periods of neutrality and war. Conditions had changed, he explained, and, in addition, all operating contracts for the Trusteeship would provide for government control should national security emergencies arise in the future. The Commerce Department readily agreed to abandon all demands for government ownership, and the Navy, too, was prepared to renounce its original desire for an intergovernmental system of wireless communications. Pointing out that American interests would control only one-fourth of the consortium, however, the Navy was at first reluctant to endorse it as a solely American enterprise privileged to government support. In addition, Assistant Secretary of the Navy Theodore Roosevelt considered the Trusteeship tantamount to a private monopoly that would give its members "unwarranted control" over South America and "restrict the development of radio communications" in the future.[34]

According to Hoover, however, the Wilson administration had "incurred certain obligations" to RCA by urging it to develop American radio abroad when government ownership appeared doomed. Despite RCA's limited share in the consortium, moreover, he favored government support for it as the "best arrangement" that American interests could get. For him, it reflected the technical and practical realities of radio enterprise, would greatly facilitate a constructive "build-up of world communications," and would be subject to competitive pressure from different modes of

ruary 1922, RG 151, file, 544–Radio, Argentina; James G. Harbord, president of RCA, to Secretary Hughes, 10 March 1923, RG 59, file, 810.74/118; Harbord to Hughes, 17 August 1923, RG 59, file, 820.74/–; memorandum for Merle-Smith, 4 February 1921, RG 59, file, 811.74/215; and Rogers, "Memorandum of a Conversation with Mr. Owen Young," 12 November 1921, RG 38, file, 120.

34. Harbord to Hughes, 10 March 1923, Hughes to the secretaries of Navy and Commerce, 14 March 1923, Hoover to Hughes, 15 March 1923, Acting Secretary of the Navy to Hughes, 19 December 1923, W. R. Vallance to Harrison, 4 February 1924, all in RG 59, file, 810.74/118, 109a, 111, 134; and Acting Secretary of the Navy to Hughes, 15 March 1923, RG 38, file, 120.

communication. Under this prodding, the Navy reversed itself and, in April 1924, endorsed RCA's membership in the Trusteeship, provided that equal opportunity was assured to other "bona fide American interests that may develop in the future."[35]

While overcoming the Navy's reluctance, the State Department was also moving swiftly to reverse Daniels's early demand for government ownership of radio facilities in the Western Hemisphere. In this connection, the United Fruit Company had joined RCA's attack on the 1916 circular as detrimental to private radio enterprise in Central and South America.[36] As a result, Hughes notified the American legations in Chile, Uruguay, Brazil, and Argentina that the United States no longer advocated government ownership.[37] In 1924, moreover, the American representative at the Mexico City Conference on Inter-American Communications affirmed the administration's commitment to "private ownership and management," insisted that government supervision of radio must not "interfere with the rights of management inherent in the ownership of property," and recommended "private initiative and the investment of private capital" as the "best" means of improving radio communications in the hemisphere.[38] And in late 1925, the Department responded to new requests from United Fruit Company for wider circulation of the Mexico City statement by soliciting new declarations from the Navy, War, and Commerce departments in favor of private management of radio facilities.[39]

As the wartime emergency passed, then, collaboration among private, multinational radio interests replaced the Navy Depart-

35. Hoover to Hughes, 15 March and 5 November 1923, and 20 March 1924, Hughes to Hoover, 11 February 1924, Vallance to Harrison, 4 February 1924, and Secretary of the Navy Curtis Wilbur to Hughes, 2 April 1924, all in RG 59, file, 810.74/111, 132, 136, 134, 137.

36. Lansing and Woolsey for the United Fruit Company to Hughes, 27 February 1923, RG 59, file, 710./Ela/81.

37. Hughes to American Legations, 20 March 1923, RG 59, file, 810.74/111.

38. Charles Warren, chairman, American Delegation to the conference, to the Secretary of State, 17 July 1924, RG 59, file, 574.D4/117.

39. Lansing and Woolsey to the Secretary of State, 28 September 1925, enclosed in Harrison to the Secretary of the Navy, 20 October 1925, and Wilbur to the Secretary of State, 23 October 1925, RG 38, file, 100; Vallance, memorandum, 9 October 1925, Harrison to the secretaries of Commerce and War, 20 October 1925, Secretary of War Dwight Davis to the Secretary of State, 7 November 1925, and Acting Secretary of Commerce Stephen Davis to the Secretary of State, 18 December 1925, all in RG 59, file, 810.74/139, 142, 143.

ment's early efforts to forge an all-American radio system under government ownership. Industry officials renounced competition as a wasteful use of resources, as incompatible with the radio art, and as detrimental to the development of an expansive radio system. The administration accepted this policy despite warnings by the Navy that such cooperative arrangements were tantamount to a dangerous private monopoly over long-distance radio. At the same time, moreover, cooperative action was spreading to other areas of the world. In China, for example, the same private, multinational interests were already pushing for similar arrangements. Here, however, their plans were stymied by the reluctance of the Japanese and United States governments to abandon all ambitions for particular advantage.

III

In China, the United States tried to balance conflicting tendencies toward independent action and cooperation. In 1921, the Federal Telegraph Company of California had signed a contract with the Chinese government, which allowed the Federal to erect a network of high-powered radio stations in China, for communication with its facilities in California and for operation under joint account with the Chinese government. This network would provide the commercial service that was needed by American traders, especially after the Navy's high-powered station in Peking was limited by international agreement to handling government traffic. Protests by the British, Japanese, and Danish governments, however, had stalled its implementation. According to these protests, the concession violated privileges previously acquired by the Marconi and Mitsui radio companies and the British Eastern Extension and Danish Great Northern cable companies. And in the face of them, the State Department had become involved in defending the Federal's contract, rejecting claims to exclusive privilege as a violation of United States treaty rights, and asserting an Open Door for communications in China.[40]

At this point, important proposals for the cooperative develop-

40. Federal Trade Commission, *Report on the Radio Industry*, pp. 59–60; Harry W. Kirwin, "The Federal Telegraph Company: A Testing of the Open Door," pp. 271–85; *Foreign Relations, 1921*, vol. 1, pp. 404–56; "Memorandum of a Conference in the Office of the Third Assistant Secretary of State," 21 January 1921, RG 43, "Communications Conference," box 100; and Nagle to Thomas Luckett, 1 November 1922, RG 151, file, 544, Radio-General.

ment of Chinese radio were advanced at both the public and private levels. Initially at least, the British took the lead. For policy-makers in the Foreign Office, it would be "most unfortunate if a comparatively small matter like [the radio controversy] should be allowed to mar Anglo-American harmony in China, to which both America and ourselves attach much importance." Accordingly, during a conversation with Butler Wright of the American Embassy, Foreign Secretary Curzon deplored the "squabbling" among the great powers over radio rights and, pointing to the new financial consortium, suggested ending the "international competition" through an "amalgamation of interests on an international scale."[41] The British Minister in Peking made a similar recommendation, although he was not certain how American officials would apply the "open door" principle "in the case of agreements covering co-operation."[42] And, at the same time, Miles Lampson of the Far Eastern Division suggested a cooperative settlement to Col. Adrian Simpson of Marconi Wireless. Lampson felt that "cut-throat international competition" was "unsound from a business point of view" and would only enable the Chinese to play "one Power against the other." Accordingly, he promised a relaxation of the monopoly over external communications from China that was claimed by the British and Danish cable companies if Marconi would discuss a cooperative settlement with its foreign rivals. Simpson agreed and wired his representative in Peking that "a pooling of all wireless interests in China" offered a "good way out" of the present difficulties.[43] Still later, Godfrey Isaacs, head of Marconi Wireless, officially notified the Foreign Office that his company was now "quite prepared to consider any pooling of interests" in China.[44]

In the United States, the Radio Corporation was urging a scheme similar to the South American consortium, including the transfer of all rights and properties claimed in China to a board of trustees consisting of British, French, Japanese, and American directors,

41. Miles Lampson, memorandum, 14 April 1921, and Curzon to Sir Auckland Geddes, British Ambassador to the United States, 20 April 1921, F.O. file: F1435/18/10. See also Lampson to F. J. Brown, General Post Office communications expert, 11 April 1921, F.O. file: F1277/181/10.
42. Alston to Curzon, 28 April 1921, F.O. file: F1614/181/10.
43. Lampson, memorandum, 20 April 1921, F.O. file: F1489/181/10; and Adrian Simpson to Ginman, 26 April 1921, F.O. file: F1575/181/10. See also Curzon to Alston, 27 April 1921, enclosing a message from Godfrey Isaacs to Ginman, F.O. file: F1569/181/10.
44. Isaacs to the Foreign Office, 27 October 1921, F.O. file: F3975/181/10.

all exercising equal authority. According to Young, China radio could not be developed "by competitive duplication of stations." Stations were "too expensive—business too meagre—wave lengths all too rare, and national feeling with reference to control of Chinese communications . . . too high" for an independent enterprise to be successful. Only a well-planned cooperative system could end the conflicts over concessions, allow prompt construction of modern radio facilities, permit "economy of capital and wave lengths," and "insure an open door policy in communications."[45]

For similar reasons, Young also supported a combination of RCA and the Federal to form the American section of the proposed consortium. Competition between weak American companies, he asserted, would fail to develop radio, would lead to uneconomical and unprofitable operations, and would hinder technological innovations. Worse, it would surrender control of American radio by allowing unified foreign systems to play one American company off against the other. It would be much better, he thought, to have a strong and unified combination subject to government supervision. Otherwise, like Daniels earlier, he favored a state monopoly.[46]

These proposals came to a head at the Washington Conference of 1921 and 1922. At that time, the British again urged a new effort "to bring some kind of order out of the present chaos" in Chinese radio. Specifically, Lord Balfour of the British delegation proposed a "consortium principle of international cooperation."[47] French officials agreed. They suggested creating a special committee to recommend procedures whereby "competition should give way to cooperation" in the development of China radio. Such cooperation would furnish China with the most modern facilities while avoiding "the waste of capital, of staff, of material and of wave-lengths"

45. Rogers, "Memorandum of a Conversation with Mr. Owen Young," 12 November 1921, RG 38, file, 120; *Foreign Relations, 1922*, vol. 1, pp. 830–35, 837–38. See also Navy Department memorandum, 3 January 1922, RG 80, file, 26509–283:23.

46. Young to Sen. Elihu Root, 12 December 1921, and Young to Hughes, 9 January 1922, in *Foreign Relations, 1922*, vol. 1, pp. 834–35, 837–38; Young to Secretary of the Navy Edwin Denby, 22 December 1921, Young Papers, box 126, file, 11–14–49–Communications, Disarmament Conference; Young to Hoover, 30 January 1922, enclosed in Hoover to Hughes, 30 January 1922, RG 59, file, 893.74/220.

47. Balfour to Curzon, 12 December 1921, F.O. file: F4605/181/10; Balfour to Curzon, 30 December 1921, F.O. file: F2/2/10; and Brown, memorandum, 16 January 1922, F.O. file: F532/2/10.

involved in competitive services. What the French had in mind
was a consortium of private British, French, Japanese, and American radio interests, which would exercise a monopoly over China
radio with the diplomatic support of their governments. The consortium would be open to participation by additional firms in the
future, but only on a basis equal to the capital invested in their
domestic facilities. This provision would assure the domination of
the large radio companies that were to organize the consortium
initially.[48]

The British and Japanese endorsed this plan and during the conference, Young and other officials of RCA urged it upon the Chinese
and American delegates. Failure to implement it, they were now
warning, could retard the development of transpacific communications, foster destructive competition among the great radio interests, and leave the Japanese in a favored position in China. Still
worse, American opposition to the scheme might result in an independent combination of British, French, and Japanese radio
companies—one powerful enough to shut Americans out of the
transpacific business. The conference, they concluded, should
either formulate a cooperative program or endorse this approach
in principle and leave the companies free to work out the details.[49]

Although they envisioned some form of cooperation, officials in
the State and Navy departments regarded such proposals as involving too many restraints on independent action. At home, they
finally agreed to support the new Federal Telegraph Company of
Delaware, the agency that RCA and the Federal had organized to

48. Balfour to Curzon, 12 December 1921, F.O. file: F4615/181/10;
"Draft of a Motion Relating to the Organization of Radio Communications in
China," submitted by M. Viviani of the French Delegation, 7 December 1921,
and draft extract from the "Minutes of the 15th Meeting of the Committee on
Far Eastern Questions," Harrison Papers, General Correspondence, box 3;
Rogers to Root, 7 January 1922, "Memorandum on Radio Consortium for
China" attached to Rogers to Root, 10 January 1922, Maj. George Squire,
memorandum for Hughes, 17 January 1922, enclosing Blancheville to Squire,
16 January 1922, and Rogers to Root, 18 January 1922, all in Record Group
43, "Conference on the Limitation of Armaments, Records of the United
States Delegation," file, 893.74/-, 2, 216 (hereafter cited as RG 43, Disarmament Conference).

49. Young to Root, 9, 12, and 25 January 1922, Young to Hoover, 27 January 1922, Lansing and Woolsey, "Memorandum on Wave Lengths," 19 December 1921, Lansing to the Chinese Minister, Washington, 20 December
1921, with enclosed memorandum dated 16 December 1921, Woolsey to Elwood, 12 January 1922, with enclosed memorandum dated 11 January 1922,
all in Young Papers, box 126, file, 11-14-49-Communications, Disarmament
Conference.

take over the latter's concession in China. Secretary of the Navy Edwin Denby had initially opposed any cooperative plan that prevented "healthy competition" in managing China traffic or barred the Federal from erecting independent stations in both China and the United States. But he became more amenable to collaboration between the American companies when he learned that Federal, acting independently, lacked the capital and technology to exploit its concession. Support for the combination was also desirable since RCA was now threatening to negotiate a separate agreement with the British, French, and Japanese. Accordingly, the Navy Department endorsed the merger while the State Department assured RCA that it anticipated no changes in China that might "jeopardize the physical safety of the investment or any rights your corporation may acquire in connection therewith." Given this assurance, RCA concluded the merger in mid-April 1922, and in September the State Department instructed the American minister in Peking to support the new combine in its negotiations with the Chinese government.[50]

In negotiating with the other powers at the Washington Conference and later, American officials also were anxious to realize their ambitions within the cooperative framework favored by the Europeans. To be sure, they would not join a Proposed Heads Agreement for a Chinese radio monopoly based on the French plan, and they still demanded an Open Door for American radio companies and execution of the Federal's original concession for transpacific traffic. But at the same time, they were ready to accept a British, French, and Japanese radio consortium that would arrange separate traffic agreements with American stations engaged in the transpacific business. A committee of experts appointed by the

50. *Foreign Relations, 1922*, vol. 1, pp. 835–36, 848–57; Young to Bullard, 6 March 1922, Young Papers, box 147, file, 11–14–65–William Bullard; Nelson T. Johnson, Acting Chief, Far Eastern Division to Harrison, 14 February 1922, Griggs of RCA to Hughes, 12 April 1922, Phillips to Griggs, 25 April 1922, Rogers to Harrison, 2 August 1922, RG 59, file, 893.74/218, 316, 247; Far Eastern Division memorandum for Harrison, 10 July 1922, RG 59, file, 574.D1/485; Rogers to Harrison, 7 June 1922, RG 43, "Communications Conference," box 130; Navy Department memorandum, 3 January 1922, RG 80, file, 26509–283:23. RCA's negotiations with the Federal Company can be followed in the Young Papers, box 125, file, 11–14–47–Far Eastern Wireless. Before proceeding with the Federal deal, RCA also obtained the approval of the American Group in the China financial consortium. See Gerard Swope, president, International General Electric Co., to Thomas Lamont, 16 March 1922, and Lamont to Swope, 24 March 1922, Young Papers, box 125, file, 11–14–47–Far Eastern Wireless.

conference and including an American representative drafted a resolution to this effect in February 1922. Under the committee's scheme, two separate radio organizations would be established, one controlled by American companies for transpacific business and the other by British, French, and Japanese interests and managing traffic between Asia and Europe. The groups would then negotiate agreements for the exchange of traffic and the joint marketing of radio equipment in China.[51]

At the Washington Conference, then, the Americans tried to accommodate a limited degree of independent action within a program for multinational cooperation in the Fast East. By mid-1923, however, the experts' plan had not been implemented. Still worse, the Chinese, under pressure from Japan, had refused to recognize the Federal-RCA agreement, and neither they nor the Japanese were paying much attention to the American claim that such obstruction contradicted the Open Door principle that was recently recognized in the Nine Power Treaty. As a result, RCA officials divided over the course to be pursued and were threatening to terminate their agreement with the Federal in favor of cooperation with the Japanese, French, and British companies.[52] Already these companies had organized a tripartite consortium, and the Japanese wanted the new agency to block the Federal's contract and shut American radio interests out of China.[53]

Confronted with these developments, the State Department utilized a fresh British proposal as a springboard for setting forth a new version of its own position, one that would allow cooperative

51. *Foreign Relations, 1922*, vol. 1, pp. 839–44; Fletcher to Hughes, 13 December 1921, with enclosures, RG 43, "Disarmament Conference," file, 893.74/5; unsigned memorandum for Fletcher, 14 December 1921, RG 43, "Communications Conference," box 129; and undated memorandum from Harrison for Hughes, Harrison Papers, General Correspondence, box 3; Balfour to Lloyd George, 4 February 1922, F.O. file: F714/2/10; and Balfour to Curzon, 7 February 1922, F.O. file: F582/2/10.

52. *Foreign Relations, 1923*, vol. 1, pp. 783–95; Harbord to Hughes, 8 February 1923, Rogers to J. V. A. MacMurray, 16 June 1923, Harbord to Hughes, 18 and 23 June 1923, and Hughes to the American Legation, Peking, 11 July 1923, all in RG 59, file, 893.74/265, 337, 325, 360, 345.

53. Foreign Office minute by Victor Wellesley, 3 September 1923, F.O. file: F1141/846/10. A copy of the agreement between Marconi Wireless, Mitsui, and the French company is attached to this minute and dated 1 February 1923. The Japanese had been trying since 1921 to organize a united front against American radio interests. See for example Ginman to Isaacs, 20 April 1921, F.O. file: F1554/181/10; Alston to Curzon, 28 April 1921, F.O. file: F1613/18/10; and Charles Eliot, British Ambassador to Japan, to the Foreign Office, 25 May 1921, F.O. file: F2336/181/10.

arrangements but reserve most United States-China traffic for American radio interests. The British wanted confirmation of the experts' plan for China together with State Department assurances regarding the nonexclusive character of the new RCA-Federal agreement. Should these be forthcoming they promised to abandon all opposition to the American radio concession in China, affirm their own commitment to the Open Door, and push forward with plans for a cooperative arrangement.[54]

Early in July the French government formally endorsed the experts' plan, and later that month the State Department followed suit.[55] All exclusive claims in China should be surrendered, American officials agreed, and the Federal-RCA group would cooperate with a British, Japanese, and French consortium so far as traffic agreements and other business arrangements were concerned. Following the experts' recommendation, however, the American group would preserve a separate identity and specialize in United States-China traffic. Such an arrangement, so Americans felt, might limit freedom of action and compromise the State Department's ability to assure equal opportunity in transpacific traffic at some future date. But it would also give the United States direct and independent communications with China, accommodate the American companies already involved, abolish all existing monopolies, and most important, avoid "friction among the several governments and their respective nationals."[56]

54. *Foreign Relations, 1923*, vol. 1, p. 793; Geddes to the Foreign Office, 16 May 1923, F.O. file: F1525/846/10; Foreign Office to Geddes, 25 May 1923, F.O. file: F1525/846/10; Foreign Office minute by Basil Newton, 25 May 1923, F.O. file: F1626/846/10; Foreign Office minute by Wellesley, 5 June 1923, F.O. file: F1690/846/10; Foreign Office minute by Ronald Campbell, 10 July 1923, F.O. file: F2074/846/10; Foreign Office to Henry Chilton, British chargé, Washington, 11 July 1923, F.O. file: F2074/846/10; MacMurray, "Memoranda (2) of Conversations with Robert Craigie, Secretary of the British Embassy," 12 and 15 May 1923, RG 59, file, 893.74/336, 338.

55. Foreign Office minute by Newton, 22 May 1923, F.O. file: F1525/846/10; and Lord Crewe, British Ambassador in Paris, to the Foreign Office, 12 July 1923, F.O. file: F2151/846/10.

56. *Foreign Relations, 1923*, vol. 1, pp. 796–821; MacMurray to Hughes, 18 May 1923, MacMurray, "Memorandum of Conversation with Mr. Harrison and Mr. MacMurray and Mr. William Brown of RCA," 14 June 1923, MacMurray to Harrison and Hughes, 29 May 1923, Harrison Papers, General Correspondence, box 5; Hughes to the American Embassy, London, 9 July 1923, "Memorandum of a Conversation with Mr. Saburi, Counselor of the Japanese Embassy on July 24, 1923," RG 59, file, 893.74/345a, 371; Henry G. Chilton to the Foreign Office, 27 July 1923, F.O. file: F2279/846/10; and Chilton to the Foreign Office, 7 August 1923, F.O. file: F2357/846/10.

The British agreed to accept the semi-independent position of the American group. They also promised to uphold the Open Door principle on a cooperative basis and to withdraw their opposition to the Federal-RCA concession.[57] This gave hope of a favorable settlement based again on Anglo-American cooperation. But this hope foundered when the Japanese rejected the American effort to reconcile cooperation and competition in the Far East. They wanted a four-power monopoly of all China radio business, one that would take in their unprofitable and inefficient Mitsui station near Peking and would operate the transpacific service as part of a larger system. When the United States balked at the latter proposition, they blocked implementation of the Anglo-American proposal.[58] The British, who had reserved the right to renew their opposition to the RCA-Federal contract should Japan reject the experts' plan, now withdrew their support as well.[59] And as a result, the situation remained deadlocked throughout the decade.[60]

IV

While these patterns of cooperation and competition were becoming established in South America and China, private spokesmen and government officials were also trying to decide upon the degree of governmental supervision that should overlay private management of long-distance radio. Although rejecting govern-

57. Foreign Office minute by Ronald Campbell, 30 July 1923, F.O. file: F2279/846/10; Wellesley to Brown, 1 August 1923, F.O. file: F2281/846/10; Chilton to the Foreign Office, 20 July 1923, Foreign Office to Chilton, 10 August 1923, and Wellesley to Brown, 2 August 1923, F.O. file: F2288/846/10.

58. *Foreign Relations, 1923*, vol. 1, pp. 822–26; *Foreign Relations, 1924*, vol. 1, pp. 570–80; Macleay, British Ambassador, Peking, to the Foreign Office, 7 August 1923, F.O. file: F2373/846/10; Macleay to the Foreign Office, 7 August 1923, F.O. file: F2374/846/10; Foreign Office minute by Campbell, 9 August 1923, F.O. file: F2374/846/10; Palairet to the Foreign Office, 26 September 1923, F.O. file: F2860/846/10. See also Ridley McLean to the Director of Naval Intelligence, 15 November 1924, and McLean, memorandum, 23 March 1925, RG 80, file, 108–19.

59. Foreign Office to the British Embassy, Washington, 29 January 1924, F.O. file: F408/63/10. See also Foreign Office minute by Newton, 22 May 1923, and Foreign Office to Geddes, 25 May 1923, F.O. file: F1525/846/10.

60. The story can be followed in *Foreign Relations, 1925*, vol. 1, pp. 890–934; *Foreign Relations, 1926*, vol. 1, pp. 1040–91; *Foreign Relations, 1927*, vol. 2, pp. 472–81; *Foreign Relations, 1928*, vol. 2, pp. 555–68; *Foreign Relations, 1929*, vol. 2, pp. 829–33; and *Foreign Relations, 1930*, vol. 2, pp. 626–27.

ment ownership or excessive statist controls, all agreed that the peculiar character of the radio business, especially the need to prevent unnecessary interference and chaotic overlapping of radio frequencies, required some form of regulation. And the best form, as industry officials saw it, was a business-government partnership that would leave ownership in private hands, rely heavily on business self-regulation through voluntary cooperation, and yet permit general governmental supervision without leading to government interference in managerial functions.[61]

With this view Secretary of Commerce Herbert Hoover agreed. Early in the decade, officials in the Commerce Department had carefully divided the areas of business and government responsibility, defining the duties of government agencies, and rejecting all proposals for greater governmental and intergovernmental regulation of commercial business. Their plan called for international reciprocity in granting radio licenses and, in theory at least, would deny government assistance to American companies seeking exclusive traffic agreements abroad, except when such agreements were the inevitable product of foreign government monopolies. In addition, it called for general government supervision but ruled out government ownership or operation of commercial radio facilities, amalgamation of the international cable and radio conventions, and federal regulation of rates.[62] The key to orderly radio operations, as they saw it, lay in developing cooperative arrangements. And in 1922, at a radio standardization conference in Washington, the industry had outlined a series of voluntary regulations to be informally enforced by Secretary of Commerce Hoover pending congressional action.[63]

61. For industry opinion see the testimony of spokesmen for the radio interests in *Hearings on H. R. 19350: Radio Communications* and *Hearings on H. R. 13159: Radio Communications.*

62. Nagle to Klein, 29 January 1923, Nagle to Hoover, 2 April 1923, Nagle to Hoover, 23 April 1923, enclosing "Memorandum A: Principles," 23 April 1923, "Memorandum B: Reassignment of Communications Activities," 23 April 1923, and "Memorandum C: Comments on Mr. Rogers' Memorandum," 24 April 1923, in HHP, Commerce, Official File, box 447. Walter Rogers, part-time communications expert for the State Department, remained the leading exponent of a larger role for the government in the field of radio. See Rogers, "Memorandum for Mr. Hoover: Electrical Communications," 10 March 1923, and Rogers to Hoover, 7 February 1923, in HHP, Commerce, Official File, box 447.

63. Herbert Hoover, *The Memoirs of Herbert Hoover*, vol. 2, pp. 140–41; and "Notes on Radio Standardization Conference," unsigned, 9 January 1923, HHP, Commerce, Official File, box 438.

Similar conferences for the "Better Voluntary Regulation of Radio" followed over the next three years. And out of them came a set of voluntary codes allocating wave lengths, classifying operators, reducing interference, and specifying interconnections between stations. This system of "industrial self-regulation," Hoover hoped, would reduce governmental regulation to a minimum and "go far to make further new legislative or administrative intervention unnecessary." The Radio Act of 1927 confirmed these expectations. It formalized the Secretary of Commerce's power to license commercial and amateur operators and authorized a Federal Commission of private radio experts to assign frequencies, limit hours of operation, and specify standards of equipment.[64]

Company officials also envisioned a similar program for the international arena. Here too, they rejected any rigorous intergovernmental arrangements that infringed on the interests of private managers. They were opposed, for example, to extending the regulations of the International Telegraph Convention to the radio field. This extension, they claimed, would subject American radio interests to control by foreign powers, impair business efficiency by undermining private initiative, and retard technological innovation by submitting the rapidly changing radio art to stultifying bureaucratic regulation.[65] At the same time, they saw a British proposal

64. Hoover, *Memoirs*, vol. 2, pp. 141–45; D. B. Carson, Bureau of Navigation, "Memorandum for the Secretary of Commerce," 28 March 1923, Department of Commerce press release, 26 August 1924, Hoover, "Address before the Third National Radio Conference," 7 October 1924, "Report of the Third National Radio Conference to the Secretary of Commerce," 10 October 1924, Hoover, "Address before the Fourth National Radio Conference," 12 November 1925, HHP, Commerce, Official File, box 438; and Hoover to Congressman Wallace White, 4 December 1924, HHP, Commerce, Official File, box 447; and Howeth, *History of Communications-Electronics*, pp. 502–6.

65. Young to Root, 25 January 1922, and Young to Hoover, 27 January 1922, Young Papers, box 126, file, 11–14–49–Communications, Disarmament Conference; Lansing and Woolsey to Hughes, 27 February and 14 March 1923, RG 59, file, 710.E1a/81, 86; Nagle, "Meeting with Elwood," 19 October 1923, Harbord to Davis, 19 October 1923, "Notes of a Conversation with General Carty of American Telephone and Telegraph Company," 25 October 1923, all in RG 59, file, 574.D4/16½, 17½; "Notes of a Conversation with General Carty," 26 August 1924, RG 59, file, 574.D5/11; Edward Wynne, State Department, "Notes on a Conversation Held in Mr. Harrison's Office," 30 April 1924, RG 59, file, 574.D3/69; Merle-Smith, "Notes of a Conference between the American Delegates to the Communications Conference and the Representatives of the Cable and Telegraph Companies," 4 November 1920, RG 43, "Communication Conference," box 98. According to Walter Rogers, the American companies were "haunted by the spectre of

to replace the practice of "preemption" with governmental allocation of wave lengths on a territorial basis as working to their dis-
advantage while benefiting the expansive British Empire.[66]

These attitudes were also reflected in official policy. Under the
Republicans, the Navy Department's early support for thoroughgoing government control gave way. In 1924, Navy officials worked
closely with industry representatives to define an American principle of regulation; one, in other words, that would affirm the "right
of owners to manage" their property subject only to general public
supervision.[67] At the same time, the State Department instructed
its delegates to the Pan American Communications Conference in
Mexico City to oppose a combined radio telegraph convention and
to delay any commitment regarding the distribution of radio frequencies.[68] Similarly, when the French suggested the communications conference that finally met in Paris in 1926, the Department
agreed to send delegates only after it was assured that telegraph,
not radio, would be discussed.[69] And at both conferences, the
American delegates successfully postponed any decision regarding
distribution of long-distance wave lengths and steadfastly dissented
from resolutions endorsing a joint radio-telegraph convention.[70]

---

government ownership." See Rogers to Hughes, 8 June 1921, RG 59, file,
574.D1/511.

66. British Embassy to Hughes, 12 April 1922, RG 59, file, 574.D2/23;
Nagle, "Meeting with John W. Elwood of RCA," 19 October 1923, Harbord
to S. B. Davis, Assistant Secretary of Commerce, 19 October 1923, RG 59,
file, 574.D4/16½; and Wynne, "Notes of a Conference Held in Mr. Harrison's Office," 30 April 1924, RG 59, file, 574.D3a/69.

67. Carty to Comdr. D. C. Bingham, Assistant Director of Naval Communications, 14 May 1924, unsigned memorandum of 11 May 1924, memorandum handed by Carty to Davis, 5 May 1924, and Charles Bracelan of
A. T. & T., to Bingham, 19 May 1924, with enclosures, RG 80, file, 12479A–
432.

68. Hughes to Charles Warren, chairman, American Delegation, 21 May
1924, RG 59, file, 574.D4/95a.

69. French Chargé to the Secretary of State, 22 September 1921, Hughes
to Harding, 22 August 1922, William Phillips to the French Chargé, 21 September 1923, French Ambassador to the Secretary of State, 15 January and
17 July 1925, Acting Secretary of State Joseph Grew to the French Ambassador, 17 August 1925, and Secretary of State Frank Kellogg to J. Beaver
White, Chairman of the American Delegation to the Paris Conference, 18
August 1925, all in RG 59, file, 574.D3/–, 6a, 68a, 95, 121, 173.

70. On the Mexico City conference see Vallance to the Secretary of State,
17, 19, and 27 June 1924, and 17 July 1924 (two telegrams), and the Secretary of State to the American delegation, 19 July 1924, all in RG 59, file,
574.D4/100, 102, 112, 117, 119, 101. On the Paris Conference see White
to the Secretary of State, 10 September 1925, and "Confidential Report Rel-

Americans hoped for an international arrangement that would protect the interests of private radio companies, leave managerial functions unencumbered by government regulations, and yet allow nonpolitical experts to devise standards for the orderly development of long-distance radio. These were the goals enunciated by Hoover and President Calvin Coolidge in opening the international radio conference in Washington in 1927. There was a need, they said, for government supervision and standardization of radio practices. This would permit orderly progress through "mutual concession and cooperation," stimulate development, and thus encourage the spread of international harmony and good will. But such regulation, Hoover warned, must be general and flexible, protecting the prerogatives of private management and guaranteeing continued innovation.[71]

In general, the conference followed these guidelines, delineating "a safe middle ground between avoidance of restrictions and the maintenance of orderly traffic." General agreement was limited to controlling interference between radio stations and standardizing operating procedures. Regulations of a managerial nature, including a provision subjecting radio to the regulations of the International Telegraph Convention, were relegated to a supplementary section, which was not to be signed by delegates from countries where the radio industry was a private enterprise. And to appease commercial radio interests in the United States, British proposals for allocating radio frequencies on a territorial basis were defeated in favor of distribution by service, a more equitable procedure and one that would also help prevent unnecessary overlapping. For Hoover, the "purely scientific" and factual approach adopted to these problems, plus a "fine spirit of cooperation," had enabled the assembled experts to devise a system of supervision and avoid political complications that could arouse emotions and stymie progress.[72]

ative to the Proposed International Radio Telegraph Conference to be held in Washington," signed by the American delegation to the Paris Conference, 19 November 1925, RG 59, file, 574.D3/195, 231.

71. Calvin Coolidge, "Address at the Opening Meeting of the International Radiotelegraph Conference," 14 October 1927, Hoover, "Address Before the International Radiotelegraph Conference," 4 October 1927, and Harbord, "Address at a Dinner Tendered to the Delegates of the International Radiotelegraph Conference," 15 October 1927, HHP, Commerce, Official File, box 439.

72. Hoover, "Address at the Final Plenary Session of the International Radiotelegraph Conference," 25 November 1927, HHP, Commerce, Official

V

In both the domestic and international spheres, then, private
and governmental policymakers emphasized business self-regulation and limited government supervision as the best way to guarantee orderly operation without infringing upon the rights of
private managers. As consolidation and collaboration proceeded
domestically, so also did combination and multinational cooperation emerge in the international arena. In South America and
China, the great British and American companies took the lead in
trying to develop such cooperative frameworks. In both areas, they
claimed that such cooperation would facilitate innovation in the
radio art, encourage an expansion of radio facilities, prevent destructive interference, and eliminate duplicate services. This, they
thought, would lay the basis for expanded trade, foster international goodwill, and eliminate the need for excessive government intervention.

In China, disagreement among Japanese and American officials
over the extent of cooperation involved in the Anglo-American
program prevented a realization of this private vision. In South
America, however, despite the Navy's fear of "monopoly," the
State Department did agree to multinational management. Here,
monopoly was garbed in the rhetoric of efficiency and service and
defended by reminders that order was essential to progress. Here
too, multinationalism was heralded as the new competition, celebrated as the best way to prevent dangerous political conflict, and
hidden behind paper concessions to conventional nationalist dog-
ma like the Monroe Doctrine. And here too, the private structure
of cooperative multinationalism added another dimension to the
informal pattern of Anglo-American entente.

File, box 439; Report of the American Delegation to the International Radiotelegraph Conference, 1927, HHP, Commerce, Official File, box 443; and
Howeth, *History of Communications-Electronics*, pp. 507–9.

CHAPTER 8

Informal Entente

Public Policy and Private Management in Anglo-American Petroleum Affairs

By focusing on the diplomatic controversies between the United States and Great Britain, previous accounts of United States petroleum policy in the postwar period have failed to illuminate the cooperative goals involved—goals that were shared by Anglo-American policymakers and industry officials alike. Nor have they appreciated the important considerations that shaped government-business relations in the United States, particularly the idea that cooperation among private petroleum interests was a more acceptable means of regulating the development of oil resources than either wide-open competition or government intervention and management. Finally, they have not understood how this private cooperation, applied internationally, worked to refashion the traditional principles of public policy.[1]

For the British, cooperation with their American counterparts was preferable to destabilizing and unprofitable competition. In the Middle East, they argued, it could also help to protect Great Britain's economic and political interests against the dual menace of Russian bolshevism and revolutionary nationalism. And for Americans, cooperation in this field, as in others, could minimize destabilizing economic conflict, promote orderly and efficient development, and reduce the demand for "statist" programs that were serious detriments to business efficiency and political stability. Accordingly, it was this cooperative approach that they tried to

1. For the best recent studies from a regional perspective see John DeNovo, *American Interests and Policies in the Middle East*, pp. 167–84, and Tulchin, *Aftermath of War: World War I and U.S. Policy Toward Latin America*, pp. 118–54. The best studies from the point of view of the oil industry are George Sweet Gibb and Evelyn H. Knowlton, *History of Standard Oil: The Resurgent Years, 1911–1927*, and Harold F. Williamson et al., *The American Petroleum Industry: The Age of Energy, 1899–1959*. Gerald D. Nash, *United States Oil Policy, 1890–1964*, is particularly good on domestic oil policy. Although all of the above deal in some respect with business-government relations, Nash and Joan Hoff Wilson, *American Business & Foreign Policy, 1920–1933*, pp. 184–200, are especially helpful.

combine with the practice of international reciprocity and the
goal of Anglo-American rapprochement. In adapting this program
to the oil arena, however, they again redefined traditional principles, especially the Open Door, in order to reconcile their competitive implications with the private vision of constructive
development through multinational management. This chapter
will describe the ideology behind United States policy, show how
policymakers tried to apply it to the Anglo-American petroleum
controversies in South America and the Middle East, and point up
the difficulties inherent in both the idea and its application.

II

As Americans perceived it, British postwar policy sought to establish a state-sponsored and preferential system of control over
the most important non-American sources of petroleum. In the
East Indies, the Dutch-Shell combine of British and Dutch capital
resisted American efforts to break its monopoly. In South America,
the same combine competed with American companies for control
of rich oil deposits. In Persia, the state-financed Anglo-Persian
Company (AP) added the disputed Khostaria concession that
covered the northern provinces to its exclusive petroleum rights in
south Persia. Through the AP, moreover, the British government
had become the majority shareholder in the powerful Turkish Petroleum Company (TPC), a multinational consortium that claimed
to possess exclusive petroleum rights in Mesopotamia and a substantial area of the old Turkish Empire. And finally, through the
San Remo Agreement of 1920, the British and French governments
had agreed to coordinate their petroleum policies for mutual advantage, not only in the Middle East, but also in Rumania, Russia,
and other areas of the world. To American officials, it seemed that
domestic producers might be excluded from the choice producing
areas of the world. And given their nearly phobic belief that domestic reserves were rapidly depleting, they were anxious to protect American interests.[2]

2. Herbert Feis, *Petroleum and American Foreign Policy*, pp. 3–8; John
DeNovo, "The Movement for an Aggressive American Oil Policy Abroad,
1918–1920," pp. 854–76; Peter M. Reed, "Standard Oil in Indonesia, 1898–
1928," pp. 311–37; Tulchin, *Aftermath of War*, pp. 118–29; and British
White Paper, "Government Investments in Registered Companies," enclosed
in Post Wheeler, Counselor of the American Embassy, London, to the Secretary of State, 1 December 1921, RG 59, file, 841.6363/185.

For some, the government itself should play a direct part in efforts to gain a large American share in foreign petroleum resources. Sen. James D. Phelan of California became the leading spokesman for this approach. In 1920, he introduced legislation calling for a United States Oil Corporation to be financed with private capital but controlled by a board of directors appointed by the President. Yet neither the petroleum industry nor the administration favored any duplication of the British system of state management. Government intervention, the American Petroleum Institute (API) argued, would undermine the "individual initiative and efficiency" that had allowed the petroleum industry to prosper. Still worse, it would substitute "a condition of government rivalries" for "fair and open commercial competition," thus transforming what had "hitherto been commercial questions" into "questions essentially political." Administration leaders agreed. State management, explained Secretary of State Bainbridge Colby in a letter attacking the Phelan plan, was counterproductive. It created "international friction embarrassing to the business itself."[3]

If state management was out, so was a return to laissez-faire or purely private initiatives. Industry officials claimed that all-out competition would only cause inefficient development, market instability, and wasteful allocation of precious oil resources. And worse, untrammeled competition discouraged investment and threatened profits by causing overproduction. Without government assistance, moreover, the industry could not overcome the restrictive and state-sponsored policies of its foreign rivals.[4]

The remaining alternative was a blend of public and private

3. DeNovo, "Movement for an Aggressive Oil Policy," pp. 872–73; "The Menace of Foreign State Monopolies to the American Petroleum Industry," a report by the Foreign Relations Committee of the American Petroleum Institute enclosed in Thomas O'Donnell, president of the Institute, to the Secretary of State, 30 September 1919, RG 59, file, 800.6363/89; Colby to Sen. Reed Smoot, 19 November 1920, RG 59, file, 811.6363/21b. The Commerce Department also attacked the Phelan Plan. See Secretary of Commerce J. W. Alexander to Smoot, 26 July 1920, and Acting Secretary of Commerce E. F. Sweet to Smoot, 28 July 1920, RG 59, file, 811.6363/25. See also in this connection Arthur Millspaugh, memorandum, 12 April 1921, RG 59, file, 811.6363/46; Millspaugh to Dearing, 10 May 1921, RG 59, file, 800.6363/328; and Ralph Arnold, American Institute of Mining and Metallurgical Engineers, to Secretary of Commerce Herbert Hoover, 23 April 1921, HHP, Commerce, Official File, box 218.

4. Norman Nordhauser, "Origins of Federal Oil Regulation in the 1920's," pp. 53–56; and Williamson, et al., *American Petroleum Industry*, pp. 300–301, 316–20.

action. Under it, the business aspects of petroleum policy, particularly the area, form, amount, and terms of investment, were to remain in private hands. But private leaders were now expected to submerge their interests in a cooperative effort to rationalize competitive activity for the sake of larger national and international goals. Such collaboration, its supporters urged, would forge controls over ruinous competition and avoid the pitfalls of government interference and inefficiency.

In the oil industry, such voluntary collaboration had been institutionalized temporarily under the National Petroleum War Service Committee. This had led, in 1919, to the formation of the American Petroleum Institute. And once organized, the new trade association had been officially encouraged by Secretary of the Interior Franklin Lane. In the future, he told the oil leaders, they must assume "the attitude of statesmen and not of selfish exploiters."[5] Mark Requa, the former head of the wartime Oil Division, also urged an abandonment of "the 'laissez-faire' doctrine."[6] In 1920, he joined with Van H. Manning of the API to work out a plan for the cooperative promotion of American oil interests under the expert tutelage of private petroleum officials. The proposal called for a cooperative marketing and producing syndicate, and when Herbert Hoover became Secretary of Commerce he promptly endorsed the cooperative approach and began soliciting industry opinion on organizing "something specific we can get behind."[7]

One result of these early initiatives was a Commerce Department

5. Lane to Van H. Manning, 24 September 1919, in Anne W. Lane and Louise H. Wall, eds., *The Letters of Franklin K. Lane, Personal and Political,* pp. 315–16; Nash, *United States Oil Policy,* pp. 23–48; Wilson, *American Business & Foreign Policy,* p. 186; and Nordhauser, "Origins of Federal Oil Regulation," pp. 54–56.

6. Mark Requa to J. Howard Pew, president of the Sun Oil Company, 12 October 1925, HHP, Commerce, Personal File, box 75. See also Requa, "The Petroleum Problem," *Saturday Evening Post* (reprint, 1920), and "Conservation," an address before the American Petroleum Institute, 19 November 1920, in HHP, Commerce, Official File, box 220.

7. The syndicate was designed for foreign operations. An outline of the company signed by Requa and dated 15 November 1920, is in HHP, Commerce, Official File, box 220. See also Requa to Hoover, 23 April and 2 May 1921, and Ira Jewell Williams to Requa, 12 May 1921, HHP, Commerce, Official File, box 251; Millspaugh, "Proposed Combination of American Oil Companies for Operation Abroad," 13 May 1921, RG 59, file, 811.6363/73; Hoover to Undersecretary of State Henry Fletcher, 14 April 1921, RG 59, file, 800.6363/272; and Wilson, *American Business & Foreign Policy,* pp. 185–87.

meeting in May 1921. There, Hoover and Secretary of State Charles Evans Hughes urged oil company officials to cooperate in a united attempt to gain a foothold in the rich oil lands of the Middle East. In return, they promised vigorous government support for the Open Door. The companies seemed amenable and, in November 1921, seven of them formed the so-called American Group led by Standard Oil Company of New Jersey. Shortly thereafter, the Group opened negotiations with the Turkish Petroleum Company for a share in Mesopotamian oil resources.[8]

In practice, to be sure, the maintenance of such cooperative mechanisms proved difficult and particular companies often resorted to individualistic and competitive action. In Mesopotamia, for example, the American Group came into conflict with the Chester Syndicate, another American combine then negotiating with the Nationalist Turks for railroad and petroleum rights.[9] In Persia, efforts to promote cooperation kept foundering on the competing claims of Jersey Standard and Sinclair Consolidated.[10] And in South America, similar outbreaks of "internecine strife" disrupted cooperative projects, hampering plans to expand American resources.[11] In such cases, the State Department generally asserted

8. On the May conference see HHP, Commerce, Official File, box 219; Bedford to Charles Evans Hughes, 21 May 1921, RG 59, file, 890g.6363/28; and DeNovo, *American Interests in the Middle East*, p. 186.

9. See Walter Teagle of Jersey Standard to Hughes, 25 August and 13 and 22 December 1922, and Hughes to Teagle, 15 and 30 December 1922, in *Foreign Relations, 1922*, vol. 2, pp. 344–45, 347–52; Allen Dulles, memorandum, 15 December 1922, Teagle to Hughes, 18 December 1922, and Dulles, "Memorandum of a Telephone Conversation with Guy Wellman," 30 December 1922, RG 59, file, 890g.6363T84/81, 82, 83, 84.

10. Stanley Hornbeck of the Economic Adviser's Office to Assistant Secretary Harrison, 22 November 1922, Assistant Secretary Phillips to Hughes, 18 August 1922, Millspaugh, "Memorandum of a Conference in Mr. Phillips' Office," 13 June 1922, and Millspaugh, "Memorandum of a Conversation with Mr. Naramore of Sinclair Company," 27 June 1922, all in RG 59, file, 891.6363 St. Oil/263, 238, 216, 231.

11. In Venezuela, lack of cooperation stalled plans for constructing facilities to transport oil across a sandbar at the mouth of Lake Maracaibo. See Harry J. Anslinger, American Vice Consul, La Guaira, to the Secretary of State, 3 July 1924, Economic Adviser's memorandum, "Petroleum Situation in Venezuela," 20 February 1925, RG 59, file, 831.6363C73/4 and 831.6363/278. In Costa Rica, there was also a clash between Sinclair Consolidated Oil Corporation, Standard Oil of California, and the United Fruit Company concerning conflicting claims to subsoil rights. See Hughes to Harding, 30 March 1921, Lester Woolsey, representing the United Fruit Company, to Hughes, 11 July 1921, and Dana Munro, "American Oil Concessions in Costa Rica,"

its doctrine of neutrality and refused to support one American faction at the expense of another.

Yet such conflicts did not mean the substitution of competitive for cooperative goals. The more "enlightened" oil leaders believed that the "future interests of the large oil concerns" really ran "parallel with each other" both at home and abroad.[12] And for men like Hoover and Hughes, the organization of these mutual interests into a pattern of "fair cooperation" was not only the key to continued modernization and expansion but also the way to eliminate one of the most "fruitful" causes of war.[13] The best system, for them and similar policymakers, was one in which government and business officials joined forces; the former creating the "opportunity" for private expansion, the latter taking responsibility for the "active and intelligent" management of their own affairs.[14]

It was this system that American officials kept urging upon the British. The oil resources of Mesopotamia and Palestine, they argued, constituted a "potential subject of economic strife." Only their "unhampered development" could satisfy world demand and avoid international friction. Yet, perversely, British military authorities in these areas seemed intent upon keeping American companies out, setting up extortionate "monopolies," and deliberately violating the theory of trusteeship explicit in the mandate principle. The latter was supposed to represent a new concept in international affairs, "formulated for the purpose of removing . . . some of the principal causes of international differences." Specifically, it was to eliminate the sources of economic warfare inherent in prewar colonialism by applying a system of fair and equal entry to the mandated territories.[15] For their part, however, the

16 February 1924, all in RG 59, file, 818.6363/107a, 93, 166. See also Tulchin, *Aftermath of War*, pp. 137, 150–52.

12. The quotation is from Heinrich Riedemann, head of Jersey Standard's German operations, speaking specifically about Jersey Standard's relations with Dutch-Shell and cited in Gibb and Knowlton, *The Resurgent Years*, p. 349.

13. See for example Hoover, "The Future of Our Foreign Trade," address at the Export Managers Club, New York City, 16 March 1926, HHP, Commerce, Personal File, box 24; and Hughes to President Coolidge, 31 October 1923, RG 59, file, 890g.6363T84/117a.

14. Phillips to Hughes, 4 May 1921, RG 59, file, 856d.6363/94.

15. Ambassador John Davis, London, to Secretary Colby, 18 June 1920, enclosing Davis to British Foreign Secretary Earl Curzon, 12 May 1920, Colby to Davis, 26 July 1920, and Colby to Davis, 23 November 1920, enclosing Colby to Curzon, 20 November 1920, in *Foreign Relations, 1920*, vol. 2, pp. 651–55, 658–59, 668–73.

British denied any discrimination against American companies. The United States, not Great Britain, they complained, dominated international oil reserves and hampered foreign competitors. And as for the Middle East, they defended rights already acquired by British companies but, like their American counterparts, affirmed the principle of equal opportunity.[16]

Yet, given the Anglo-American character of postwar oil conflict, the actions urged in the name of open entry and enlightened cooperation often came out as reciprocal bargaining between the two major powers and their private firms. In the background here was the Mineral Lands Leasing Act passed by Congress in 1920. Under it, the Interior Department could bar foreign nationals, whose governments denied equal opportunities to American citizens, from access to petroleum resources in the United States. The act was applied against the Dutch because of their discrimination against American companies in the East Indies.[17] And similar restrictions might be applied against the British unless they adopted a reciprocal policy toward American firms in the Middle East and elsewhere. Of equal importance was a fear of destabilizing competition and a willingness to trade concessions in South America for alterations of British policy in the Middle East. In February 1921, Arthur Millspaugh, the State Department's oil expert, outlined this strategy in a long memorandum for the Secretary of State. Since the petroleum question was primarily an Anglo-American issue, he argued, it could be resolved on a world basis through international reciprocity between the two countries. If the United States fairly accommodated the British in areas under its "diplomatic influence," he later explained, then it could expect reciprocal benefits in countries like Persia. And eventually the two countries could forge a world-wide pattern of political and economic cooperation that would allow each to satisfy its needs and permit a joint defense of common interests against revolutionary and nationalist governments.[18]

16. Curzon to Colonel French, Cairo, 30 August 1919, Curzon to Grey, 30 October 1919, Curzon to John Davis, 21 November 1919, in *Documents on British Foreign Policy*, First Series, vol. 5 (London, 1952), pp. 366, 501–3, 541–42; Curzon to Geddes, 7 May 1920, in ibid., vol. 13 (London, 1963), pp. 256–57; Curzon to Davis, 28 February 1921, and Curzon to Geddes, 21 May 1921, in *British and Foreign State Papers, 1921*, vol. 114 (London, 1924), pp. 409–14, 30–35.

17. See DeNovo, "Movement for an Aggressive Oil Policy," pp. 867–73; and Reed, "Standard Oil in Indonesia," pp. 311–37.

18. Millspaugh, "Informal and Provisional Memorandum on the General

Consequently, it was this reciprocity approach that provided the framework within which American and British oil interests would eventually join forces, institutionalize a petroleum entente at the private level, and celebrate the results as superior to either "statism" or the "old individualism." And since previous accounts have largely missed this Anglo-American collaboration in both Latin America and the Middle East, it seems advisable to examine the results in some detail.

II

Before the armistice, the United States had attempted to convert large areas of Latin America, especially the sensitive Panama Canal region, into a preferential petroleum sphere. In 1918, when an investigation by the State Department disclosed that British capital controlled John H. Amory and Son, a nominally American firm seeking petroleum concessions in Costa Rica, Secretary of State Robert Lansing ordered the American chargé at San José to oppose the grant on grounds that oil exploration in the "neighborhood of the Panama Canal" should be restricted to American citizens. Subsequently, when Amory received the concession, Lansing again complained that it violated the traditional policy of the United States toward the canal region.[19] Still later, the British would reply to American protests concerning the Middle East by claiming discrimination against British interests in Costa Rica.[20]

In conjunction with this policy of preference in the canal area, the State Department also attempted to discourage American capital from entering joint ventures under British leadership. Organizations like the Caribbean Petroleum and the Colon Development

---

Petroleum Situation, Outstanding Petroleum Questions, and the Position Taken by the Department Relative Thereto," 19 February 1921, RG 59, file, 800.6363/325; and "Memorandum of a Conference on December 15, 1921, attended by Dearing, J. B. Moore, Robbins, Kornfeld, and Millspaugh," 16 December 1921, RG 59, file, 891.6363 St. Oil/71.

19. Stewart Johnson, American chargé, San José, to Lansing, 6, 24, 26 June and 31 August 1918, and Lansing to Johnson, 1 July 1918, 29 August, and Lansing to consul Chase, 9 December 1918, in *Foreign Relations, 1918*, vol. 1, pp. 872–76. See also Tulchin, *Aftermath of War*, pp. 135–36.

20. Curzon to Ambassador Davis, 9 August 1920, in *British and Foreign State Papers, 1921*, vol. 114, pp. 399–404; Davis to the Secretary of State, 1 March 1921, in *Foreign Relations, 1921*, vol. 2, p. 84; and Curzon to Geddes, 7 May 1920, in *Documents on British Foreign Policy*, First Series, vol. 13, pp. 256–57.

companies[21] were seen as efforts to use American investors for British purposes.[22] As a consequence, the Department instructed its foreign agents to support only those companies incorporated in the United States "and actually controlled by United States capital."[23]

The Department's unilateralism remained in effect in 1920, when Venezuela and Costa Rica instituted ouster proceedings against the Colon, Caribbean, and Amory companies. The American interests involved in Venezuela immediately turned to the Department for protection, in effect asking it to support a joint Anglo-American enterprise at a time when independent American firms were hoping to obtain exploration rights that covered areas entailed in the contested concessions.[24] The British also asked the Department to support Amory and Son in Costa Rica, and Congressman George Graham filed a similar petition in behalf of the American interests involved there.[25] The Department reacted by

21. Caribbean Petroleum was a subsidiary of the General Asphalt Company of Philadelphia, which, in turn, was controlled by Dutch-Shell through its Burlington Investment Company. The Colon Development Company was also a subsidiary of Burlington, but one in which Henry Doherty, J. P. Morgan & Co., and other Wall Street interests held a minority share through their Carib Syndicate. See Latin American Division memorandum, unsigned, 15 February 1918, Preston McGoodwin, American Minister, Venezuela, to Lansing, 5 and 19 January 1920, Polk to McGoodwin, 29 February 1920, Adee to McGoodwin, 28 April 1920, C. K. MacFadden, of the Carib Syndicate, to Colby, 3 May 1920, Polk to McGoodwin, 29 May 1920, MacFadden to Colby, 16 June 1920, and "Statement of Facts with Respect to the Colon Development Company, Ltd., and the Interests of the Carib Syndicate Limited Therein," unsigned, 1 February 1928, all in RG 59, file, 831.6363/17, 19, 20, 31, 22, 27, 31, 25, and org. See also Tulchin, *Aftermath of War*, p. 147.

22. See for example McGoodwin to Lansing, 21 November 1919, and Breckinridge Long to McGoodwin, 1 April 1920, RG 59, file, 831.6363/18.

23. Adee to the diplomatic and consular officers, 16 August 1919, RG 59, file, 800.6363/16a. These instructions corresponded with recommendations by the State Department's Economic Liaison Committee. See Economic Liaison Committee Report, 11 July 1919, RG 59, file, 811.6363/45.

24. McGoodwin to the Secretary of State, 7 and 26 April and 11 June 1920, and MacFadden to the Secretary of State, 3 May and 16 June 1920, RG 59, file, 831.6363/22, 26, 33, 27, 35.

25. Geddes to the Foreign Office, 9 April 1921, F.O. file: A2459/291/32; Foreign Office minute, 12 April 1921, ibid., Geddes to Hughes, 9 May 1921, F.O. file: A3589/291/32; Geddes to the Foreign Office, 24 May 1921, F.O. file: A4099/291/32; Geddes to Hughes, 23 March 1921, in *Foreign Relations, 1921*, vol. 1, p. 649; George Graham to Colby, 2 July 1920, and Colby to Graham, 20 July 1920, RG 59, file, 818.6363Am6/41. See also Tulchin, *Aftermath of War*, p. 137.

attempting to defend the equity rights of American investors in the Colon Company, which indirectly contributed to British success in revalidating the entire concession.[26] For the Latin American Division, the incident proved conclusively that the Department "should pay no attention to Americans" who held a minority interest in foreign-controlled companies and were "used as cats-paws" in the struggle for oil. And again the Department's Latin-American agents were instructed not to support British-owned or controlled companies.[27]

In addition, when the British requested that the Amory claims be arbitrated by a neutral agent, Stewart Johnson of the Latin American Division insisted that the arbiter be limited to assessing monetary damages should he find that Costa Rica had illegally terminated the contract. Restoration of the concession was to be ruled out. Johnson's position was supported by his colleague, Sumner Welles. According to both men, the strategic interests of the United States, especially its interests in building a new canal across Nicaragua, were reason enough to exclude the British.[28]

Millspaugh disagreed and recommended in his memorandum of February 1921 that the United States "use its influence with the governments" of Latin America in order to guarantee equal opportunity for all foreign petroleum interests.[29] In a series of memoranda the following May and July, he again tried to bring the Depart-

26. Norman Davis to McGoodwin, 24 June 1920, McGoodwin to Hughes, 25 March, 4 May, and 14 June 1921, RG 59, file, 831.6363/33, 53, 54, 58, 63; Henry Beaumont, British Minister, Caracas, to the Foreign Office, 26 March 1921, F.O. file: A2618/316/47. Revalidation of the Colon concession, moreover, set a precedent for reconfirmation of another disputed British concession in Venezuela—that of the Venezuelan Oil Concessions Company. See Beaumont to the Foreign Office, 4 May 1921, F.O. file: A3939/316/47.

27. Latin American Division memorandum, 27 April 1921, Dearing to McGoodwin, 6 May 1921, RG 59, file, 831.6363/93, 33; and Hughes to diplomatic and consular agents in Latin America, 26 August 1921, RG 59, file, 810.6363/5a.

28. The Costa Rican affair can be followed in Foreign Relations, 1921, vol. 1, pp. 649, 661–63. On Stewart Johnson and Summer Welles see Johnson to Hughes, 10 September 1921, and Welles to Hughes, 8 April 1921, RG 59, file, 818.6363/Am6/107, 121.

29. Millspaugh, "Informal and Provisional Memorandum on the General Petroleum Situation . . . ," 19 February 1921, RG 59, file, 800.6363/325. In the margin of this memorandum, Assistant Secretary Van S. Merle-Smith noted the significance of Millspaugh's recommendations, commenting that they ran "counter" to the usual "strategic considerations" in the Panama Canal area.

ment's Latin-American policy into line with the strategy of Anglo-American cooperation based on private management and reciprocity. In the "long run," he argued, the soundest position was neither to support nor oppose British enterprises in the Western Hemisphere so long as they were not exclusive and did not violate the Monroe Doctrine. If the Amory concession represented a *bona fide* commercial enterprise under private management and was not subject to control by the British government, the United States should not interfere with a determination of the disputed contract in a manner acceptable to both parties. It should open Latin America to private British and joint British-American petroleum interests, and, in return, the British might be expected to alter their policies in the Middle East.[30]

Hughes accepted Millspaugh's recommendations. In August 1921, he dispatched a circular to the Department's Latin-American representatives instructing them to respect the rights of foreign nationals. And while he rejected a British request for official support, he did inform the British Ambassador that he would not oppose arbitration of the disputed Amory concession. This decision reversed the Department's earlier insistence on settlement through the Costa Rican courts, ignored Johnson's recommendation for restrictions on the terms of arbitration, and allowed Great Britain to pressure Costa Rica into arbitration without arousing American hostility.[31]

This shift in attitude was also apparent in Venezuela. There, the British Foreign Office had decided to support the Caribbean Petroleum Company when the Venezuelan government challenged its concession in the courts. The Caribbean was a multinational enterprise controlled by British, American, and Dutch capital, and

30. Millspaugh to Hughes, 2 May 1921, Millspaugh to Dearing, 14 May 1921, and Millspaugh to Welles, 8 July 1921, RG 59, file, 818.6363Am6/124, 85, 93. With reference to proposals for making the Western Hemisphere a preferred field for American oil interests, Millspaugh wrote Dearing that he did not think that the solution to the international oil problem was to be found in partitioning the world into oil zones but rather in reaching an understanding with the French and British. See Millspaugh to W. W. Cumberland and Dearing, 23 April 1921, RG 59, file, 810.6363/12.

31. Hughes to American diplomatic and consular officers in Latin America, 26 August 1921, RG 59, file, 810.6363/5a; Munro, "American Oil Concessions in Costa Rica," 16 February 1924, RG 59, file, 818.6363/166; *Foreign Relations, 1921*, vol. 1, pp. 646–68; and Andrew Bennett, British Minister, Costa Rica, to the Foreign Office, 17 December 1921, F.O. file: A9370/291/32.

the Foreign Office hoped for a cooperative defense of the interests involved. In 1922, the Dutch government agreed to this strategy.[32] And later that year the State Department also instructed its Minister at Caracas to support the British and Dutch representations for a fair determination of the contested concession.[33]

At the same time, when Venezuela threatened to cancel the Buchivacoa concession of the British Controlled Oilfields Ltd., a subsidiary of the Dutch-Shell group, the Department again fell in line with the cooperative thrust of private policy. In this case, Dutch-Shell had agreed to divide the concession with Jersey Standard; an agreement that "fairly well mapped out" Venezuela among the "great oil groups, American, Dutch, and British."[34] And following the new line, American diplomats joined with their British associates in obtaining a complete reaffirmation of the concession. Cooperation had replaced conflict on both the diplomatic and private levels, and as if to signify this change, Jersey incorporated a new Venezuelan subsidiary appropriately named the American-British Oil Company.[35]

In Latin America, then, the State Department acceded to the cooperative thrust of private policy, reversing its original decision to endorse only wholly American concerns and agreeing to support cooperation and combination among British and American capital. The merging of this capital, which was already in progress, made

32. Petroleum Department to the Foreign Office, 23 June 1922, F.O. file: A4013/2715/47; Foreign Office minute, 28 June 1922, ibid.; Foreign Office to Beaumont, 7 July 1922, ibid.; Petroleum Department to the Foreign Office, 6 July 1922, F.O. file: A4350/2715/47; Rowland Sperling to Beaumont, 13 July 1922, ibid.; and Board of Trade to the Foreign Office, 9 November 1922, F.O. file: A6815/2715/47.

33. Hughes to American Minister Willis Cook, 25 September 1922, RG 59, file, 831.6375C23/29a; Beaumont to the Foreign Office, 13 December 1922, F.O. file: A83/83/47; Bennett to the Foreign Office, 7 February 1924, F.O. file: A1334/1334/47; and Tulchin, *Aftermath of War*, p. 149.

34. Charles DeVault, American Vice Consul, London, to Hughes, 6 April 1923, and Robert Skinner, American Consul General, London, to the Secretary of State, 2 May 1922, RG 59, file, 831.6363/132, 98; Geddes to the Foreign Office, 13 April 1922, F.O. file: A2715/2715/47; and Geddes to the Foreign Office, 2 May 1922, F.O. file: A3212/2715/47.

35. Hughes to Cook, 28 July 1923, Bedford of Jersey Standard to Hughes, 21 August 1923, Solicitor's Office memorandum, 31 August 1923, Economic Adviser's Office memorandum, 11 September 1923, Phillips to Cook, 19 September 1923, Munro, memorandum, 16 February 1924, Francis White of the Latin American Division, memorandum, 20 March 1924, Frederick Chabot, American chargé, Caracas, to Hughes, 7 June and 9 August 1924, and American Consul, Venezuela, to the Secretary of State, 12 February 1926, all in RG 59, file, 831.6363/140, 142, 231, 205, 230, 313.

complete unilateralism impossible, and what remained of that policy was abandoned in expectation of reciprocal treatment by the British elsewhere. Indeed, by this time the move toward cooperative arrangements in the Middle East was well underway. As in Latin America, unilateralism was abandoned, and as the British accepted the idea of development through multinational firms, the State Department proceeded to redefine the neutrality doctrine and the Open Door in such a way as to remove most of their competitive implications.

III

In 1921, Jersey Standard, with assistance from the State and Commerce departments, had won a tentative concession over Persia's northern provinces in exchange for a $5 million loan to the Persian government.[36] But the proposed grant conflicted with rights claimed by the Anglo-Persian Company under the Khostaria concession—rights the Persians considered invalid but which the British vowed to defend.[37] Already in 1920, when a British official in Teheran had suggested that Anglo-American cooperation in Persia would dispel rumors that Great Britain wanted to monopolize the world's petroleum resources, the Foreign Office had labeled the proposal inopportune and had told the Persian Minister in London that Great Britain would tolerate only a symbolic American participation in Persian oil development.[38]

By 1922, however, a union between AP and Jersey Standard had gradually come to seem highly advantageous to both sides. American policymakers hoped that a conciliatory attitude in this British stronghold would gain reciprocal benefits in Mesopotamia and would avert costly competition in which American interests would

36. Millspaugh, "Memorandum of a Conversation with the Persian Minister and the Counselor of the Legation," 17 December 1920, and Hoover to Hughes, 28 November 1921, RG 59, file, 891.6363 St. Oil/16, 49½.

37. Sir Charles Greenway, head of AP, to G. P. Churchill of the Foreign Office, 24 August 1921 and Curzon to Henry Norman, British Minister, Teheran, 29 August 1921, F.O. file: E9826/76/34; Curzon to Sir Percy Cox, British Minister, Teheran, 9 April 1920, and Curzon to Geddes, 30 August 1920, in *Documents on British Foreign Policy*, First Series, vol. 13, pp. 465–66, 600.

38. Norman to Curzon, 26 October 1920, Curzon to Norman, 8 November 1920, and Curzon to Cox, 10 April 1920, in *Documents on British Foreign Policy*, First Series, vol. 13, pp. 621–22, 636–37, 466–67.

certainly be the losers.[39] Operating independently, Jersey Standard officials also decided that they lacked the facilities needed to transport crude produced in the northern provinces to the Persian Gulf.[40] Moreover, they needed help from AP if they were to advance the risky loan demanded by the Persian government in exchange for an oil concession.[41] And if they were to invest large sums, they wanted the security that British protection could provide.[42]

Similar considerations influenced the British. For them, Persia had vast strategic as well as economic importance. And since their position in the area was threatened less by an independent American commercial thrust than by Russian expansion and left-wing nationalists in Teheran, the Foreign Office preferred to cooperate with American interests. "Better Americans than Bolsheviks," exclaimed Sir Eyre Crowe regarding Jersey Standard's proposed oil loan to the Persian government. "After all," another Foreign Office official explained, the Americans "will be on our side against the Bolsheviks who are the sole real peril."[43]

39. Dulles to Phillips and Harrison, 14 August 1922, and Phillips to Hughes, 18 August 1922, RG 59, file, 891.6363 St. Oil/237, 238.

40. Unsigned memorandum of a conference attended by John Bassett Moore and Millspaugh, 9 December 1921, RG 59, file, 891.6363 St. Oil/63; and Gibb and Knowlton, *The Resurgent Years*, p. 310.

41. The problem was that virtually all revenues available as security for a loan, except the royalties on the oil produced by AP in south Persia, were already pledged for the redemption of bonds held by the British. This obstacle was removed when AP and Jersey agreed to support a Persian loan jointly, using the south Persian oil royalties as security. See Geddes to the Foreign Office, 15 January 1922, Foreign Office to Geddes, 18 January 1922, and Foreign Office minutes by Churchill, Lancelot Oliphant, and Ronald C. Lindsay, 7 January 1922, F.O. file: E578/7/34; unsigned "Memorandum of a Conference on December 15, 1921," dated 16 December 1921, Moore to Hughes, 20 December 1921, Robbins to Dearing and Millspaugh, 16 January 1922, Millspaugh, "Memorandum of a Conference with Dearing, Bedford, and Millspaugh of January 16, 1922," dated 17 January 1922, Hughes to Ambassador Geddes, 30 January 1922, Geddes to Hughes, 31 January 1922, Bedford to Hughes, 21 February 1922, all in RG 59, file, 891.6363 St. Oil/71, 77, 105, 108, 104, 128, 142.

42. Dulles, memorandum for Phillips and Hughes, 30 January 1923, RG 59, file, 890g.6363T84/79; Moore to E. J. Sadler, 16 December 1921, enclosed in Moore to Hughes, 20 December 1921, American chargé, Teheran, to Hughes, 27 November 1921, Hoover to Hughes, 22 December 1921, all in RG 59, file, 891.6363/77, 70, 81.

43. Crowe's remark is a comment on a Foreign Office minute by Lindsay, 23 November [1921], F.O. file: E12845/76/34; and Foreign Office minute, 29 July 1921, F.O. file: E8788/76/34. See also memorandum by Curzon, 1 March 1922, enclosed in American Minister Joseph Kornfeld, Teheran, to Hughes, 5 September 1922, RG 59, file, 891.6363 St. Oil/246.

Initially, the British wanted Jersey Standard to acquire a 50 percent share in the Khostaria concession. This, they hoped, would "make for greater political stability" in Persia and discourage American companies from demanding a foothold in either southern Persia or Mesopotamia.[44] To be sure, the Foreign Office continued to oppose confirmation of Jersey Standard's tentative concession by the Persian Medjliss. But this opposition was intended to smooth the way for American participation in the Khostaria concession on terms favorable to the AP.[45] In November 1921, however, the Medjliss officially approved Jersey Standard's independent grant. The British Minister in Teheran opposed this action, but policymakers in London lamented the sudden infirmity of AP's negotiating position with Jersey Standard. "Our position is untenable," confessed one Foreign Office official. Pointing to anti-British sentiment in Teheran, he now thought the "best thing" was to "encourage the Americans to come in" even if the terms worked out involved "matters going beyond the mere Khostaria concession."[46]

Accordingly, in late 1921, Sir John Cadman, a British oil expert, suggested an amalgamation of private British and American capital in the Middle East. Shortly thereafter, negotiations between Jersey Standard and AP got underway, and, by early 1922, they had successfully concluded an arrangement that was fully supported by the Foreign Office. Under it, the two companies formed a new Perso-American Petroleum Company, effectively controlled by American interests and entrusted with the tentative concession assigned to Jersey Standard by the Persian government. Should the Medjliss refuse to accept joint control of this concession, the agreement also provided Jersey Standard with an equal share in the disputed Khostaria grant claimed by AP.[47] Pleased with the deal, Sir

44. Petroleum Department to the Foreign Office, 21 June 1921, F.O. file: E7134/76/34; Greenway to Oliphant, 9 November 1921, and Oliphant to Greenway, 11 November 1921, F.O. file: E12436/76/34.

45. Foreign Office minute by Oliphant, 10 November 1921, and Oliphant to Greenway, 11 November 1921, F.O. file: E12436/76/34.

46. Reginald Bridgeman, British chargé, Teheran, to the Foreign Office, 22 November 1921, Foreign Office to Bridgeman, 24 November 1921, and Foreign Office minutes by Churchill and Lindsay, 23 November 1921, all in F.O. file: E12845/76/34.

47. Greenway to Oliphant, 28 November 1921 (with enclosures), F.O. file: E13201/76/34; Petroleum Department to the Foreign Office, 9 December 1921, F.O. file: E13568/76/34; Greenway to Oliphant, 14 December 1921, F.O. file: E13802/76/34; Petroleum Department to Churchill, 31 January 1922, enclosing Sir John Cadman to AP Co., 28 January 1922, F.O. file: E1193/7/34; Geddes to Curzon, 16 February 1922, F.O. file: E1803/7/34;

Charles Greenway, who headed both the Anglo-Persian Company and the Persian Railways Syndicate, called for a "British-American entente" and joined the Syndicate's directors in suggesting joint financing of the Persian railway system, joint efforts to reorganize Persia's finances, and the appointment of American citizens to replace the British financial advisers who were recently dismissed by the Persian government.[48]

While these negotiations were underway at the private level, an exchange of notes between the State Department and the British Embassy in Washington signaled the beginning of an informal entente at the diplomatic level. The British proposed a united front in Persia—one based on the Jersey-AP combine and designed to prevent the Persian government from causing friction between the two great powers. Hughes agreed with the British. Since Sinclair Consolidated was competing with Jersey Standard for control of the northern fields, he could not formally support the arrangement. But he did assure the British that he approved the Jersey Standard-AP deal and would not permit the Persian government to use American interests in a fashion detrimental to Anglo-American relations. He also agreed that continued discussions would be useful, welcomed cooperation between the two governments, and suggested that its durability required British concessions to American initiatives in Mesopotamia and Palestine. For his part, Ambassador Geddes warmly endorsed this "informal understanding." And at the Foreign Office, Lancelot Oliphant confidently expected the "common interests between [the] Anglo-Persian and American companies" in Persia would "greatly increase our good relations with the [American government] even in the matter of the Mesopotamian oil fields." Nothing, he warned, "should be done . . . to hinder the object in view."[49]

---

and AP Co. to the Foreign Office, 17 February 1922, F.O. file: E1859/7/34. See also Bedford to Hughes, 21 February 1922, RG 59, file, 891.6363 St. Oil/142.

48. Kornfeld to Hughes, 20 January 1922 (quoting Greenway), RG 59, file, 891.6363 St. Oil/111; and Oliphant, memorandum, 20 January 1922, F.O. file: E798/7/34.

49. Geddes to the Foreign Office, 23 December 1921, enclosing a memorandum by Chilton, British chargé, of an interview at the Department of State, 17 December 1921, Foreign Office minute by Oliphant, 11 January 1922, F.O. file: E329/7/34; Geddes to the Foreign Office, 15 January 1922, F.O. file: E578/7/34; and Geddes to Hughes, 13 January 1922, F.O. file: E1340/7/34; memorandum by Dearing and Fletcher, 22 December 1921, Geddes to Hughes, 31 December 1921, in *Foreign Relations, 1921*, vol. 2,

Subsequently, British officials complained of ineffective support by the State Department for the Jersey Standard-AP combine. When the Persian government refused to recognize the new Perso-American Company and turned instead to Sinclair Consolidated, the Foreign Office strongly objected on behalf of the Anglo-American group at Teheran.[50] But the corporation's involvement, British policymakers believed, forced the State Department to remain impartial. According to Ronald Lindsay of the Foreign Office, the "American attitude here is nothing more than their regular traditional attitude whenever such a case as this arises. The Govt. is so much afraid of being accused of favoring 'the interests' that it has had to adopt the rule that when two rivals are competing for one concession, it will be 'impartial'—which *means* 'impotent'— and it can never be brought to depart from this rule."[51] As a result, another official explained, the British government found itself in an "invidious position [as the] sole protector of the Standard Oil Company's interests against the activity of Sinclair Corporation."[52]

Despite these complaints, however, the possibility of an independent American concession in north Persia did not greatly disturb the British. To be sure, they still hoped to defeat Sinclair Consolidated and to confirm the Khostaria concession. But they were ready to accept an independent American enterprise. As they saw it, AP already controlled the south Persian fields, and any "extension of their interests into the northern provinces would . . . lead sooner or later to conflict with Persia's northern neighbour." Under these circumstances, it was "politically advantageous to have an independent American interest in a position to act as a buffer between our interests and those of Russia." Moreover, even if Persia awarded an independent grant to Sinclair Consolidated or to Jersey Standard, they reasoned that oil produced in the north could be marketed only through south Persia. This would require some arrangement with AP, and this, in turn, would produce the desired

pp. 653–55; Fletcher, "Memorandum of a Conversation with Mr. Chilton," 10 January 1922, Hughes to Geddes, 11 January 1922, and Geddes to Hughes, 16 January 1922, RG 59, file, 891.6363 St. Oil/86, 104.

50. In making these representations to the Persian government, the Foreign Office was responding to requests from AP. This can be followed in F.O. file: E44/E59/E827/E965/E1244/44/34.

51. See Foreign Office minute by Lindsay, 27 June 1922, F.O. file: E6317/7/34. See also Churchill minute, 21 June 1922, F.O. file: E6226/7/34.

52. Sir Percy Loraine, British Minister, Teheran, to the Foreign Office, 24 June 1922, and Foreign Office minute by Churchill, 26 June 1922, F.O. file: E317/7/34.

Anglo-American cooperation. What the British really envisioned, then, was any arrangement that would insure American collaboration in stabilizing Persia against bolshevism.[53]

Although officials in the Foreign Office believed otherwise, the State Department did staunchly defend the Jersey Standard-AP deal against Persian objections to including the British in any concession that covered the northern provinces. When the Persian government threatened to terminate discussions with Jersey Standard and conclude new arrangements with Sinclair Consolidated, it quickly was warned that no American company would "buck the British Government" and that collapse of the Jersey Standard deal would make it impossible for Persia to find a new source of foreign financial assistance.[54] And to the British, Assistant Secretary Fred Morris Dearing gave assurances that "after a while the Persian Government if it continued to need money badly would probably become more receptive."[55] The State Department, Ambassador Geddes wrote to his superiors in London, shares "my own opinion that the Persian government could scarcely hope to raise another loan here if the Standard Oil Company loan fell through. This last mentioned factor, when realised by the Persian government may lead them to a more reasonable attitude."[56]

Firmly committed to the new policy, the State Department also refused to be moved when officials of Sinclair Consolidated bitterly bemoaned the lack of government support for their enterprise. A British-supported combine, they charged, was given equal if not better treatment than a purely American company.[57] In response, Assistant Secretary Leland Harrison told the complainants that an association of American and foreign capital did not in itself relieve the Department of its obligation to assist such American interests impartially. Further explaining the circumstances controlling the

53. See Foreign Office minute by Churchill, 16 May 1924, F.O. file: E4282/44/34; and J. J. Clarke, Board of Trade, memorandum, 20 May 1924, F.O. file: E4661/44/34.

54. Dearing to Millspaugh, 2 March 1922, RG 59, file, 891.6363 St. Oil/ 153. See also Millspaugh to Dearing, 11 February 1922, Dearing to Fletcher, 1 March 1922, RG 59, file, 891.6363 St. Oil/137, 130, 148.

55. Dearing to Millspaugh, 13 March 1922, RG 59, file, 891.6363 St. Oil/ 160. See also Dearing to Millspaugh, 4 and 7 March 1922, RG 59, file, 891.6363 St. Oil/156, 158.

56. Geddes to the Foreign Office, 8 March 1922, F.O. file: E2654/7/34.

57. R. Crandall to Hughes, 6 September and 9 October 1922, Dulles to Harrison, 27 September 1922, William Heroy of Sinclair to Hughes, 12 March 1923, and Dulles to Hughes, 5 November 1923, RG 59, file, 891.6363 St. Oil/247, 255, 254, 276, 304.

Department's policy, both Hughes and Allen Dulles of the Near Eastern Division noted the need for multinational cooperation in the Middle East and their reluctance to embroil the United States in political conflicts on behalf of independent and competitive American enterprises.[58]

Indeed, despite assurances of impartial support for both Jersey Standard and Sinclair Consolidated, the Department was deliberately scuttling the neutrality doctrine for the sake of Anglo-American cooperation. Although Harrison told Sinclair Consolidated that support would go to any firm possessing valid rights, the Department kept postponing an investigation of the contested Khostaria claim—the concession upon which the future of the new Perso-American Company would depend should Persia cancel Jersey Standard's 1921 contract.[59] Millspaugh also warned the Persian Minister that its alleged illegality could not outweigh the reasons for Anglo-American cooperation. And reflecting anything but neutrality, Hughes rejected a request by the Persian Minister that he refute press reports claiming Department support for the validity of the concession.[60]

Not until Sinclair Consolidated's independent action threatened to disrupt Anglo-American cooperation did Dulles and Assistant Secretary William Phillips urge a solicitor's examination of the concession. Clearly they hoped it would uphold the concession's validity, leaving Sinclair Consolidated "high and dry" and relieving the Department of any potential "embarrassment."[61] Later, moreover,

58. Harrison to the Sinclair Consolidated, 6 October 1922, Hughes to Harding, 28 October 1922, Harding to Hughes, 30 October 1922, and Dulles to Hughes, 5 November 1923, RG 59, file, 891.6363 St. Oil/247, 256a, 257, 304; and Hughes to Coolidge, 8 November 1923, in *Foreign Relations, 1923*, vol. 2, pp. 717–18.

59. On the Department's alleged neutrality see Hughes to American legation, Teheran, 8 November 1923, RG 59, file, 891.6363 St. Oil/304. See also Millspaugh to Phillips and Hughes, 14 June 1922, Millspaugh, "Memorandum of a Conversation of the Secretary with Bedford and Wellman," 12 June 1922, Harrison to Sinclair Consolidated, 6 October 1922, RG 59, file, 891.6363 St. Oil/219, 229, 247; and "Memorandum of an Interview with Thomas Lamont by Telephone," 24 March 1923, Harrison Papers, General Correspondence, box 6.

60. For Millspaugh and Hughes on the Khostaria concession see Millspaugh to Dearing and Fletcher, 19 December 1921, Millspaugh to Dearing, 3 January 1922, Millspaugh to Fletcher, 9 January 1922, Millspaugh, memorandum, 1 March 1922, Persian Minister to Hughes, 14 March 1922, all in RG 59, file, 891.6363 St. Oil/145, 74, 88, 92, 149, 157.

61. Dulles to Phillips and Harrison, 14 August 1922, and Phillips to Hughes, 18 August 1922, RG 59, file, 891.6363 St. Oil/237, 238.

when a preliminary report from the Solicitor's Office indicated that the concession was indeed invalid, Hughes failed to order a follow-up investigation or to make the preliminary findings available to Sinclair Consolidated.[62] Support for the company was clearly not going to be forthcoming and this, together with the Teapot Dome scandal, was the major factor in finally knocking that company out of the Persian competition.[63]

IV

In Mesopotamia, as in Persia, the British abandoned early efforts to monopolize valuable petroleum resources and agreed to accept a significant American participation in the rights claimed by the Turkish Petroleum Company. In this case, the State Department had refused to admit the validity of the TPC's concession and had attacked its exclusive features as incompatible with the concept of trusteeship inherent in the mandate system. This convinced the British that American collaboration in petroleum development would be necessary to protect the TPC's stake in Mesopotamian oil and to assure American support for British mandates in the Middle East. In February 1922, Colonial Secretary Winston Churchill summarized this view in a memorandum to Foreign Secretary Earl Curzon. According to Churchill, the legality of TPC's concession probably could not survive if arbitrated. More important, so long as "Americans are excluded from participation in Iraq oil we shall never see the end of our difficulties in the Middle East." With American oil interests satisfied, on the other hand, "such pressing questions as the ratification of the mandates by the League of Nations, etc., will prove comparatively simple" and "even the

62. A copy of the solicitor's report dated 25 August 1922 can be found in RG 59, file, 891.6363 St. Oil/243½.
63. The Department failed to remain neutral in many other ways. As late as January 1924, for example, Dulles was suggesting to Jersey officials that the Department had not yet investigated the Khostaria claim. Also in January 1924, Dulles authored a memorandum for Hughes specifying the several occasions on which the Department had assured Jersey officials and others of its warm support for the Jersey Standard-AP combine. Indeed, the American Minister in Teheran apparently advised the representative of Sinclair Consolidated there that he was wasting his time trying to get a concession over the northern provinces. See Dulles, "Memorandum of a Conversation with Wellman," 24 January 1924, Dulles to Hughes, 29 January 1924, and Millspaugh, "Memorandum of a Conversation with Chester Naramore of the Sinclair Company," 25 May 1922, RG 59, file, 891.6363 St. Oil/328, 331, 206.

Kemalist situation" might be "appreciably relieved." The benefits to be derived from cooperation seemed "so great," in fact, that Churchill was ready "to pay a high price for it."[64]

Churchill followed closely the progress of negotiations between AP and Jersey Standard, hoping that collaboration between these companies in Persia would "lead to similar co-operation in Iraq." Officials in the Foreign Office shared this hope, and in March they joined with the Colonial Office and the Petroleum Department in urging this policy on the Cabinet.[65] Their memorandum, drafted by Churchill, recommended American participation in the TPC's concession as the best way to terminate the Anglo-American dispute over mandates and the TPC's oil monopoly.[66]

In the United States, oil policy was following a similar evolution. Here too, the seven companies in the American Group modified an early proclivity for independent action in favor of consolidation and cooperation with the Turkish Petroleum Company. According to Millspaugh, the Group originally favored an "actual division of the territory" in Mesopotamia, "not merely a share of the dividends" of a multinational consortium.[67] And initially, Millspaugh also supported this approach. Fearing that a proposal by Hoover for a multinational combine in the area could not guarantee the American Group a "fair share," he persuaded Hughes to veto the idea and block efforts to hold an international conference on the question.[68]

Once negotiations got underway, however, both Millspaugh and the American Group became amenable to a joint venture, provided that the profits and the product were fairly divided. They were insisting now upon an equal division of the shares and an equal voice in management, and they were pushing particularly an operational plan that would limit the consortium's function to the production of oil that was to be divided among the shareholders

64. Churchill to Curzon, 1 February 1922, F.O. file: E1195/32/65.

65. Foreign Office minute by Ernest W. Weakley, Eastern Department, 4 February 1922, minute by Lindsay, 6 February [1922], and Curzon to Churchill, 8 February 1922, F.O. file: E1195/132/65.

66. Churchill, "Memorandum to the Cabinet," 13 March 1922, F.O. file: E2902/132/65.

67. Millspaugh, memorandum for Dearing and Hughes, 20 October 1921, and Millspaugh, "Memorandum of Conversations in New York on November 26, 1921," RG 59, file, 890g.6363/49a, 76.

68. Hoover to Hughes, 17 April 1922, Millspaugh, "Memorandum on the Proposed Letter to the Secretary of Commerce," 29 April 1922, Hughes to Hoover, 2 May 1922, RG 59, file, 890g.6363/96, 181.

in proportion to their stock participation. In this way, it seemed, they were trying to balance conflicting tendencies towards cooperation and competition.[69]

As in Persia, the State Department quickly followed the cooperative thrust of private policy. Just as the Persian situation resulted in the Department's scuttling of the neutrality doctrine, so the developments in Mesopotamia led it to redefine the historic meaning of the Open Door, bringing that concept into line with the consolidation of British and American capital. In one sense, the Department became a captive of its own world view. While the distinction between governmental and business spheres of responsibility authorized the government to protect basic ground rules of the market place, particularly the Open Door, the ban on state management made the Department reluctant to intervene in practical business issues. In effect, this meant surrendering to private initiative the final right to determine whether these ground rules accommodated the business realities of international enterprise.

Throughout the Mesopotamian negotiations, Hughes studiously labored to maintain a semblance of the earlier position on the Open Door. He argued, for example, against any monopolization of Mesopotamian resources and demanded that all interested firms be invited into the American Group. He also refused to formally support the so-called self-denying ordinance—a clause that would prohibit parties to the proposed oil agreement from acting independently of their partners in the old Turkish Empire. Yet at the same time, he acknowledged the Group's right to limit its own activities as a business proposition.[70] The Department, he repeatedly declared, was not interested in "particular business arrangements." And while Hoover might argue that "national pride" demanded at least a 25 percent share in any Mesopotamian consortium, Hughes took the position that once the Department had assured American companies the opportunity of membership, any question concerning the particular division of shares was "one of business rather than one involving the policy of the Government." Once the gov-

69. Millspaugh, "Memorandum on the Proposed Letter to the Secretary of Commerce," 29 April 1922, RG 59, file, 890g.6363/181; Gibb and Knowlton, *The Resurgent Years*, pp. 294–95, 298–307.

70. Millspaugh," Memorandum of a Conversation of the Secretary with Bedford and Wellman of Standard Oil," 22 June 1922, RG 59, file, 890g.6363/147; Dulles, memorandum, 20 December 1922, RG 59, file, 890g.6363T84/; and Hughes to Teagle, 22 August, 15 and 30 December 1922, in *Foreign Relations, 1922*, vol. 2, pp. 342–44, 348–49, 351–52.

ernment had opened the door, he told Walter Teagle, president of Jersey Standard, the oil companies must make their own "business arrangements."[71]

As in other areas, the result was that business arrangements quickly undercut the older principle of equal opportunity. In theory at least, this nineteenth-century concept embodied the laissez-faire notion of equal and wide-open competition among the interests of all countries in the markets of the world; a notion that TPC and American Group members considered incompatible with contemporary economic realities. Effective and efficient oil development, they argued, required massive combinations of capital and technology. Hence, the only businesslike solution to the Mesopotamian muddle was a multinational monopoly. As Guy Wellman of Jersey Standard put it in late 1923 and early 1924, the need for large investments when coupled with the risks of loss involved made a monopoly economically imperative to justify the venture.[72]

The chief concession that business leaders were willing to make to the Open Door principle was the incorporation of a subleasing scheme that would limit the area that the proposed consortium could develop and commit it to dispose of the remaining territory through public subleasing to the highest bidder.[73] This, they argued, would allow for practical implementation of the Open Door.[74] But clearly, there would be large elements of monopoly involved, and the extent to which the door remained open would depend upon the policies of the consortium.

Consequently, the arrangement sparked an important debate within the administration. As Dulles noted, it brought the Department "face to face" with the "practical proposition" as to whether the TPC proposal was "consonant with the principle of the Open Door." And for H. C. Morris, chief of the Petroleum Division of the

71. Hoover to Hughes, 19 August 1922, HHP, Commerce, Personal File, box 47; Hughes to Hoover, 31 March 1923, and Dulles, memorandum, 15 December 1922, RG 59, file, 890g.6363T84/91a, 81.

72. Dulles to Hughes, 26 October 1923, RG 59, file, 890g.6363T84/117; and Dulles, memorandum, 22 January 1924, in *Foreign Relations, 1924*, vol. 2, pp. 224–25. See also "Comments on the General Oil Controversy Between the United States and Great Britain," an address by Manning at the International Chamber of Commerce Conference, London, 27 June–2 July 1921, HHP, Commerce, Official File, box 192.

73. See draft agreement of April 1923 and the proposed convention between the new consortium and the government of Mesopotamia (Iraq), in *Foreign Relations, 1923*, vol. 2, pp. 224–25.

74. See again the first two items cited in Note 72.

Bureau of Foreign and Domestic Commerce, the answer was no. Why should the government, he asked, endorse an attempt by a group originally organized "to gain an independent concession" in Mesopotamia to "force its way into the Turkish Petroleum Company as the easiest means to an, at best, only partially satisfactory end?" The agreement, he contended, was "an evasion and not a confirmation (satisfaction) of our open-door policy."[75]

Refusing to equate independent action with the Open Door, however, opinion in the State Department favored the agreement as a realistic fulfillment of that principle. While neither Stanley Hornbeck of the Economic Adviser's Office nor Dulles considered the subleasing provision an application of the traditional Open Door, both accepted the argument of the American Group and recommended it as a practical resolution of the Mesopotamian issue. "It is not easy to apply a theoretical principle like the Open Door to a practical situation like that in Mesopotamia," conceded Dulles. "From a practical standpoint," added Hornbeck, "first-comers must enjoy preference over subsequent applicants. It cannot be expected that equal commercial opportunity can be extended throughout an indefinite period of time."[76]

Economic Adviser Arthur Young agreed. "Although as a general rule monopolies are reprehensible," he noted, "I do not see how the Department can in all instances rigidly oppose monopolistic enterprises." And according to Young, the Mesopotamian arrangement was not entirely incompatible with past precedent. Like the China financial consortium, he argued, it attempted to protect the Open Door by creating a multinational, big-company oligopoly. In both cases, to be sure, there were elements of monopoly involved. In the China consortium, they derived from the exclusive diplomatic support given to the groups involved, and in Mesopotamia they were inherent in exclusive concessions supported by govern-

75. Dulles to Hughes, 26 October 1923, RG 59, file, 890g.6363T84/117; and H. C. Morris to Christian Herter, 23 November 1923, HHP, Commerce, Official File, box 219.

76. Dulles to Hughes, 26 October 1923, and Stanley K. Hornbeck, memorandum, 26 April 1923, and Hornbeck to Dulles, 8 February 1924, RG 59, file 890g.6363T84/117, 142. The economic reasoning behind the American Group's argument had been expressed earlier by Foreign Trade Adviser Wesley Frost. "To my mind," he wrote in late 1920, "the open door formula does not aid very materially because in most countries the supply of petroleum is so limited that the door cannot remain open except until two or three companies have actually taken control of the resources." See Frost to Manning, 27 November 1920, RG 59, file, 800.6363/205a.

ment power. Yet in each case, there were also elements of openness that created an atmosphere conducive to fairness and efficiency. The China consortium was both multinational in character and so organized that each national group included the major firms of good standing. The same was true of the Mesopotamian arrangement; and in its case there was the added factor of the subleasing provision permitting future participation by additional interests.[77]

Having told the American Group that he would not be "so impractical" as to prevent a happy conclusion to the Mesopotamian dispute, Hughes also fell in with this logic. If the government was to be of "real assistance to American business interests," he told President Calvin Coolidge in October 1923, it was necessary to deal with the Mesopotamian matter from a "practical rather than from a theoretical" point of view. And practically speaking, an arrangement that combined a limited form of monopoly with open entry for new lessees and a multinational membership seemed to represent a businesslike application of the Open Door principle. The alternative, he thought, was a form of political and economic competition that would be injurious to world peace.[78] And when Coolidge agreed, he notified Teagle that while the proposed concession was "in technical form" monopolistic, the multinational character of the consortium and the subleasing provision accorded "satisfactory recognition" to the Open Door principle.[79]

The British had anticipated the American reaction. Throughout the negotiations, policymakers in London had taken the lead in convincing the European companies involved to concede the American Group a 20 percent share in the enterprise. This was necessary, they repeated, to "secure American assent" to the British mandate in Mesopotamia, for "without that it would probably be impossible to get the Turkish Petroleum Company really going." As they saw it, substantial American participation would also be a useful antidote against independent action by American companies and a rebellious Iraq government. After all, there was always "the risk that the Iraq Government would decline to leave themselves

77. Arthur N. Young, memorandum, 10 May 1923, RG 59, file, 890g.6363T84/92.

78. Millspaugh, "Memorandum of a Conversation of the Secretary with Bedford and Wellman," 22 June 1922, RG 59, file, 890g.6363/47; and Hughes to Coolidge, 31 October 1923, RG 59, file, 890g.6363T84/117a.

79. Coolidge to Hughes, 31 October 1923, RG 59, file, 890g.6363T84/118; and Hughes to Teagle, 8 November 1923, in *Foreign Relations, 1923*, vol. 2, pp. 257–59.

indefinitely in the hands of His Majesty's Government; would claim
that the oil was Iraq oil and ought to be developed; and would
simply scrap the Turkish Petroleum Company" and dispose of its
resources as it saw fit. A 20 percent share also could be easily divided among the companies in the American Group which, in turn,
could satisfy potential claims by outside American interests. And
this, the British assumed, would make it easier for the State Department to accept the limitations on the Open Door entailed.[80]

This assumption proved correct, for the State Department did
not alter its positive opinion when the business aspects of the arrangement between TPC and the American Group were finally
completed in 1928. The delay had resulted from a dispute over the
share to be assigned to G. S. Gulbenkian, an independent stock-
holder in the original TPC who demanded a 5 percent interest in
the new combine. The companies involved had at first refused to
concede, but as negotiations wore on and Gulbenkian's determination showed no sign of wilting they finally forged an agreement
that awarded him a 5 percent interest and equally divided the remaining shares in the new Iraq Petroleum Company among themselves. The agreement also incorporated the subleasing provision
and the restrictions on independent action within the old Turkish
Empire that had been embodied in the original understanding. Yet
despite these restrictions, the State Department supported the new
combine when the American Group presented the final agreement
for approval in April 1928.[81]

V

In Mesopotamia, when the distinction between private and governmental responsibility blurred, the State Department was forced
to redefine the Open Door, bringing it into line with the realities
of business enterprise as defined by private petroleum officials. This
permitted the institutionalizing of Anglo-American cooperation at
the private level, allowed American interests a share in Middle
Eastern resources, preserved the ban on state management, and

80. Geddes to the Foreign Office, 12 January 1923, Foreign Office minute
by Weakley, 15 January 1923, F.O. file: E582/91/65; and R. C. Vernon of
the Colonial Office, to Weakley, 4 August 1922 (with enclosure), F.O. file:
E7739/132/65.

81. See Economic Adviser's memorandum, 13 April 1928, G. Holland
Shaw to Wellman, 16 April 1928, RG 59, file, 890g.6363T84/321, 320; and
Gibb and Knowlton, *The Resurgent Years*, pp. 298–308.

avoided politically destabilizing economic competition. In effect, the Mesopotamian settlement followed a pattern also established in Latin America and Persia. In each case the Department abandoned unilateralism in favor of a policy that encouraged multinational, especially Anglo-American, management of petroleum resources by private business leaders. In each case, it claimed that such an arrangement would help to maximize development and avoid economically inefficient and politically injurious state management. And in each case, concepts derived from the older competitive model—such concepts as aggressive nationalism, the neutrality doctrine, and the Open Door—were redefined to accommodate the new vision of expert management and cooperative capitalism. From seemingly opposite positions, America and Britain had moved toward a common approach in their solutions to the international petroleum problem, and through reciprocal trading they had made this approach applicable to all the major oil regions. In practice, the dream of an "all-British" system and the American vision of an Open Door world had come out as an informal Anglo-American entente, institutionalized at the private level, surrounded with the mystique of enlightened capitalism, and masked behind tortured concessions to competitive symbols.

CHAPTER 9

Retreat From Cooperation

The Conflict of Goals in Anglo-American Resource Policy

During the 1920s British and American leaders also tried to extend the sphere of Anglo-American cooperation to include resource allocation in general. As elsewhere, American officials opposed state-sponsored and preferential programs. Such programs, they argued once more, replaced the kind of business efficiency and technological change that was stimulated by private initiative with the type of political conflict that hampered development and jeopardized world peace. Cooperative arrangements based upon enlightened private management, so it seemed, could do a much better job of developing and allocating the world's resources. Yet, in this area the cooperationists had much less success than in others. Here the aspirations for independent sources of supply were particularly strong, and these competitive desires were exacerbated by the reluctance of British authorities to abandon restrictionist schemes in favor of an Anglo-American understanding that did not include concessions on tariff and commercial policy. The result was a deadlock at the governmental level, rejection of several suggestions for organizing private cooperation, and the adoption by the United States of a more nationalistic policy than was apparent in the fields of finance, communications, or petroleum.

Attempts to secure a general agreement on resource allocation came during an Anglo-American controversy over rubber policy in the last half of the postwar decade. In this controversy, the conflicting strains that characterized American resource policy are evident—strains that were less obvious in the American approach to other issues. An examination of it can also show how the resulting tensions, if left unreconciled, could stymie the cooperative program, prevent market integration through multinational regulation, and undermine efforts to enlarge the area of Anglo-American understanding.

I

In the postwar decade, Americans came to appreciate the importance of foreign raw materials to continuing prosperity in the United States. The wartime need for adequate supplies of critical materials had pointed up their strategic significance.[1] And despite the abundance of rich domestic resources, American industry had become increasingly dependent upon foreign sources of supply. From 1925 to 1929, the United States was the world's largest user of every important metal and of a host of other raw materials. It consumed over 60 percent of the world's output of eight critical materials, 40 percent of ten additional materials, and 20 percent of still another fourteen.[2]

In view of these strategic and economic needs, Allied plans to control both domestic and foreign sources of vital raw materials added to American anxiety. Such control had been a central feature in the recommendations of the Paris Economic Conference of 1916. In 1918, it had reappeared in British plans to shut American capital out of the British Empire and pool postwar resources for the preferential benefit of Allied industries. And at the Paris Peace Conference, the French and British had again proposed combining resources in a postwar inter-Allied raw-material cartel.[3]

1. During the war, the Shipping Board's Bureau of Planning and Statistics had worked on the problem of raw materials, especially the connection between shipping facilities and access to foreign sources of raw materials. See Edwin F. Gay, director of the Bureau of Planning and Statistics, "Economic Defensive: Strategic 'Key' Resources and the 'Master Key' Shipping, Summary," 11 June 1918, RG 32, "Subject-Classified General File," 34514; and "Relation Between the United States and Other Countries Regarding Important Raw Materials," a report prepared by the American Section of the Allied Maritime Transport Council, n.d., RG 32, "Records of the Division of Planning and Statistics, General File," 084.08.

2. Eugene Staley, *Raw Materials in Peace and War*, p. 15; Jacob Viner, "National Monopolies of Raw Materials," and Josiah Edward Strong, "Steel-Making Minerals," both in *Foreign Affairs: An American Quarterly Review*, pp. 585–600.

3. On the Paris Economic Conference of 1916 and the subsequent British and French proposals for a postwar economic alliance see Chapter 2. For British plans to close the empire to American capital see Hoover to Lansing, 10 May 1918, attached to C. D. Snow of the Bureau of Foreign and Domestic Commerce (BFDC) to B. S. Cutler, chief, BFDC, 27 May 1918, RG 40, file, 77270. For the British proposal to pool raw materials see Colville Barclay to Lansing, 12 June 1918, RG 40, file, 77270. For the British and French proposals at the Paris Peace Conference see "Minutes of the Raw Material Section of the Supreme Economic Council," 4 April 1919, minute 5, vol. 9,

To be sure, these early plans had failed to materialize. But in the postwar period, the Allies had sponsored and encouraged new restrictive raw-material cartels. French potash producers combined with their German rivals to restrict the marketing of potash used in fertilizer compounds needed by American farmers. British interests controlled nitrate production in Chile and regulated the industry through their domination of the Nitrate Producers Association and its London Nitrate Committee. And the British Rubber Growers Association, representing planters in Ceylon and Malaya, controlled over 70 percent of the world's rubber and attempted to regulate prices through an export restriction scheme. By 1923, moreover, similar cartels were limiting the production and thus raising the price of six other basic commodities. As American critics saw it, these cartels levied a several billion dollar annual "supercharge" on American consumers. And worse, they were threatening to return the world to "medieval" trade policies that might curtail consumption, cripple industry, and leave millions of American workers unemployed.[4]

In response to such policies, one group of American officials had long been discussing a defensive strategy for the United States. In May 1918, for example, Shipping Board Chairman Edward Hurley had urged President Woodrow Wilson to arm the United States for the inevitable resumption of commercial competition after the war by securing control over foreign sources of key raw materials. He envisaged a billion dollar government cartel that could purchase deposits of essential resources, especially in South America and Asia.[5] Similarly, J. E. Spurr, a mining engineer attached to the

---

pp. 25–32, Supreme Economic Council Papers, and unsigned memorandum (probably by Lamont) 13 June 1919, Lamont Papers, Series 4-A, file, 165–10.

4. Unsigned "Abstract of a Report on the German-French Potash Combine," n.d., and Charles C. Concannon, chief, Chemical Division, BFDC, 28 November 1925, HHP, Commerce, Official File, box 232; Col. S. Heintzelman, "Report by the G-2 Division of the War Department General Staff," 11 May 1922, attached to Kenzie Walker, acting budget officer, War Department, to the Secretary of War, 15 May 1922, and unsigned "Memorandum on National Control of Chilean Nitrate Production," 15 February 1923, HHP, Commerce, Official File, box 214; Paul L. Palmerton, chief, Rubber Division, BFDC, to the Secretary's Office, 23 December 1925, HHP, Commerce, Official File, box 128; and House, Committee on Interstate and Foreign Commerce, *Hearings on H. R. 59: Crude Rubber, Coffee, Etc.*, 6–22 January 1926, pp. 1–7.

5. Hurley to Bernard Baruch, 21 May 1918, RG 40, file, 77270. Hurley forwarded a copy of this letter to President Wilson on 22 May 1918. See Woodrow Wilson Papers, Series 5–A, box 3.

Shipping Board, suggested forming a number of raw-material corporations to be controlled by a holding company organized under the Treasury Department. These corporations could gain financial control over important mineral deposits in the Western Hemisphere, thus creating an American commercial sphere that would be useful in bargaining for access to raw-material sources controlled by other commercial blocs.[6]

Most Wilsonians, however, rejected this strategy because it interjected the government into the private economy and contradicted their hope for progress through an expanding world economy. Anglo-German commercial rivalry, they believed, had resulted in war precisely because government intervention in the market had escalated economic competition between private interests into political and military conflict. Therefore, the United States government must not behave like a "benevolent monopolist" for private commercial interests abroad.[7] It must not endorse foreign-trade tactics that it had "been condemning when practiced by the Germans."[8] And it must make others realize that such tactics would "inevitably lead to wars without end."[9] Instead of Hurley's scheme, therefore, Secretary of Commerce William Redfield wanted the government to fully develop unexploited domestic resources, turning this enterprise over to private commercial interests after the war. He also favored multinational consultation on the best way for using these resources to meet postwar shortages abroad.[10]

6. J. E. Spurr's ideas are discussed by Lester H. Woolsey, State Department solicitor, in a memorandum to the Secretary of State, 25 May 1919, enclosed in Lansing to William Redfield, 6 June 1918, RG 40, file, 77270.
7. Redfield to Hurley, 28 May 1918, RG 40, file, 77270.
8. Frank Taussig of the Tariff Commission to Redfield, 30 November 1918, RG 40, file, 78075. Taussig's remark was in connection with a proposal by Secretary of the Navy Josephus Daniels that the government-owned merchant marine carry American exports at cost. In conveying the suggestion to Taussig, Redfield also protested that such methods would "out-German the Germans." See Redfield to Taussig, 16 November 1918, RG 40, file, 77270.
9. Gay, "Economic Defensive: Strategic 'Key' Resources and the 'Master Key' Shipping, Summary," 11 June 1918, RG 32, "Subject-Classified General File," 34514.
10. Redfield to Wilson, 29 May 1918, Wilson Papers, Series 2, box 177; Redfield to Hurley, 28 May 1918, Redfield to Baruch, 29 May 1918, Redfield to Hurley, 6 June 1918, B. S. Cutler to Redfield, 27 June 1918, unsigned memorandum for W. S. Gifford, BFDC, 3 July 1918, Redfield to Baruch, 15 July 1918, and Redfield to Secretary of the Interior Franklin Lane, 15 and 19 July 1918, all in RG 40, file, 77270; and Redfield to Wilson, 11 November 1918, RG 40, file, 77977.

Republican policymakers shared these assumptions, attacking government-sponsored raw-material monopolies as economically unsound and injurious to world peace. Such price-fixing cartels, they insisted, undermined efficient business practices, discouraged innovative improvements, and distorted normal market operations. Although intended to stabilize prices, they actually injured consumers and producers alike by invariably leading to "extortionate" demands, thereby reducing consumption, promoting the use of substitutes, and stimulating the development of new sources of supply. And worse, by substituting state management for the "higgling of producers and merchants," they lifted commercial matters "into the realm of international relations," made government officials "bargainers in the market on behalf of whole countries," and thus posed "broad dangers to wholesome international relations."[11]

One line of Republican policy emerged as a joint effort by business and government to force the abandonment of undesirable foreign cartels. When appropriate, the government was to file protests against exorbitant prices, block American capital from underwriting the foreign combinations, encourage conservation and the use of substitutes, and support the development of independent sources of supply free from manipulation by foreign interests. At the same time, business was to organize for the cooperative defense of American interests by creating buying pools and fostering the cooperative promotion of new supply lines. Here, as in other fields, the success of wartime collaboration had provided an important precedent, and after the war trade bodies like the Rubber Association of America hoped to act as "cooperative agent[s]" between the government and the consumer in protecting American interests.[12]

11. Herbert Hoover, "America Solemnly Warns Foreign Monopolists of Raw Materials," pp. 307–11; E. Dana Durand, BFDC, "Economic and Political Effects of Government Interference with the Free International Movement of Raw Materials," pp. 25–34; Julius Klein, "International Cartels," pp. 448–58; Department of Commerce, press release, 23 December 1925, HHP, Commerce, Official File, box 128; and Hoover, "The Future of Our Foreign Trade," 16 March 1926, HHP, Commerce, Personal File, box 24.

12. Hearings on H. R. 59: Crude Rubber, Coffee, Etc., pp. 4–7, 286–89; Hoover, "Foreign Combinations Now Fixing Prices of Raw Materials Imported Into the United States," an address before the Chamber of Commerce of Erie, Pennsylvania, 31 October 1925, HHP, Commerce, Official File, box 128; Everett G. Holt, chief, Rubber Division, BFDC, "Foreign Government Price Fixing of Our Import Raw Materials," 25 October 1926, HHP,

Most Republican policymakers, however, hoped that this attack on foreign practices, with its "atmosphere of contention and dispute," was only temporarily necessary. Their ultimate solution was one that would combine collectivist programs at home with cooperative multinationalism abroad. This was the reasonable way to proceed, and once the foreign governments that were involved, particularly the British, had been persuaded to abandon their monopoly practices, an enlightened system of raw-material development and allocation might be adopted. This system would be based on equal opportunity and scientific management and, in operation, could eliminate politically dangerous trade wars, stimulate business efficiency and "progressive production," and increase the standard of living for all people.[13]

Government policy, then, tried to balance contending strategies, fostering cooperative business self-regulation and government-business collaboration in promoting national self-sufficiency while, at the same time, seeking a broader multinationalism founded on private management. And while, in theory, equality of opportunity was to be a major factor in any multinational formula, as in other areas cooperative regulation clearly limited the competitive implications of that principle. These conflicting goals help to account for the tension between independent action and multinationalism, competition and monopoly that underlay the American attitude toward raw-material cartels. And nowhere was this tension more apparent than in the pattern of policy toward the production of rubber and the British efforts to stabilize prices.

II

After the war, overproduction and declining prices for crude rubber had led British planters in Ceylon and Malaya to adopt a voluntary scheme to stabilize prices by restricting production and marketing. This voluntary arrangement had failed to work, however, and with the price of rubber continuing to decline the British

Commerce, Official File, box 256; A. L. Viles, general manager of the Rubber Association of America, to Hoover, 18 April 1921, HHP, Commerce, Official File, box 257.

13. Hoover, "Foreign Combinations Now Fixing Prices of Raw Materials Imported Into the United States," 31 October 1925, HHP, Commerce, Official File, box 128; and unsigned "Outline of an Address by Herbert Hoover to a Conference of Rubber, Oil, and Automotive Men," n.d., HHP, Commerce, Official File, box 128.

Colonial Office had appointed an Advisory Committee to study the situation and formulate recommendations. In 1922, this committee, which was led by Sir James Stevenson, had suggested a compulsory restriction plan whereby each plantation could export only 60 percent of its standard production for 1920. Growers exporting above this level were to be assessed an additional, prohibitive duty on their entire shipment.[14] This scheme, it was hoped, would increase the price of crude rubber and save the planters from financial ruin. By "making the Americans pay" more for rubber imports, as Colonial Secretary Winston Churchill pointed out, it would also "contribute materially to stabilizing the dollar exchange." For these reasons, the Foreign Office, the Board of Trade, and the Colonial Office had endorsed the Stevenson Plan and it was subsequently enacted into law.[15]

Despite provisions that would allow adjustments to changed market conditions, Americans considered the plan too inelastic. They feared exorbitant price increases and, more important, artificial shortages of rubber supplies needed by domestic industry. Already in 1922, the United States was consuming over 70 percent of the world's annual rubber output, and in subsequent years the automobile would create an ever-growing market for the rubber tire industry. According to industry reports, moreover, the artificial shortage engendered by the Stevenson scheme soon would be compounded by an absolute shortage of rubber. The Rubber Association of America predicted that by 1929 world demand would reach 672,000 tons as against potential production of only 657,000 tons. According to Americans, there was a need for unlimited, not restrained, production.[16]

14. Palmerton to the Secretary's office, 23 December 1925, HHP, Commerce, Official File, box 128; Rubber Association of America, "Memorandum for the Secretary of State," 17 July 1925, in *Foreign Relations, 1925*, vol. 2, pp. 245–53; and *Hearings on H. R. 59: Crude Rubber, Coffee, Etc.*, pp. 11–15, 18–23.

15. Gerald Villiers, Assistant Secretary, Foreign Office, "Account of a Meeting Held at the Colonial Office on the Subject of the Rubber Restriction Scheme," 20 September 1922, F.O. file: W7858/3414/29; "Proposals of the Colonial Office for the Stabilization of the Rubber Industry," 7 October 1922, F.O. file: W8445/3414/29; and Ronald Campbell to Sir Gilbert Grindle, Colonial Office, 9 October 1922, F.O. file: W8445/3414/29.

16. Hoover to Sen. Medill McCormick, 2 February 1923, Holt, "Foreign Government Price Fixing of Our Import Raw Materials," 25 October 1926, HHP, Commerce, Official File, box 256; Rubber Association of America, "Memorandum for the Secretary of State," 17 July 1925, and F. A. Sterling, counselor, American Embassy, London, to the Secretary of State, 23

To meet this need, American officials had begun looking into the possibility of developing independent sources of supply. In 1922, Herbert Hoover had dispatched Assistant Secretary of Commerce Claudius Huston to survey conditions in the Far East. In 1923, he gained congressional funding for investigations in the Philippines, the Middle East, and the Amazon Valley, and to conduct these investigations he established a division of crude rubber in the Bureau of Foreign and Domestic Commerce. Eventually, when the studies were completed, they formed the first really exhaustive report on the rubber situation ever available to American industry.[17]

It was also Hoover who took the lead in trying to mobilize investment capital through cooperative projects. He encouraged, for example, legislative efforts to legalize buying pools for the cooperative purchase of raw-material imports. He supported a $10 million combine sponsored by the American Automobile Chamber of Commerce to produce, buy, and sell rubber. This combine, he thought, would help to free the consumer of rubber from "unreasonable prices." And along the same lines, he lauded a plan by the tire manufacturers for a $50 million corporation that was to engage largely in developing new plantations abroad.[18]

At the same time, the State and Commerce departments vigorously supported plans by the Firestone Tire & Rubber Company to open new plantations on the West Coast of Africa. Convinced that British growers would ignore the "complaints of American manufacturers," Harvey Firestone had early decided to conduct his own surveys into new sources of supply. And in 1924, after unsuccessful investigations in the Philippines, Mexico, and Panama, he turned to Liberia, secured an initial ninety-nine-year lease on some two thousand acres of plantation property, and subsequently arranged for a private loan to the Liberian government and another ninety-nine-year lease on one million acres of land. The loan was intended both to rehabilitate Liberia's finances and to guarantee the kind of control over its internal economy that Firestone be-

---

July 1925, in *Foreign Relations, 1925*, vol. 2, pp. 245–56; and *Hearings on H. R. 59: Crude Rubber, Coffee, Etc.*, pp. 206–7.

17. Hoover to Senator McCormick, 2 February 1923, HHP, Commerce, Official File, box 256; Hoover to Albert Reeves, Automobile Chamber of Commerce, 5 March 1923, HHP, Commerce, Official File, box 128; and *Hearings on H. R. 59: Crude Rubber, Coffee, Etc.*, pp. 3–4, 226, 309–11.

18. Hoover to Sen. Wesley Jones, 21 April 1924, HHP, Commerce, Official File, box 226; and *Hearings on H. R. 59: Crude Rubber, Coffee, Etc.*, pp. 277, 280, 282, 286.

lieved was essential for the protection of his investment. At first, the Liberian legislature was reluctant to accept the arrangement, but in December 1926 it ratified a somewhat revised loan contract under pressure from the State Department.[19]

These and similar schemes, however, were largely unsuccessful. Despite the Commerce Department's encouragement, the new combines launched by the rubber manufacturers and the Automobile Chamber of Commerce were reluctant to undertake important investment operations abroad. At a meeting of rubber manufacturers in New York in May 1924, Hoover outlined the findings of his crude rubber survey but found that most of the manufacturers preferred allowing British growers to continue raising the rubber needed by American industry. Only Firestone advocated new acquisitions of land that was not under British control. Yet, his Liberian adventure did not get off the ground until the 1930s. A Ford Motor Company project in Brazil also made little progress. And while Goodyear and United States Rubber added slightly to their acreage in the Far East, this gain was offset by the reduced holdings of the Intercontinental Rubber Company.[20]

Even in the Philippines, where the Commerce Department's report had been highly favorable, there was little new investment. In this case, American companies refused to act unless changes were made in the Philippine laws that limited the size of holdings and prohibited the use of imported coolie labor. As in other areas, they also wanted government guarantees for the security of their investments. Perhaps if the government had subsidized expansion, the story might have been different. And there were proposals for doing so, with one scheme calling for a tax of two cents a pound on

19. *Hearings on H. R. 59: Crude Rubber, Coffee, Etc.*, pp. 249–53; Cleona Lewis, *America's Stake in International Investments*, p. 286; *Foreign Relations, 1925*, vol. 2, pp. 367–459; *Foreign Relations, 1926*, vol. 2, pp. 503–97; Palmerton to the Secretary's Office, 23 October 1925, HHP, Commerce, Official File, box 526; and Frank Chalk, "The United States and the International Struggle for Rubber, 1914–1941" (Ph.D. dissertation), pp. 77–95, 130–50.

20. Geddes to the Foreign Office, 29 March 1923, F.O. file: W2854/47/29; Lewis, *America's Stake in International Investments*, pp. 284–87; unsigned, "Memorandum on a Conference at the Lotus Club, New York," 20 May 1924, HHP, Commerce, Official File, box 127; O. P. Hopkins, acting director of the BFDC, "Notes on Conference," n.d., unsigned, "Memorandum on Conference with Rubber, Automotive and Oil (?) Representatives regarding Rubber Position," n.d., RG 151, file, 621.2, Investigation General; and Chalk, "The United States and the International Struggle for Rubber," pp. 69–72.

crude rubber imports and using the proceeds to subsidize private planting abroad. Such proposals, however, went further than Hoover was willing to go. It was "much better for our industries to solve these matters than to lay down upon the Government," he argued; and following the ban on state management he continued to confine his efforts to urging private action, conducting surveys, and forwarding information on investment possibilities to interested American groups.[21]

Another reason for the failure to develop new sources of supply was the division among American manufacturers over an appropriate response to the Stevenson scheme. To Firestone it was anathema, and after learning that the India Rubber Manufacturers Association of Great Britain was seeking to bring about its repeal, he set out to organize an international front of manufacturers that could bring pressure on the British Foreign Office. In February 1922, a representative of the British manufacturers attended a conference of rubber consumers that Firestone had convened in Washington. The result was a series of resolutions endorsing the Commerce Department's proposed survey of new sources of supply and recommending cooperation between American and British users in defeating the Stevenson scheme.[22]

Other American rubber manufacturers, however, led by U.S. Rubber, Goodyear, and Goodrich, rejected Firestone's plan. After boycotting the Washington conference, they proceeded to launch a publicity campaign that was designed to undermine Firestone's strategy and inform American consumers of the need for market stability that had prompted the Stevenson scheme. Most members of the Rubber Association, Ambassador Geddes reported to London, "show a most friendly disposition" and "are sharply op-

---

21. *Hearings on H. R. 59: Crude Rubber, Coffee, Etc.*, pp. 108, 114–15, 117, 119, 136–37, 252, 286; F. A. Seiberling, Seiberling Rubber Co., to Hoover, 28 December 1925 and 21 January 1926, HHP, Commerce, Official File, box 257; Hoover to Phil Bennett, Lieutenant Governor of Missouri, 20 September 1926, HHP, Commerce, Official File, box 256; Palmerton to the Secretary's office, 11 December 1925, RG 151, file, 621.2, Dutch East Indies; and Palmerton to Commercial Attaché Hugh Butler, London, 3 February 1926, RG 151, file, 621.2, Straits Settlement.

22. Geddes to the Foreign Office, 2 March 1923, F.O. file: W1980/42/29; *Hearings on H. R. 59: Crude Rubber, Coffee, Etc.*, pp. 249–51; Alfred Lief, *The Firestone Story: A History of the Firestone Tire & Rubber Company*, pp. 147–49; and Chalk, "The United States and the International Struggle for Rubber," pp. 58–59.

posed to Firestone's activities." Indeed, as a result of this opposition, Firestone resigned from the association in May 1923.[23]

The leading figures in the Rubber Association hoped to collaborate with British growers rather than British manufacturers. Already in 1922, Edgar Davis of the rubber industry had suggested an international rubber combine dominated by British and American interests. This cooperative organization, he believed, could consolidate existing rubber production, develop new sources of supply, and coordinate growing and marketing programs. This, in turn, would bring stability, efficiency, and rapid technological advance to all segments of the rubber business. Initially at least, officials in the Commerce Department had considered a similar program. As they saw it, unified production and marketing arrangements could "reduce production costs," guarantee "an adequate supply of rubber," utilize "surplus production in new channels," and substitute "scientific control over production" for the "unscientific methods at present in vogue."[24]

Even after enactment of the Stevenson scheme, both public and private officials wanted to collaborate with the British in adjusting the export restrictions to consumer demand in the United States market. In January 1923, Assistant Secretary Huston impressed upon the British Commercial Counselor in Washington the "importance of Anglo-American co-operation and close understanding." The need, he insisted, was for price stability in the rubber industry and for assurances that British restrictions would be tailored to American consumption.[25] At the same time, the Rubber Association invited a British delegation to the United States for discussions, and after admitting the need for stabilization measures to protect the growers, asked for guarantees that additional exports would be allowed should the present allotment schedule

23. *Hearings on H. R. 59: Crude Rubber, Coffee, Etc.*, p. 251; Geddes to the Foreign Office, 22 June 1923, F.O. file: W5200/47/29; J. Joyce Broderick, Commercial Counselor, British Embassy, Washington, to the Foreign Office, 15 August 1923, F.O. file: W6439/47/29; Geddes to the Foreign Office, 2 March 1923, F.O. file: W1980/47/29; and Firestone to Viles, 8 May 1923, HHP, Commerce, Official File, box 128.

24. James Lawrence, *The World's Struggle with Rubber, 1905–1931*, pp. 30–31, 111–12; Chalk, "The United States and the International Struggle for Rubber," pp. 28–31; and "Memorandum on Conference with Rubber, Automotive and Oil (?) Representatives regarding Rubber Position," n.d., RG 151, file, 621.2, Investigations General.

25. Memorandum by the British Commercial Counselor, n.d., enclosed in Geddes to the Foreign Office, 19 January 1923, F.O. file: W886/47/29.

prove too inflexible. These were given on an informal basis, and the rubber manufacturers then agreed to supply the growers with periodic market reports depicting consumption and outlining future requirements.[26]

By mid-1925, however, this informal understanding had broken down. A heavy reduction of rubber stocks in London had forced a rapid upward fluctuation in the price of crude, and British officials in Washington began reporting new agitation among American consumers, including the more moderate members of the Rubber Association.[27] Indeed, during a meeting with Secretary of State Frank Kellogg in July, representatives of the Rubber Association outlined the crisis facing their industry and asked the Department to intervene in their behalf with the British government. They also met privately with officials of the British Embassy, repeating their complaints and asking for relief. Specifically, they wanted an immediate increase in the exportable allowance of crude rubber, a replenishment of the depleted rubber stocks on hand in London, and a revision of the Stevenson scheme to make the exportable allowances automatically adjustable to changing market requirements.[28]

In London, American Ambassador Alanson Houghton urged this program on officials at the Foreign Office. Excessive demands on American consumers, he warned, would force a use of substitutes,

26. Geddes to the Foreign Office, 9 February 1923, F.O. file: W1434/47/29; Geddes to the Foreign Office, 2 March 1923, F.O. file: W1980/47/29; "Report of Delegates From the Rubber Growers Association (Inc.), London, On Their Visit to the Rubber Association of America (Inc.), New York, January-February, 1923," F.O. file: W2408/47/29; Viles to Palmerton, 28 February 1923, HHP, Commerce, Official File, box 128; "Memorandum Submitted by the Rubber Association of America Inc. With Reference to the Effect Upon America's Crude Rubber Supply of the British Stevenson Scheme Under which the Export of Crude Rubber From British Possessions is Restricted," in Foreign Relations, 1925, vol. 2, pp. 245–53; and the testimony of Viles in Hearings on H. R. 59: Crude Rubber, Coffee, Etc., p. 35.

27. Howard, British Ambassador to the United States, to the Foreign Office, 5 June 1925, F.O. file: W5894/5208/50; and Howard to the Foreign Office, 14 June 1925, F.O. file: W5208/5208/50.

28. Frank B. Kellogg to Ambassador Alanson Houghton, London, 18 July 1925, and Houghton to Kellogg, 23 July 1925, in Foreign Relations, 1925, vol. 2, pp. 253–56; Frederic C. Hood of the Rubber Association of America to Wallace McClure of the State Department's Economic Adviser's Office, 17 July 1925, McClure, memorandum, 23 July 1925, and Kellogg to Houghton, 18 July 1925, RG 59, file, 841.6176/8, 5, supp.; H. G. Chilton to the Foreign Office, 19 July 1925, F.O. file: W6898/5208/50; and Chilton to the Foreign Office, 19 July 1925, F.O. file: W6909/5208/50. See also Chilton to the Foreign Office, 12 June 1925, F.O. file: W5895/5208/50.

the development of new sources of supply, and, even worse, possible retaliation against the free export of American commodities to England. He pointed up the significance of American assistance and Anglo-American collaboration to European stabilization, and he argued that international conditions "made it more than ever necessary that we should co-operate." Given this need, he concluded, it would be deplorable "if conflict over a trading question made such assistance and co-operation impossible." [29]

Although the British rejected the American plan, they did modify the export restrictions in a modest attempt to allay American fears. The object, as Foreign Secretary Austin Chamberlain explained, was to preserve the spirit of the Stevenson scheme but "avoid the dangers which must arise to our international relations from the growing agitation in America." In August, they increased by ten points the percentage of standard production that might be exported at minimum duty. Subsequently, they raised the percentage by another five points and released several thousand pounds of stored Malayan rubber. The result, they claimed, was an overall increase to roughly 80 percent of standard production. And this, they insisted, would prevent any immediate shortage yet maintain price stability and assure adequate future supplies by guaranteeing growers a return sufficient to stimulate additional investment in new plantations. [30]

The rubber manufacturers, however, insisted that these measures were insufficient and requested the State Department to seek further relief. But Kellogg and Houghton worried that a formal protest would arouse public opinion in England and make it difficult for the Foreign Office to take ameliorative action. Hoover agreed, preferring to await full market developments under the adjusted Stevenson scheme before lodging new complaints. Consequently, Kellogg instructed Houghton to discuss the matter informally with British officials, asking only if additional relief measures had yet been determined. This was done and the response

29. Austin Chamberlain, memorandum, 22 July 1925, F.O. file: W7067/5208/50; Houghton to Kellogg, 23 July 1925, enclosing Aide-Memoire to the British Foreign Office, 22 July 1925, in *Foreign Relations, 1925*, vol. 2, pp. 254–56; and Houghton to Kellogg, 23 July 1925, RG 59, file, 841.6176/6.

30. Chamberlain, memorandum, 22 July 1925, F.O. file: W7067/5208/50; Sterling to Kellogg, 17 August 1925, enclosing Chamberlain to Ambassador Houghton, 15 August 1925, in *Foreign Relations, 1925*, vol. 2, pp. 256–59; Houghton to Kellogg, 1 and 17 August 1925, and Sterling to Kellogg, 18 August 1925, RG 59, file, 841.6176/13, 19, 22.

from the Foreign Office was a promise to reassess the situation with a view to remedial action should it be desirable.[31]

While negotiations proceeded at the governmental level, several proposals were offered for patching up the 1923 understanding on a private and cooperative basis. In January 1925, Foreign Secretary Chamberlain urged informal conferences between British growers and American manufacturers in order to remove any misunderstanding. At the same time, British Ambassador Esme Howard recommended a similar course as the best method of undercutting new criticism by Hoover and safeguarding the growers "without incurring the resentment of one of the strongest industries" in the United States. And in November, Ambassador Houghton suggested that American consumers might participate in the Stevenson Advisory Committee. This, he assumed, would "bring the opposing factors of supply and demand together," allow for "adequate consideration of present and future needs," and promote "satisfactory development of the rubber industry as a whole."[32]

Later that same month, representatives of the Rubber Association began negotiating with British growers for renewed regulation of the rubber market. The plan, as originally suggested by Churchill, had called for an American banking syndicate to cover the long-term demands of Goodyear, Goodrich, U.S. Rubber, and Fisk Rubber Company. But as later revised, it contemplated removing all export restrictions and allowing British and American rubber interests, supported by their financial backers, to fix the price of rubber at a series of downward rates until a "base" price was reached that all would agree to maintain. The British favored the plan, Houghton reported, but would implement it only with the cooperation and consent of the State Department.[33]

---

31. Kellogg to Houghton, 21 November 1925, and Houghton to Kellogg, 24 November 1925, in *Foreign Relations, 1925*, vol. 2, pp. 261–62; Kellogg to Houghton, 10 October 1925, and Houghton to Kellogg, 12 and 13 October 1925, RG 59, file, 841.6176/26, 27, 28; and Kellogg to Hoover, 10 October 1925, enclosing Viles to Kellogg, 7 October 1925 with attached memorandum submitted by the Rubber Association of America, n.d., and Hoover to Kellogg, 13 October 1925, HHP, Commerce, Official File, box 129.

32. Howard to Chamberlain, 18 January 1925, F.O. file: W11864/5208/50; and Houghton to Kellogg, 9 November 1925, in *Foreign Relations, 1925*, vol. 2, pp. 259–61.

33. L. S. Amery, Colonial Secretary, to Chamberlain, 7 December 1925, F.O. file: W11150/5208/50; and Houghton to Kellogg, 24 and 25 November 1925, in *Foreign Relations, 1925*, vol. 2, pp. 261–62, 263–64.

Although the British proposal was similar to the Commerce Department's earlier idea for multinational cooperation in regulating the rubber market, policymakers considered its provisions for price fixing and governmental sanctions as economically unsound, contrary to the ban on state management, and a threat to peaceful trade relations. Price fixing of this sort, Hoover and Kellogg agreed, would "discourage progress in production methods, stifle consumption, increase the use of less efficient substitutes, [and] stimulate abnormal production in non-price-fixing areas where production cannot exist on a sound economic basis." The proposal would also undermine the "whole fabric" of international relations by promoting excessive government intervention in economic affairs. As a result, they warned, "discussions, which should be kept to the markets," would be "elevated into international negotiations between governments." And this, in turn, would add "innumerable conflicts" and arouse "bitter public sentiments." Consequently, they refused to countenance cooperation by private American interests in any price-fixing scheme and instead urged the British to join them in blocking the spread of such schemes before similar policies were forced upon the administration by agricultural interests in the United States. As a first step in this new cooperation, they suggested eliminating all restrictions on rubber exportations and banning all private loans designed to underwrite other price-fixing cartels. Cooperation on this basis promised important benefits; as the world's "greatest importers of raw materials," the United States and Great Britain had the "most to lose" from the spread of such state-sponsored cartels in the underdeveloped world.[34]

British reaction was mixed. To appease American fears, they agreed to raise the exportable percentage of rubber to 100 percent of standard production for the quarters beginning in February and May 1926. They also adopted a more lenient policy on rubber produced by small estates, a policy that theoretically increased total

34. Kellogg to Houghton, 24 November and 1 December 1925, in *Foreign Relations, 1925*, vol. 2, pp. 262, 264–65; Kellogg to Hoover, 27 November 1925, Hoover to Kellogg, 28 November 1925, enclosing draft of a letter to Houghton, 28 November 1925, and Kellogg, "Conversation with the British Ambassador," 7 January 1926, RG 59, file, 841.6167/40, 42, 57; and Kellogg to Hoover, 2 December 1925, HHP, Commerce, Official File, box 129. See also in this connection Hoover to Kellogg, 25 September 1925, enclosing "Memorandum on Dispatches from the American Embassy in London Relative to the Rubber Situation," n.d., HHP, Commerce, Official File, box 129.

exports to 105 percent of standard production.[35] But at the same time, they resented Hoover's attack on government-sanctioned price-fixing arrangements and rumors that Congress would soon investigate the British rubber cartel. Great Britain was "still an independent country," fumed Robert Vansittart of the Foreign Office, and "we will not stand being 'investigated' by anybody." For Robert Craige, price fixing did for agriculture what a tariff did for industry, and accordingly he thought that Hoover's arguments would carry more weight if they had not emanated from such a staunch protectionist. Given the American tariff, moreover, many British officials were now insisting that export restrictions on rubber not only salvaged the flagging rubber industry but also helped Great Britain to earn the dollar exchange needed to liquidate its war debt to the United States.[36]

In part, these criticisms were shared by influential American leaders. Houghton complained that domestic price-support policies made American opposition to "price-fixing a bit ludicrous in English eyes." Assistant Secretary of State William Castle worried that Hoover's public attacks on foreign monopolies would "make the conduct of our foreign relations more difficult." And for Owen D. Young, official criticism of European trade restrictions would be more effective "if we did not indulge in them ourselves, and at the same time demand extraordinary [debt] payments." Although he agreed with Hoover that government intervention could "lead the whole world to disaster," Young was equally troubled by an American program that exacted "amounts from our debtors up to the breaking point" while simultaneously "excluding their goods" from the United States. And given these circumstances, he even confessed a "certain sympathy with [the European] effort to get as much" as possible from American consumers.[37]

35. Houghton to Kellogg, 4 December 1925, in *Foreign Relations, 1925,* vol. 2, pp. 265–67; and Houghton to Kellogg, 30 April 1926, RG 59, file, 841.6176/85.

36. Foreign Office minute by Vansittart, 23 December 1925, F.O. file: W11722/5208/50; and Robert Craige, minute, 7 December 1925, F.O. file: W11150/5208/50. For other samples of British resentment see also Vansittart to Howard, 4 January 1926, F.O. file: W11722/5208/50; Foreign Office minutes by Campbell, 12 December 1925 and 22 January 1926, F.O. file: W11150/W11722/5208/50; and Brandes, *Hoover and Economic Diplomacy,* pp. 91–94.

37. Houghton to William R. Castle, 7 December 1925, and Castle to Houghton, 7 January 1926, William R. Castle Papers, Folder, England; and

When the British responded to the Hoover-Kellogg proposal for
a cooperative attack on trade restrictions, American tariff policy
played a large role in their calculations. Although refusing to block
foreign cartels from borrowing in the London market, they did admit the need for reducing all governmental barriers to international
trade. And despite the difficulty in deciding upon general principles, they were ready to begin a discussion of the problem with
a view toward some Anglo-American understanding. But they insisted that this discussion include both import and export barriers,
because high tariffs afforded "perhaps the most powerful support
given by governments to price-fixing combinations."[38] Although
"sympathetic in form and substance," Craige explained, this reply
was actually "destructive of the United States proposal." It would
be addressed "to a highly protectionist government which has not
the slightest idea of effecting any . . . reduction in its tariff rates."[39]

In the United States, however, a group of policymakers, led by
Wallace McClure of the State Department's Economic Adviser's
Office, wanted to adapt the British plan to American needs. As
early as 1925, McClure had urged the Department to consider the
"larger aspects" of the rubber controversy, especially the depen-
dence of industrial nations like the United States upon foreign
sources of raw materials. And while pointing out that increasing
restrictions abroad might force the United States to adopt similar
policies, he favored instead negotiating bilateral treaties that provided reciprocal assurances of free access to raw materials.[40]

A year later, McClure proposed bilateral discussions with the
British on raw-material problems. Such discussions, he hoped,
could avoid commercial policy in general or tariff policy in particular. Although agreeing with the British contention that import
and export duties related alike to the problem of governmental restraints on trade, he considered the tariff as being beyond the

Young to Hoover, 5 January 1926, Owen D. Young Papers, box 9, file, 1–73–
Herbert Hoover.

38. Sterling to Kellogg, 7 April 1926, enclosing British Secretary of State
for Foreign Affairs to the American chargé, 6 April 1926, in *Foreign Relations,
1926*, vol. 2, pp. 358–61. The British proposal was based on a draft prepared
by the Board of Trade. See Board of Trade to the Undersecretary of State,
16 January 1926, F.O. file: A315/10/45.

39. Foreign Office minute by Craige, 25 January 1926, F.O. file: A351/
10/45. See also minutes by Campbell and Vansittart, 22 and 25 January 1926,
F.O. file: A351/10/45.

40. Economic Adviser's memorandum, "The Rubber Situation," 3 August
1925, RG 59, file, 841.6176/25.

Department's authority to negotiate and involving an area so comprehensive as to make effective agreement impossible. The British should be amenable to this limitation, he felt, because it also ruled out imperial preference and other protectionist measures recently enacted or discussed by Parliament. And the United States, he thought, should tolerate such forms of government intervention as the Stevenson Act where they were necessary to protect consumers and producers from destructive economic forces. The Stevenson scheme, he insisted, was not bad because it entailed state intervention but because it did not work effectively. And like Houghton earlier, he proposed correcting it by allowing consumer representatives from the United States to participate in its management.

Eventually, McClure envisioned a general Anglo-American understanding regarding the development and exportation of raw materials. Noting that the manufacturing interests in industrial countries had historically opposed any restraints that hampered their access to essential resources, he saw the Anglo-American rubber controversy as an opportunity to forge a new alliance against excessive restrictions that might be imposed by developing countries. This alliance, he contended, should be founded on equal access to sources of raw materials, the free movement of these materials across national boundaries, and some definition of the rights of those engaged in developing raw materials around the world. An Anglo-American agreement on these and other matters, he hoped, could then serve as a model for other nations. And this, in turn, would be the forerunner of a stable and lasting peace.[41]

However sensible this approach seemed to McClure, his recommendations were overwhelmed by the general feeling that Great

41. Wallace McClure to Arthur Young, 23 August 1926, McClure, "Memorandum: Raw Material Policy," 24 August 1926, McClure, "Considerations in Respect of the Connection or Lack of Connection Between the Doctrines of Free Movement of Raw Materials and Protective Duties Upon Imports of Merchandise in General," 25 August 1926, and McClure, memorandum for Young, "Relations Between the United States and Great Britain in Respect of Coal, of Rubber and of Raw Materials Generally," 5 November 1926, RG 59, file, 841.6167/105, 107, 108, 115. See also unsigned memorandum (probably by McClure), "Rubber—Raw Material Situation and the British Notes," 24 September 1926, and Young, "Raw Material Problem . . . ," 23 August 1926, RG 59, file, 841.6176/19, 106. William S. Culbertson of the Tariff Commission favored a similar policy, including the negotiation of commercial treaties that would include equal access to raw materials. See Culbertson to Harding, 13 December 1921, and Culbertson to Hughes, 19 February 1923, William S. Culbertson Papers, boxes 46 and 49.

Britain was not prepared to compromise on the rubber issue. According to Hoover, the British position offered "no hope" for a settlement. Like officials in the State Department, he did not believe that the administration had the freedom to discuss import duties. At the same time, he refused to agree that tariff barriers, which primarily affected domestic consumers who had participated in their erection, were equivalent to export restrictions that injured foreign interests who had no voice in their formulation. For officials in the Commerce Department and the rubber industry, moreover, the tariff had not hampered European trade with the United States and unlimited, rather than restricted, exportation of rubber was the best method of earning the dollars needed to liquidate the war debt. Accordingly, when the British requested that all diplomatic correspondence regarding the rubber debate be published, Hoover refused to consent on grounds that the United States considered the British position too far removed from a constructive solution to warrant pursuit through full exposition of the American program.[42]

The result, then, was neither the independent development of new sources of supply nor American membership in governmental price-fixing arrangements. Instead, Hoover turned next to cooperative action by American consumers and financiers. He won the voluntary cooperation of American bankers in banning loans to foreign cartels, defending this program as guarding the consumer against any action that would help perpetuate unreasonable prices and protecting the banker against a "storm of criticism" far "more costly than the loss of a few commissions."[43] In conjunction with the rubber and automobile manufacturers, he also launched a publicity campaign to stimulate rubber conservation and the use of synthetic substitutes. By the summer of 1926, he claimed, tire

42. Hoover to Kellogg, 18 May 1926, unsigned memorandum to Young, 22 June 1926, British Ambassador to Kellogg, 30 July 1926, Hoover to Kellogg, 12 August 1926, RG 59, file, 841.6176/93, 99, 104; Harold Haskell of Hood Rubber Co. to McClure, 18 July 1925, RG 59, file, 841.6176/9; and unsigned memorandum, 18 January 1926, HHP, Commerce, Official File, box 129.

43. Hoover to Kellogg, 13 November 1925, enclosing draft letter, n.d., and Hoover to George Carson, Johnson County Savings Bank, Iowa City, Iowa, 5 January 1926, HHP, Commerce, Official File, box 129; Hoover testimony in *Hearings on H. R. 59: Crude Rubber, Coffee, Etc.*, p. 4. See also in this connection the administration's attitude toward loans that would underwrite the Brazilian coffee cartel and the German potash cartel in *Foreign Relations, 1925*, vol. 2, pp. 533–35, and *Foreign Relations, 1926*, vol. 2, pp. 205–13.

sales to dealers had already declined by 25 percent while rubber consumption generally had declined by over seventy thousand tons from the previous year. The result, he argued, was an overall reduction in the price of rubber of more than 50 percent—a reduction that could be disastrous to British growers should they continue their restrictionist policies.[44]

In addition, Hoover sought to counter British restrictions by organizing a cooperative buying pool in the United States that would help to drive down prices. This could work, he thought, if the Webb-Pomerene Act were amended, allowing consumers to eliminate competitive bidding in favor of collective purchasing arrangements and depending upon open participation, profit restrictions, and other appropriate restraints to safeguard the antitrust laws and protect the buying public. Early in 1924, he persuaded Sen. Arthur Capper to introduce the required legislation in Congress.[45] Despite endorsements by industry representatives, however, Congress did not act on the proposal. In December 1925, a similar appeal by Hoover again failed to generate congressional support, as did fresh recommendations by the rubber interests the following January.[46]

As a result, Hoover came to rely chiefly on government-business collaboration and informal cooperation at the private level. In 1926, he began sending periodic market analyses to the leading rubber manufacturers. This, as one manufacturer explained, helped the companies to "influence the London market" through joint action based on common information.[47] At the same time, Hoover met privately with industry officials to organize a "protective plan" under which the rubber manufacturers would incorporate a common purchasing agency. Each manufacturer was to hold an interest

44. Hoover to Houghton, 1 May 1926, in Hoover to Kellogg, 30 April 1926, HHP, Commerce, Official File, box 129; Hoover to Kellogg, 18 May 1926, RG 59, file, 841.6167/93; Everett G. Holt, "Foreign Government Price Fixing of Our Import Raw Materials," 25 October 1926, HHP, Commerce, Official File, box 256; *Hearings on H. R. 59: Crude Rubber, Coffee, Etc.*, pp. 207, 227; and Brandes, *Hoover and Economic Diplomacy*, pp. 107–8.

45. Hoover to Arthur Capper, 6 March 1924, and Capper to Hoover, 8 March 1924, HHP, Commerce, Official File, box 129.

46. Hoover to Capper, 10 December 1925, HHP, Commerce, Official File, box 126; Capper to Hoover, 15 December 1925, HHP, Commerce, Official File, box 129; *Hearings on H. R. 59: Crude Rubber, Coffee, Etc.*, pp. 50, 110–11, 116, 137–38, 226–27.

47. Unsigned memorandum for Harold Stokes, Secretary's office, 17 June 1926, HHP, Commerce, Official File, box 127; F. A. Seiberling to Hoover, 1 January 1926, HHP, Commerce, Official File, box 257.

in the combine proportionate to its 1925 consumption schedule. But participation by outside interests was also to be solicited. The result, so its supporters claimed, would be an agency that could protect consumers from restrictionist schemes by stabilizing prices at a "fair" level, creating a national crude rubber reserve, and encouraging investment in foreign rubber plantations. The Justice Department apparently agreed that any restrictions entailed did not violate the antitrust laws because, at a meeting with industry officials in August, it gave its consent to the proposal.[48] And one result was the $50 million combine organized by the rubber manufacturers.

Collective purchasing arrangements, however, ran into stiff opposition from congressional defenders of the antitrust tradition. Although the rubber combine did not stimulate important new investments in rubber holdings, it did work successfully as a buying pool throughout 1927. And in February 1928, the Commerce Department won renewed approval for its operation from the Attorney General. Hoover, though, still had hopes of securing congressional authorization. In January 1928, he once more joined with industry officials in supporting a new bill that would amend the Webb Act to permit cooperative buying of rubber, potash, and sisal—all commodities under "monopoly" control by foreign governments. But again, opponents of the bill, led by the Democratic minority, had blocked passage of the measure. It was, they claimed, contrary to the antitrust laws and designed to protect, not the consumer, but the large profits of the rubber industry. Given this opposition, Hoover again was forced to skirt Congress and win Justice Department approval for renewing the informal and voluntary arrangements worked out earlier.[49]

The defeat of Hoover's program by antitrusters in Congress was

48. Viles to William J. Donovan, assistant to the Attorney General, 2 August 1926, HHP, Commerce, Official File, box 256; Hoover to John J. Raskob, General Motors Corporation, 4 August 1926, Raskob to Hoover, 18 August 1926, HHP, Commerce, Official File, box 127. The British, of course, followed these developments with some interest. See for example Broderick to the Foreign Office, 30 December 1926, F.O. file: A6935/10/45.

49. Holt to Nash, 24 February 1928, HHP, Commerce, Official File, box 127; Holt to Donald Renshaw, American Trade Commissioner, Singapore, 20 March 1928, Klein to William Cooper, Commercial Attaché, London, 31 July 1928, RG 151, file, 254, Straits Settlement; House, Committee on the Judiciary, *Hearings on H. R. 8927: A Bill to Amend the Webb-Pomerene Act*, 9, [19] January 1928, pp. 20–33; and Brandes, *Hoover and Economic Diplomacy*, pp. 100–101.

matched by the failure of the Stevenson scheme in England. For British growers, market conditions and rubber prices remained destructively unstable throughout the 1920s. The Netherlands government had refused to participate in the Stevenson scheme and, as Hoover had predicted, American manufacturers gradually shifted as much of their purchasing as possible to the lower-priced rubber produced by Dutch growers. As a result, the share controlled by British planters declined to less than half of the world's rubber output, a decline of over 20 percent in ten years. Finally admitting these unfortunate results, the British government abandoned the scheme late in 1928.[50]

III

In rubber policy, then, American officials continued their search for a new era of peace, prosperity, and progress. They ruled out a policy of preference and state management and attacked foreign raw-material "monopolies" as harmful to business efficiency, injurious to technological change, antithetical to the best interests of both consumer and producer, and bound to introduce a disturbing political element detrimental to the peaceful development of trade. Yet, at the same time, they rejected laissez-faire, conceded the need for market stability and regulation, and wanted to achieve this through private and cooperative arrangements at both the domestic and international levels. This, they believed, would facilitate the development of new supply lines, regularize marketing procedures, and foster increased innovation. Such an approach, however, required a change of attitude on the part of the British, and by 1928 efforts to secure this change had failed. In addition, Hoover's call for new investments in foreign sources of supply had been largely ignored. The conservation campaign, although immediately successful, had offered no solution to the problem of expanding needs. And the attempt to develop cooperative buying pools, successful in the short run, had been stymied by unsympathetic antitrusters in Congress.

More important, all of these policies had made it more difficult

50. Foreign Office memorandum, "A Short History of the Rubber Restriction Scheme," February 1928, Foreign Office minute by T. M. Snow, 19 April [1928], F.O. file: A1967/507/45; and F. L. Belin, First Secretary of the American Embassy, London, to the Secretary of State, 5 April 1928, RG 59, file, 841.6176/142.

to attain the larger goal of international harmony and cooperation. The British continued to think in terms of government-supported price-fixing schemes or arrangements that would include American tariff concessions. But since American commitments allowed little freedom of maneuver on these matters, the cooperative arrangements that had taken shape in other areas failed to materialize in the rubber field. Instead, the acrimony created by the dispute, coming as it did in the midst of new controversies over war debts and naval limitations, preserved an area of tension in the emerging Atlantic alliance. "The Stevenson Plan," complained Angus Fletcher of the Foreign Office, "proved very costly to us and, like the Geneva Naval Conference, has made quite disproportionate inroads on the credit balance which the Irish settlement, the Washington Conference and the Debt settlement had provided."[51]

51. Fletcher to Sir Arthur Willert, 13 April 1928, F.O. file: A2766/507/45. "For my own part," Sir Esme Howard wrote after the Stevenson scheme had been abandoned, "I may say that I received the news . . . with some relief, since it removes a source of misunderstanding and continual bickering between the United States and ourselves." See Howard to Chamberlain, 26 April 1928, F.O. file: A2814/507/45.

CHAPTER 10

Conclusion

The Limits of Cooperation in the New Era

As apparent in the rubber controversy, the policy of the United States was less than wholly consistent. Instead, often disparate ideas competed in the policymaking process, resulting in an alternating emphasis on independent action and multinationalism, private initiative and state management. In part, this reflected the search for an approach that best fulfilled American interests and ambitions. Yet to say that expediency alone determined which approach was adopted is misleading. For in part, this wavering also indicated that Americans had not yet reconciled older ideals with contemporary perceptions of economic realities. With individual enterprise being displaced by large concentrations of corporate power both at home and abroad, the conventional precepts of laissez-faire (and isolationism) so engrained in the consciousness of the American people appeared increasingly inappropriate. And for many the success of wartime economic collaboration among businessmen and between business and government seemed to symbolize the benefits to be derived from some kind of centralized planning and control.

This strain of thought had two offshoots. One was the notion of private planning and industrial collaboration in regulating economic development—a notion already well established in the domestic economy before the war. The other was the idea of state or state-supported management and planning, an alternative foreign to American experience but one that gained widespread, if short-lived, support after the war. Outside this strain, however, persisted important support for the competitive ideal so deeply embedded in American tradition. Despite the tendency toward consolidation and cooperation, proponents of this ideal were suspicious of collective action among private interests, relied on competitive activity to regulate economic behavior, and depended on the state to prohibit unfair collusion and to insist upon equal opportunity.

Advocates of state management vied weakly for attention during the economic controversies of the postwar decade. Their case rested in part on the spread of state capitalism abroad and on the aggressiveness of foreign governments in promoting their commercial interests overseas. To them, it was necessary to establish similar programs at home, for only the enormous resources of the government could protect American interests and allow the United States to compete effectively in world markets against the state-sponsored and preferential policies of its foreign rivals. Taking the war government as a model, moreover, advocates of government management envisioned a bureaucratic state, which would plan and coordinate the efficient and rational use of scarce resources and protect the public interest by insuring the kind of constructive development abroad, which was so vital to prosperity at home. This was the rationale behind proposals for a federally subsidized European recovery program, state management of foreign loans, government control and ownership of radio and cable facilities, and state-sponsored oil and raw-material cartels.

For most, however, the liabilities of state management outweighed the benefits. Thus, proposals for a larger governmental role stood little chance of receiving a full hearing. They contradicted the private character of the American political economy and were staunchly opposed by powerful interests in the private sector. To the extent that private interests contemplated a direct governmental role in commercial affairs, they usually supported public subsidies for private enterprise or endorsed the kind of general government supervision that was needed to reform, rationalize, and integrate otherwise chaotic areas of the international economy. Neither function required the participation of the state in managerial activity. And those who thought along these lines could offer strong reasons why the state should not enter the managerial realm. Government, they claimed, was particularly ill equipped to manage commercial affairs without the waste, instability, and bureaucratic paternalism that hampered efficiency, growth, and innovation. Still worse, so most agreed, government intrusion escalated economic competition into political conflict and threatened world peace. These were the views shared by most American officials; and in the period under discussion such views led them to terminate precipitously their participation in the wartime inter-Allied councils, to reject Allied proposals for state financing of European recovery, and to advocate instead private assistance through normal banking and commercial channels. Their beliefs also led them to reject all proposals for state management and financing in cable, radio, oil, and rubber policy, and they influenced the State Department's decision to ignore Hoover's pleas for more rigorous control over capital exports.

If state management was unacceptable though, so was a policy based on the competitive ideal. In an age of large-scale operations, of cartels and state financing, of economic interdependence and capital shortage, a return to laissez-faire could have little appeal. In financing world development, for instance, the large demands on American capital and the need to make efficient use of available resources required some form of cooperative action and supervision. In certain sectors of the international economy, particularly radio and cable development, competition hampered the extension of existing facilities, resulted in a wasteful duplication of services, and caused destructive interference. In other areas, competition increased costs, reduced incentive, prevented the consolidation of capital and technology that was needed to develop resources, dislocated rather than harmonized supply and demand factors, and prevented market integration and development. Moreover, excessive competition could escalate into political contests between governments seeking to protect their interests in world markets. And this, in turn, could lead to further instability and new threats to world peace.

With both state management and laissez-faire ruled out, policymakers shifted toward a third alternative—one that adapted older ideals to contemporary circumstances. In theory, this approach would preserve private incentive through collective action and reconcile the need for order and stability with such traditional virtues as individualism and equal economic opportunity. It would also apply the legacy of progressive ideas to the solution of postwar problems. On the one hand, it would eliminate destructive competition, guarantee stability, reduce costs, and increase efficiency. But, it would also leave managerial functions to be handled by private business leaders supposedly skilled in scientific management and dedicated to peace and prosperity for all. And by encouraging these private leaders to cooperate in fostering constructive development, it would maximize growth, raise living standards across the globe, and limit the need for government intervention and regulation.

Such an approach certainly was flexible enough to include government action. Government could provide encouragement and useful information, and it could protect private interests abroad. Through reciprocal bargaining with other nations, it could open previously restricted areas to private expansion, and through business-government collaboration and the regulation of loans it could promote the right kind of private development. But government action was not to replace private leadership and initiative. The new order was to be regulated by enlightened private managers and avoid the pitfalls of either ruinous competition or paternalistic and oppressive government.

In addition, whether by design or concession, the government helped private leaders to construct a rationale that made appropriate gestures to traditional ideals and symbols, especially to such old slogans as equality of opportunity, the Open Door, and the Monroe Doctrine. In this way, for instance, equality of opportunity in Latin America was redefined to mean promotion of collaboration among British and American oil, cable, and radio interests. In this way, too, inserting a subleasing provision in the Mesopotamian oil arrangement, or referring to the Monroe Doctrine in the South American radio consortium seemed to convert essentially multinational monopolies into guardians of the Open Door and agents of uniquely American interests.

II

Applied internationally, the theory of cooperative capitalism required important concessions by the great powers to a broader community of interests along with enlightened action by private leaders in managing the international economy. And in many respects, developments at middecade seemed to be fulfilling these requirements. British and American interests were working out cooperative arrangements in oil, radio, and cable policy. Following the logic inherent in the private approach, these arrangements were giving full vent to business demands for consolidation and collaboration in the interest of stability, efficiency, and rational development. At the same time, a second financial consortium had been launched in China. And in Europe, Anglo-American compromise and collaboration had seemingly set the stage for steady expansion managed through private and central bank cooperation. There, the Anglo-American debt settlement, the Austrian and German reconstruction schemes, and sterling's return to the gold standard gave rise to new hopes for lasting stability and progress.

In the second half of the decade, there were still other signs that the postwar clash of world views was giving way to a larger community of interests. The Locarno Conference followed the Dawes Plan by one year. It produced a series of European arbitration conventions and a Treaty of Mutual Guarantee among the great Continental powers. Under this treaty Germany, France, and Belgium renounced war as an instrument of policy against each other and, along with Great Britain and Italy, guaranteed the demilitarization of the Rhineland and the territorial status quo of the Franco-German and German-Belgian borders. Although not participating directly in the Locarno negotiations, the American government had helped to insure their success through subtle warnings that new loans for European recovery depended on a favorable outcome.[1]

The Locarno Conference had been followed by new collaboration at the central and private bank level. In 1926 and 1927, the New York Federal Reserve Bank and the Bank of England, together with leading British and American investment houses, launched successful stabilization schemes in Belgium and Italy.[2] At the same time, they collaborated with the Reichsbank and the Bank of France to relieve new pressure on pound sterling. This pressure arose in 1927 when the Bank of France began selling its sterling balances for gold in order to force an increase in British discount rates and curb the volume of low-interest borrowings in the London market. As the French saw it, these borrowings were fueling speculation in francs and threatening domestic inflation. A substantial drain on British reserves, however, could drive pound sterling off the gold standard, while protecting sterling by raising rates would discourage industrial growth and exacerbate England's already serious unemployment problems. Accordingly, Benjamin Strong engineered a new cooperative program at a meeting of central bankers in New York in July 1927. Under this program, France and Germany agreed to purchase their gold from New York instead of London, and, as in 1924, Strong and Montagu Norman of the Bank of England agreed to coordinate their rate policies, lowering

1. *Documents on British Foreign Policy*, Series 1a, vol. 1, (London, 1966), pp. 1–17; Jon Jacobson, *Locarno Diplomacy: Germany and the West, 1925–1929*, p. 3; and Frank C. Costigliola, "The Politics of Financial Stabilization: American Reconstruction Policy in Europe, 1924–1930," pp. 156–63.

2. Henry Clay, *Lord Norman*, pp. 256–58.

American discount rates in order to center the world's gold demands on New York and alleviate pressure for an increase in British rates. The result, or so it seemed at the time, was another victory for the kind of private and cooperative multinationalism so celebrated by American leaders. "How could these great, these vital" and "most difficult operations" in Austria, Germany, Belgium, and Italy "have been carried through," asked Thomas Lamont, "if financial leaders on both sides of the water had not sunk their individual interests and worked together for the benefit of the countries involved?"[3]

Despite these successes, however, flaws were already appearing in the American vision of constructive development through enlightened cooperation. In dealing with the rubber situation and radio communications in China, policymakers allowed narrow national ambitions to block the search for stability and order through multinational collaboration and managerial regulation. And in the Far East, where American ideas were implemented, they proved less than adequate to solve the problems of the postwar era. There, the Wilson administration had counted on the second financial consortium to neutralize China for development and stimulate quality investment. The Harding administration shared these expectations, and during the Washington Disarmament Conference Hughes had achieved great power approval for the (modified) Open Door as the basis for cooperation in the Orient. Yet, with political instability persisting in China, the bankers were reluctant to undertake important operations. And their conservative approach not only alienated American manufacturers, it also failed to stimulate the political and economic reforms that were considered necessary to stabilize China and bring peaceful trade expansion. Still later, with Chinese nationalism leaving the Japanese with apparently no peaceful alternative for satisfying their economic needs on the Asian mainland, the American plan would collapse. Unwilling to condone Japanese aggression, the United States was also unprepared to resort to military action in defense of its Far Eastern objectives.

Policymakers also had great difficulty in forging restraints on competition among American concerns. Although expected to sub-

3. Ibid., pp. 232–37; Lester V. Chandler, *Benjamin Strong, Central Banker*, pp. 372–77; Stephen V. O. Clarke, *Central Bank Cooperation, 1924–1931*, pp. 111–27; and Thomas Lamont address, "International Finance and World Trade," 18 November 1927, HHP, Commerce, Official File, box 17.

merge their particular interests in common programs, American bankers and exporters shared different opinions on the investment program needed to expand trade and stimulate constructive development abroad. Exporters charged the bankers with hampering commercial expansion, and the bankers paid slight attention to the financial needs of commercial interests. In South America, it was easier to forge cooperative arrangements among British and American oil companies than to maintain a united front among American concerns. And in Persia, the State Department was forced to choose between Sinclair Consolidated and Jersey Standard. In addition, suspicion characterized the relationship among American cable companies and, despite Hoover's efforts, American rubber interests remained badly divided on the correct response to British restrictionism.

There were other signs that enlightened action by private leaders was falling short of expectations. American bankers opposed even the mild form of governmental intrusion into their investment activities as defined in the loan control program. And while they were conservative in their approach to investment in China, the bankers followed a policy of reckless lending in other areas of the world. During the second half of the decade, for instance, they were negotiating excessive loans for dubious projects with such South American countries as Peru and Colombia.[4] And in Europe, as with the loans to German municipalities, they were poorly employing their capital in unreproductive enterprises. To Hoover and others the situation called for more rigorous federal supervision. But given the attitudes in both the private and public sectors, this control was not forthcoming. Instead, the Commerce Department could only continue its efforts at persuasion, distributing information on loan proposals and campaigning for the high investment standards that would promote trade on a sound basis by stimulating constructive improvements abroad.[5]

In applying their programs, moreover, policymakers often ended up with new forms of restrictionism. This was clearly the case with the Fordney-McCumber Tariff of 1922. The Harding administration considered the high protective tariff as necessary to protect "infant industries" and prevent the American market from being

4. Carl P. Parrini, *Heir to Empire: United States Economic Diplomacy, 1916–1923*, pp. 273–74.

5. Joseph Brandes, *Herbert Hoover and Economic Diplomacy: Department of Commerce Policy, 1921–1928*, pp. 155–57, 187.

inundated by European commodities that were made unfairly
cheap because of the depreciated character of European currencies.
At the same time, however, by protecting workers and industries
in the United States, Hoover and other leaders believed that it
would also raise living standards and stimulate an ever-expanding
market for European luxury items and foreign raw-material imports. This expansion would offset the restrictive effects of the tariff
and, along with continued lending by private investors, promote
international economic equilibrium and European recovery.[6] In
addition, they hoped that the unconditional most-favored-nation
clause in commercial treaties would expand international markets,
while Section 317 of the Fordney-McCumber act would encourage
equality of treatment by permitting retaliation against nations that
adopted discriminatory tariff policies.[7] This retaliation could work
fairly, they argued, because disinterested experts on the Tariff
Commission would administer the act's provisions scientifically.[8]
Like the Federal Lands Leasing Act and the Kellogg Cable Landing Act, then, the tariff was to serve as a lever for promoting the

6. See the excellent work on the tariff by Joan Hoff Wilson, *American
Business & Foreign Policy, 1920–1933*, pp. 65–100; Parrini, *Heir to Empire*,
pp. 212–47; and Melvyn P. Leffler, "The Struggle for Stability: American
Policy Toward France, 1921–1933," pp. 278–355. See also Hoover, "The
Future of Our Foreign Trade," 16 March 1926, HHP, Commerce, Personal
File, box 24; and Warren G. Harding, message to Congress, 12 April 1921, in
Foreign Relations, 1921, vol. 1, p. ix. As the American standard of living in-
creases, Grosvenor Jones, chief of the Finance and Investment Division of the
BFDC, explained, "our importations of foodstuffs, raw materials, and semi-
manufactured goods will increase, both actually and relatively to our exports. Such a tendency has been in process for some years and is likely to
continue for years to come in an increasing degree. This will make it easier
for the world at large to pay its debts to this country." See Jones to Drake, 12
November 1925, RG 151, file, 254, Straits Settlement.

7. William S. Culbertson diary, 27 January 1920 and 30 January 1923, Wil-
liam S. Culbertson Papers; Culbertson, "Commercial Agreements and the
Development of Foreign Trade," a preliminary report submitted to the Tariff
Committee of the National Foreign Trade Council, n.d., Culbertson Papers,
Bound Correspondence, 1917–1918; Culbertson to Charles Evans Hughes, 14
December 1922, Culbertson Papers, Bound Correspondence, 1922; Wallace
McClure to the Foreign Trade Adviser, Secretary of State, and Assistant
Secretary of State, 27 May 1921, W. W. Cumberland, Foreign Trade Adviser's
Office, to Fred Morris Dearing, 18 June 1921, Dearing to Hughes and Henry P.
Fletcher, 21 June 1921, and Culbertson to Hughes, 29 September 1922, all in
RG 59, file, 611.003/841, 842, 844, 1141; and Arthur N. Young to Hughes,
21 October 1922, RG 59, file, 611.0031/179.

8. Culbertson diary, 7 December 1921 and 28 May 1922, Culbertson Papers. See also Melvyn P. Leffler, "Herbert Hoover, the 'New Era,' and American Foreign Policy."

market expansion and integration considered necessary for world prosperity.

Yet, despite the rhetoric of scientific administration, flexibility, and equal opportunity, policymakers never fully reconciled the high tariff with their goal of a peaceful and prosperous global trading community. As Melvyn P. Leffler and Joan Hoff Wilson have pointed out, tariff bargaining proved a long and cumbersome process subject to developments in the domestic economy, congressional logrolling, and pressure from vested interests, especially small businessmen who favored protectionism. Despite contrapuntal arguments by large industries and other export interests, most policymakers also considered the domestic market too important to make meaningful concessions, and the emphasis always remained on the import of non-competitive commodities.[9] As a result, although the volume of European imports increased throughout the decade, the tariff made it difficult for the Allies to earn enough dollars to liquidate their war debts to the United States.

The American tariff was only the most obvious sign of the kind of market restrictions that emerged in the postwar decade. In oil, cable, and radio affairs, the outcome of American policy was the creation of multinational monopolies dominated by British and American interests—monopolies that helped to reduce Anglo-American conflict but at the same time destroyed the broad equality of opportunity that was believed to be essential for economic peace. Such monopolies, of course, were defended as practical and businesslike applications of conventional ideals, essential to efficiency, stability, and market development. But they were also developing new sources of political friction by making the commercial interests of other nations largely dependent upon the enlightened goodwill of private Anglo-American business leaders.

III

Instead of the wide great-power community envisioned by Col. E. House in 1916, an informal Anglo-American economic entente had emerged by middecade. Through compromise and collaboration, the United States and Great Britain had forged new cooperative programs, with other powers either excluded from the final

9. Leffler, "The Struggle for Stability," pp. 301–8; and Wilson, *American Business & Foreign Policy*, pp. 86–100.

arrangements or included as junior partners. Even in Europe, the multinationalism that produced the Austrian stabilization scheme and the Dawes settlement was founded too narrowly on Anglo-American cooperation. In this sense, Walter Hines Page's vision of an Anglo-American partnership as the cornerstone of a wider community of interests came closer to reality. Yet not close enough, for the Anglo-American partnership faltered in the second half of the decade and this hampered progress toward a final resolution of the German issue—the central pillar in the edifice of European recovery.

As the British found it increasingly difficult to maintain pound sterling at par, stabilize their domestic economy, and protect London's position as a center of international finance, Anglo-American collaboration on war debts and European recovery began to dissolve. In 1926, British attacks on American debt policy provoked a brief but bitter Anglo-American debate. Chancellor of the Exchequer Winston Churchill blamed the Treasury Department for absorbing in debt payments funds needed to reconstruct Europe. And Secretary of the Treasury Andrew Mellon charged the British with using American war loans for selfish commercial rather than joint military purposes. According to Mellon and other officials, the British were again trying to organize a debtor coalition against the United States and to undermine the Treasury's funding negotiations with its European debtors, especially the French.[10] In 1927 and 1928, Norman and Strong also differed over Franco-American schemes for the financial stabilization of Poland and Rumania—schemes that avoided the British-dominated financial section of the League of Nations, and, in the case of Poland at least, stymied Norman's plans to use economic assistance to force a revision of the Versailles settlement that was favorable to Germany.[11]

In other areas as well, new disputes weakened the Atlantic partnership that had emerged in the first half of the postwar decade. Most important, an Anglo-American controversy over the limitations to be placed on cruisers and armaments scuttled the Geneva Naval Disarmament Conference in 1927. Great Britain and France subsequently negotiated a bilateral arms agreement that supported

10. Costigliola, "The Politics of Financial Stabilization," pp. 259–61. See also the extract from the House of Commons Debates, 24 March 1926, F.O. file: C3893/7/62, and British Ambassador Esme Howard to the Foreign Office, 9 September 1926, F.O. file: A5006/3895/45.

11. Clay, *Lord Norman*, pp. 259–64; and Chandler, *Benjamin Strong*, pp. 390–422.

the British position on the cruiser issue—an agreement that Americans viewed as a surreptitious effort to protect Britain's supremacy on the seas at the expense of naval parity for the United States.[12] The resulting acrimony severely strained the Atlantic partnership and brought relations between the two countries to their lowest point in the postwar decade.

These controversies certainly did not represent a clear reversal of British policy toward the United States. There were new cooperative initiatives, as with the Belgian and Italian stabilization schemes and the successful efforts to protect pound sterling in 1927. Norman also put aside his disappointment over the Polish stabilization scheme and participated in extending a central bank credit to the Bank of Poland. And later, he agreed with Strong that constructive cooperation between central bankers was more important than any dispute over the Rumanian stabilization program.[13] Moreover, while Churchill moved toward an open repudiation of the Anglo-American debt accord, others considered this approach counterproductive; it would hamper Anglo-American cooperation and make the United States less amenable to some future revision of the debt settlement.[14] British opinion also divided on the controversial question of naval limitations. Leaders of the Labour and Liberal parties criticized the government for the failure of the Geneva Conference, and the subsequent Anglo-French arms accord, they complained, alienated German and American opinion and restored the secret diplomacy and alliance system of the prewar period. Robert Craige, American specialist in the Foreign Office, worried that the naval controversy would prejudice Anglo-American relations, stymie the evolution of a more lenient American attitude on the debt question, and strain relations with the Dominions, especially Canada, which felt that "the orientation of our policy should be towards, rather than away from America."[15]

In 1928, Craige authored an important memorandum pleading for a policy of reconciliation and continued cooperation with the

12. David Carlton, "Great Britain and the Naval Disarmament Conference of 1927," pp. 573–98; and David Carlton, "The Anglo-French Compromise on Arms Limitation, 1928," pp. 141–62.

13. Clay, *Lord Norman*, pp. 260, 264–66.

14. British Ambassador Esme Howard to the Foreign Office, 9 April 1926, Foreign Office minute by Robert Craige, 29 April 1926, F.O. file: C4809/7/62; minute by Craige, 8 August 1926, and minute by Robert Vansittart, 9 August 1926 (initialed by Austen Chamberlain), F.O. file: A4144/3895/45.

15. Craige, memorandum, 3 October 1928, F.O. file: A7132/39/45; and Jacobson, *Locarno Diplomacy*, pp. 189–90.

United States. As he saw it, a spirit of Anglo-American cooperation had dominated the middle years of the decade when "the Mesopotamian oil question was settled, the Irish Free State was created, the Washington Naval Treaty was signed, the Anglo-Japanese Alliance was abrogated and the debt settlement took place." By 1927, however, new disputes over war debts and naval limitation had seriously depleted the stock of goodwill accumulated earlier. Relations between the two countries were now "unsatisfactory" and war was "*not* unthinkable." But for Craige, continued estrangement would injure British interests. Commercially, the United States was Great Britain's "best customer so far as direct exports are concerned," and in financial affairs "good relations" seemed so "valuable as to be almost essential." The "friendly attitude of American banks" had helped to maintain British credit and restore pound sterling to the gold standard, and "friendly co-operation" between the Federal Reserve Board and the Bank of England could prevent fluctuating exchange rates in New York and London. Good relations also increased British "influence and prestige in the councils of Europe," where the "aid and co-operation of American finance" seemed essential to any further adjustment of the reparation problem. Under these circumstances flexibility and "timely" concessions were in order, for in "almost every field, the advantages to be derived from mutual cooperation are greater for us than for" the United States.[16]

In the second half of the decade, then, cooperative efforts coexisted with new strains in Anglo-American relations. To be sure, Craige and other officials urged appeasement and continued cooperation. But for his part, Churchill belittled anything that smacked of "obsequiousness" in British policy toward the United States.[17] Indeed, Churchill's attack on American debt policy weakened the creditor alliance that was worked out in 1923, while the Anglo-American naval controversy at Geneva undermined the gains made at the Washington Conference six years earlier. Disputes over the Polish and Rumanian stabilization schemes also injured the fragile framework of private and central bank cooperation that had been so successful in the Austrian, German, Belgian, and Italian stabilization programs. Still worse, Anglo-American conflict

    16. Craige, "Outstanding Problems Affecting Anglo-American Relations," 12 November 1928, F.O. file: A7895/39/45.
    17. Craige, minute, 26 November 1928, F.O. file: A8067/39/45.

over reparations stymied new initiatives on the German issue as well.

In 1924, all appreciated that the Dawes Plan promised only a temporary reprieve—a moratorium during which a lasting solution to the German issue could be devised. And at Thoiry in 1926, the French and German governments negotiated an agreement that took a step in this direction. The French agreed to return the Saar to Germany and to evacuate the Rhineland immediately. In return for these and other concessions, France was to receive reparation payments in advance of its Dawes annuities through the capitalization of German railway bonds that were pledged to the Allied governments as security against reparation transfers. If implemented, this agreement would have eased the tensions in Franco-German relations and provided the French with capital needed to stabilize the franc. But the United States government would not permit the German bonds to be floated in the New York market unless the French ratified the Mellon-Berenger debt funding agreement negotiated earlier that year. The British took a similar position on the previously negotiated Churchill-Caillaux debt agreement. Unlike the French, moreover, they felt that nothing was to be gained from the Thoiry scheme. The German bonds could be marketed only at a substantial discount; therefore forfeiting future British income under the reparation schedule and undermining the prospects for a "successful development of the Dawes Plan."[18] In 1926, then, the Anglo-American creditor alliance that had worked to promote a moderate reparation settlement two years earlier was now hampering any extension of the cooperative spirit embodied in the Dawes Commission and the Locarno Conference.

In large part, British objections to the Thoiry scheme stemmed from a fear that further reductions in German transfers would jeopardize the Treasury's ability to meet its obligations to the United States. As a result, the British preferred to stand by the Dawes Plan—a preference that worked against American efforts to further rationalize the reparation problem. As German pressure for French withdrawal from the Rhineland mounted and as the

18. The Thoiry negotiations and the Anglo-American response can be followed in Jacobson, *Locarno Diplomacy*, pp. 84–90; and *Documents on British Foreign Policy*, Series 1a, vol. 2 (London, 1969), especially pp. 393–445. The quotation is from ibid., pp. 414–18.

reparation authorities became increasingly concerned about Germany's public finances and borrowing practices, American officials endorsed an old solution—one calling for a commission of private experts to arrange a "definitive settlement" of the German problem. S. Parker Gilbert, the American agent general for reparations, wanted to eliminate the machinery for transfer protection established under the Dawes Plan and fix the total amount of indemnity at a sum below the standard Dawes annuities. According to him, this action would provide Germany with the incentive to meet its obligations and undertake necessary fiscal reforms, prevent a possible conflict between reparation transfers and the amortization of foreign, primarily American, loans, and facilitate the commercialization of German reparation bonds. The latter, in turn, would help depoliticize indemnity payments and expedite a general liquidation of both reparations and war debts.[19]

The French were amenable to the American plan. Commercialization of the reparation bonds, they believed, would help to prevent future defaults and expedite payments. But they would only support the plan if German liabilities were fixed at a sum sufficient to cover their debts to the United States and Great Britain and offset part of the cost that was involved in reconstructing the devastated regions. Such a settlement would enable the French government to ratify the British and American debt funding agreements—a consideration of some importance since a war stocks debt of $400 million to the United States would be due for repayment in August 1929 unless the French had ratified the Mellon-Berenger accord. The British took a similar position. Initially at least, they suggested that the best solution to their own and Europe's problems was to cancel both war debts and reparations. Since cancellation was unlikely, however, they soon reasserted the strategy of the Balfour note. This tactic required reparation transfers that, together with Allied debt payments, would enable the British to liquidate their American debt. Prior to 1924, this strategy had been thwarted by the French, whose policy hampered German recovery and reparation transfers. This had led to Anglo-American cooperation in demanding the modified reparation program that was eventually embodied in the Dawes Plan. But in 1928, this strategy worked against the American plan. Worried that new American

19. Leffler, "The Struggle for Stability," p. 356; Costigliola, "The Politics of Financial Stabilization," pp. 428–36; and Clarke, *Central Bank Cooperation*, p. 145.

initiatives might reduce the Dawes annuities below the sum needed to satisfy their debt payments to the United States, the British now cooperated with the French and agreed to a new experts' inquiry only when assured that reparation transfers would be sufficient for them to meet their debt obligations.[20]

Still, in many ways the Young Commission and its findings seemed to confirm the American faith in scientific management and cooperative multinationalism at the private level. The commission terminated Allied controls over Germany and French occupation of the Rhineland, and it modified the Dawes schedule of indemnity payments. In addition, during subsequent negotiations at The Hague the governments involved organized the Bank for International Settlements. The Bank was to replace the existing reparation machinery, facilitate German transfers, insure currency stability, and protect the gold standard. In operation, so Americans hoped, it would also institutionalize the central bank cooperation that had emerged since 1923, eliminate unnecessary political intervention in financial affairs, and allow semiprivate bankers to organize the world economy on a business basis.[21]

Despite these successes, however, the "definitive settlement" worked out in 1929 fell short of expectations. The new Bank for International Settlements claimed only marginal support from the British, who worried that it would not only be dominated by French and American interests but also would undermine their efforts to reestablish London's position as an international financial center and diminish their role as a leading promoter of central bank cooperation in European stabilization. Given the Anglo-French position on war debts and reparations, moreover, the modified reparation schedule devised by the experts sorely disappointed the Germans, who had hoped for a substantial downward adjustment. To be sure, President Herbert Hoover had refused to accept an official link between German transfers and Allied debt payments to the United States. Under his prodding, Owen D. Young, the

20. *Documents on British Foreign Policy*, Series 1a, vol. 5, (London, 1973), pp. 347–48, 353–54, 358–86, 391–94, 432–36; Jacobson, *Locarno Diplomacy*, pp. 215–28; Clay, *Lord Norman*, p. 267; Leffler, "The Struggle for Stability," pp. 365–67; Costigliola, "The Politics of Financial Stabilization," pp. 442–51; and Clarke, *Central Bank Cooperation*, p. 145.

21. Harold G. Moulton and Leo Pasvolsky, *War Debts and World Prosperity*, pp. 188–223; Clay, *Lord Norman*, p. 269. On the American view of the Bank for International Settlements see also Lamont to Philip Snowden, British Chancellor of the Exchequer, 20 August 1929, Lamont Papers, Series 4–C, Germany and Reparations.

private American delegate who headed the experts' inquiry, had eliminated such provisions from the commission's report. But the reparation schedule devised assured the Allies of receipts equal to their net debt payments, and a "concurrent memorandum" appended to the report tied any future reduction of German annuities to a similar reduction of inter-Allied war debts.[22]

More important, successful implementation of the Young Plan required private financial assistance in underwriting the German economy. And as in 1924, American bankers took the lead in floating a $300 million loan to the German government. Yet, this private approach to European recovery could work only so long as American gold and capital moved abroad. In part this flow required appropriate rate policies in the United States. Such policies had been the basis of the successful cooperative programs worked out in 1924 and 1927, when low rates in the United States seemed desirable to stabilize pound sterling and stimulate domestic economic activity. Appropriate rate policies, however, could not guarantee continued American assistance should economic conditions at home and abroad discourage investors or should private resources be diverted elsewhere. Between July 1928 and October 1929, for example, the stock-market boom had kept surplus American funds at home. Moreover, it eventually drove up interest rates and drew gold back to New York. This had put pressure on the Germans, who counted on large sums of American capital to finance their reparation obligations, and on the British, who were compelled to tighten their monetary policy despite the debilitating effect of higher rates on their domestic economy. To be sure, the stock-market crash in October 1929 reduced rates in New York, and this reduction, together with the international loan under the Young Plan, provided temporary relief for the British and the Germans. But as the economic crisis deepened all hopes for further American assistance collapsed.[23]

Even without the depression, loans by private bankers offered only a partial solution to reconstruction. The toothless loan control program left the American government with no way to insure that

22. Costigliola, "The Politics of Financial Stabilization," pp. 483–84; Leffler, "The Struggle for Stability," pp. 370–75; Moulton and Pasvolsky, *War Debts and World Prosperity*, pp. 189–93; and Jacobson, *Locarno Diplomacy*, pp. 275–76.

23. Clarke, *Central Bank Cooperation*, pp. 142–71; and Clay, *Lord Norman*, pp. 238–55.

capital exports really contributed to economic recovery. And as Parrini has argued, even had private loans flowed uninterruptedly into reproductive enterprises, this could have worked to stimulate German recovery only if commodities produced by German industries found markets abroad. A trade surplus would provide Germany with the foreign exchange needed to pay reparations and thereby facilitate a liquidation of war debts as well. But increasingly, the European powers were erecting trade barriers that shut Germany out of world markets and hampered economic integration and expansion.[24] They were determined, it seemed, to block a resurgence of German competition, especially after the crash of 1929 and the consequent shrinkage of world markets.

On the other hand, the United States did not follow a more enlightened policy. The Hawley-Smoot tariff of 1930 raised rates across the board. And in Europe, the United States government opposed the commercial reintegration of Russia. In this connection, American officials had long appreciated that Russian integration would help stimulate European recovery and ease the pressure on the United States for reconstruction capital.[25] But fear of bolshevism and the ban on dealings with a radical government that did not recognize the sanctity of property rights and past debts had led them to reject all proposals for the reintegration of Russia into Europe. During the Genoa Conference of 1922, for example, Hughes won support for a temporary ban on private negotiations with the Soviets pending a meeting of experts at The Hague to survey Russia's economic needs. He then refused to send an official American representative to the Hague conference, encouraged the French to push a ban on all commercial negotiations with the Soviets until their government had settled with the previous owners of confiscated property, and when this had been introduced, cabled his support and won its adoption.[26] As the Europeans were intent upon preventing a revival of German competition, so it seemed that the Americans were determined upon policies that hampered

24. Parrini, *Heir to Empire*, p. 269.

25. As early as March 1920, for example, Assistant Secretary of the Treasury Russell Leffingwell had written that nothing would "reduce the demand upon the United States for credits for Europe as effectively as the restoration of trade relations between Russia and Western Europe, thus rendering possible the exchange of foodstuffs from Russia for manufactured products from Western Europe." See Russell C. Leffingwell to Secretary Carter Glass, 13 March 1920, Russell C. Leffingwell Papers, Letterbooks, vol. 42b.

26. Parrini, *Heir to Empire*, pp. 163–68.

Russian integration. Ruling out these avenues to recovery, however, merely increased the pressure for cancellation of war debts
and reparations. And because this action was unacceptable, Americans had to rely on private loans, the effectiveness of which was
drastically limited by the lack of adequate regulation and, especially after 1929, the spread of market restrictions and economic
depression both at home and abroad.

While the Young Commission and the new bankers' loan to Germany seemed to reinforce the American faith in private programs,
they were clearly a case of too little, too late. A fair-weather approach, the theory of private and cooperative multinationalism
could not withstand the onslaught of hard times. As Moulton and
Pasvolsky have shown, the world-wide depression that began in
1929 and the changing political conditions on the Continent, particularly in Germany, made the "definitive settlement" unworkable
after all. Even the Bank for International Settlements, the creation
of which culminated nearly a decade of private and central bank
cooperation, fell prey to the resurgence of statism and economic
nationalism during the 1930s.

IV

Contemporary observers can find much to contemplate in the
mixture of success and failure evident in the postwar efforts of
policymakers to forge cooperative, private programs for regulating
economic change. No one can challenge their vision of a peaceful
and expansive world economy nor their understanding that, in an
economically interdependent world, constructive development
abroad can encourage prosperity and progress at home. Yet one
can see in the experience of the period how difficult it is to control
nationalist pressures or to balance a faith in private leadership and
industrial self-government against the proper degree of public control needed to gain the larger goals of peace and prosperity for all.
And these insights may prove useful. For now, as then, policymakers find it difficult to strike a creative balance between national
autonomy and international cooperation. Despite the world-wide
collapse in 1929 and the subsequent growth of industrial consolidation and government regulation, they also persist in believing that
private officials can serve as agents for a broader community of interests, a belief that continues to inhibit effective public regulation

and limit the area of public control. And like policymakers in the New Era, they too readily abandon hopes for fostering growth and stability at home without the kind of monopoly controls abroad that stymie world-wide development and breed war and revolution.

Bibliography

1. Primary Sources

A. Private Manuscript Collections

Baker Library, Harvard University, Boston, Mass.
    Thomas W. Lamont Papers

Herbert Hoover Presidential Library, West Branch, Iowa
    William R. Castle Papers
    Herbert Hoover Papers
        Commerce Period, Official File
        Commerce Period, Personal File
        Pre-1921 Material
    Vance McCormick Diary
    Benjamin Strong—Montagu Norman Correspondence
    Supreme Economic Council Papers

Library of Congress, Washington, D. C.
    Chandler P. Anderson Papers
    Tasker H. Bliss Papers
    Bainbridge Colby Papers
    William S. Culbertson Papers
    Josephus Daniels Papers
    Norman H. Davis Papers
    Henry P. Fletcher Papers
    Charles Hamlin Diary
    Leland Harrison Papers
    Charles Evans Hughes Papers
    Robert Lansing Papers
    William Gibbs McAdoo Papers
    Henry White Papers
    Woodrow Wilson Papers

Ohio Historical Society, Columbus, Ohio
    Warren G. Harding Papers

University of Notre Dame Archives, Notre Dame, Ind.
    Edward N. Hurley Diary
Van Horne House, Van Hornesville, N. Y.
    Owen D. Young Papers

B. Government Archives

Public Record Office, London, Eng.
    Cabinet Papers (Minutes)
    General Records of the Foreign Office (Record Group 371)
    Records of the Treasury

National Archives of the United States, Washington, D. C.
    Record Group 32, "General Records of the United States Shipping Board"
        "Official Minutes of the Proceedings of the United States Shipping Board"
        "Records of the Division of Planning and Statistics"
        "Shipping Board General File"
        "Subject-Classified General File"
    Record Group 38, "General Records of the Department of the Navy"
        "Correspondence of the Director of Naval Communications"
    Record Group 40, "General Records of the Department of Commerce"
    Record Group 43, "General Records of the United States Participation in International Conference, Commissions, and Expositions"
        "Conference on the Limitation of Armaments, Records of the United States Delegation"
        "Records of the Preliminary International Conference on Electrical Communications, 1920"
    Record Group 56, "General Records of the Department of the Treasury"
    Record Group 59, "General Records of the Department of State"
    Record Group 80, "General Records of the Department of the Navy"
        "Office of the Secretary of the Navy"
    Record Group 151, "General Records of the Department of Commerce"
        "Bureau of Foreign and Domestic Commerce"
    Record Group 256, "General Records of the American Commission to Negotiate Peace, Paris Peace Conference"

Federal Record Depository of the United States, Suitland, Md.
    Record Group 39, "General Records of the Department of the Treasury, Bureau of Accounts"

C. Published Government Documents

1. Great Britain

Foreign Office

British and Foreign State Papers, *1921*, vol. 114, London, 1924.
British and Foreign State Papers, *1922*, vol. 116, London, 1925.
Documents on British Foreign Policy, *1919–1939*.
  London: H. M. S. O., 1946–.

Parliament

Parliamentary Papers (Commons), vol. 43 (1921) (*Accounts and Papers*, vol. 24), Cmd. 1214.
Parliamentary Papers (Commons), vol. 23 (1922) (*Accounts and Papers*, vol. 13), Cmd. 1621, 1650, 1667.
Parliamentary Papers (Commons), vol. 24 (1923) (*Accounts and Papers*, vol. 12), Cmd. 1812.
Parliamentary Papers (Commons), vol. 25 (1923) (*Accounts and Papers*, vol. 13), Cmd. 1943.

2. United States

Congress

House of Representatives. Committee on Interstate and Foreign Commerce, *Hearings on H. R. 59: Crude Rubber, Coffee, Etc.*, 69th Cong., 1st sess., Washington: GPO, 1926.
——. Committee on the Judiciary, *Hearings on H. R. 8927: A Bill to Amend the Webb-Pomerene Act*, 70th Cong., 1st sess., Washington: GPO, 1928.
——. Committee on the Merchant Marine and Fisheries, *Hearings on H. R. 19350: A Bill to Regulate Radio Communications*, 64th Cong., 2d sess., Washington: GPO, 1917.
——. Committee on the Merchant Marine and Fisheries, *Hearings on H. R. 13159: A Bill to Further Regulate Radio Communications*, 65th Cong., 3d sess., Washington: GPO, 1919.
——. Committee on the Merchant Marine and Fisheries, *Hearings on H. R. 15430: A Bill Continuing the Powers and Authority of the Federal Radio Commission*, 70th Cong., 2d sess., Washington: GPO, 1929.
Senate. Committee on Interstate Commerce, *Hearings on S. 6: A Bill to Provide for the Regulation of the Transmission of Intelligence by Wire or Wireless*, 71st Cong., 1st and 2d sess., Washington: GPO, 1930.
——. Subcommittee of the Committee on Commerce, *Hearings on S. 1651: A Bill Providing for the Construction of a Pacific*

Cable and for Other Purposes, 66th Cong., 1st sess., Washington: GPO, 1919.

————. Subcommittee of the Committee on Foreign Relations, *Hearings on S. C. R. 22: Relative to Engaging the Responsibility of the Government in Financial Arrangements Between Its Citizens and Sovereign Foreign Governments*, 68th Cong., 2d sess., Washington: GPO, 1925.

————. Subcommittee of the Committee on Interstate Commerce. *Hearings on S. 4301: A Bill to Prevent the Unauthorized Landing of Submarine Cables*, 66th Cong., 3d sess., Washington: GPO, 1921.

Department of the Navy

Annual Reports of the Secretary of the Navy, 1916–1920, Washington: GPO, 1917–1921.

Department of State

Papers Relating to the Foreign Relations of the United States, 1916–1929, 36 vols., Washington: GPO, 1925–1944.

Papers Relating to the Foreign Relations of the United States: Paris Peace Conference, 1919, 13 vols. Washington: GPO, 1942–1947.

Papers Relating to the Foreign Relations of the United States: The Lansing Papers, 1914–1920, 2 vols. Washington: GPO, 1939–1940.

Federal Trade Commission

Report on Cooperation in the American Export Trade, Washington: GPO, 1916.

Report on the Radio Industry, Washington: GPO, 1924.

Post Office Department

Annual Reports of the Postmaster General, 1916–1920, Washington: GPO, 1917–1920.

D. Memoirs, Diaries, Collected Documents, Contemporary Accounts, and Studies by Participants

Baker, Ray Stannard. *Woodrow Wilson and World Settlement.* 3 vols. Garden City: Doubleday, Page & Co., 1922–1923.

————. *Woodrow Wilson: Life and Letters.* 8 vols. New York: Doubleday, Doran & Co., 1927–1929.

Baker, Ray Stannard, and Dodd, William E., eds. *The Public Papers of Woodrow Wilson.* 6 vols. New York: Harper & Brothers, 1925–1927.

Bane, Suda Lorena, and Lutz, Ralph H., eds. *The Blockade of Germany*

After the Armistice, 1918–1919. Stanford, Calif.: Stanford University Press, 1942.

————. *The Organization of American Relief in Europe, 1918–1919.* Stanford, Calif.: Stanford University Press, 1943.

Baruch, Bernard. *The Making of the Reparations and Economic Sections of the Treaty.* New York: Harper & Brothers, 1920.

————. *Baruch: My Own Story.* New York: Henry Holt & Co., 1957.

————. *The Public Years.* New York: Holt, Rinehart & Winston, Inc., 1960.

Brown, F. J. *The Cable and Wireless Communications of the World.* London: Sir Isaac Pitman and Sons, Ltd., 1927.

Burnett, Philip M., ed. *Reparations at the Paris Peace Conference from the Standpoint of the American Delegation.* 2 vols. New York: Columbia University Press, 1940.

Clark, Keith. *International Communications: The American Attitude.* New York: Columbia University Press, 1931.

Clarkson, Grosvenor B. *Industrial America in the World War: The Strategy Behind the Line, 1917–1918.* Boston: Houghton Mifflin Co., 1923.

Cronon, E. David, ed. *The Cabinet Diaries of Josephus Daniels, 1913–1921.* Lincoln: University of Nebraska Press, 1963.

Culbertson, William S. *International Economic Policies.* New York and London: D. Appleton and Company, 1925.

"Dangers of the Proposed New Radio Bill." *The Wireless Age* No. 4 (March 1917):374–87.

Daniels, Josephus. *The Wilson Era: Years of War and After.* Chapel Hill: The University of North Carolina Press, 1946.

Davenport, E. H., and Cooke, Sidney Russell. *The Oil Trusts and Anglo-American Relations.* New York: Macmillan, 1924.

Dawes, Charles G. *A Journal of Reparations.* London: Macmillan, 1939.

Durand, E. Dana. "Economic and Political Effects of Governmental Interference with the Free International Movement of Raw Materials." *International Conciliation* No. 226 (January 1927):25–34.

Fischer, Louis. *Oil Imperialism: The International Struggle for Petroleum.* New York: International Publishers Co., Inc., 1926.

"Government Ownership of Wireless." *The Wireless Age* No. 4 (February 1917):300–308.

Grew, Joseph C. *Turbulent Era: A Diplomatic Record of Forty Years, 1904–1945.* Edited by Walter Johnson. 2 vols. Boston: Houghton Mifflin Co., 1952.

Hendrick, Burton J., ed. *The Life and Letters of Walter H. Page.* 3 vols. Garden City: Doubleday & Co., Inc., 1925.

Hoover, Herbert. *American Individualism.* Garden City: Doubleday & Co., Inc., 1922.

————. "America Solemnly Warns Foreign Monopolists of Raw Materials." *Current History* 33 (December 1925):307–11.

————. *The New Day: Campaign Speeches of Herbert Hoover.* Stanford, Calif.: Stanford University Press, 1928.

————. *The Memoirs of Herbert Hoover.* 3 vols. New York: Macmillan, 1951–1952.

————. *The Ordeal of Woodrow Wilson.* New York: Popular Library Paperback Edition, 1961.

House, Edward M., and Seymour, Charles, eds. *What Really Happened at Paris: The Story of the Paris Peace Conference, 1918–1919.* New York: Charles Scribner's Sons, 1921.

Houston, David F. *Eight Years with Wilson's Cabinet, 1913–1920.* 2 vols. Garden City: Doubleday, Page & Co., 1926.

Hughes, Charles Evans. *The Pathway of Peace: Representative Addresses Delivered During His Term as Secretary of State, 1921–1925.* New York: Harper & Brothers, 1925.

————. *Our Relations to the Nations of the Western Hemisphere.* Princeton: Princeton University Press, 1928.

Hull, Cordell. *The Memoirs of Cordell Hull.* 2 vols. New York: Macmillan, 1948.

Hurley, Edward N. *Bridge to France.* Philadelphia: J. B. Lippincott Co., 1927.

Inman, Samuel Guy. "Imperialistic America." *The Atlantic Monthly* 134 (July 1924):107–16.

Keynes, John Maynard. *The Economic Consequences of the Peace.* New York: Harcourt, Brace & World, Inc., 1920.

Klein, Julius. "International Cartels." *Foreign Affairs: An American Quarterly Review* 6 (April 1928):448–58.

Lamont, Thomas W. *Across World Frontiers.* New York: Harcourt, Brace & World, Inc., 1951.

Lane, Anne W., and Wall, Louise H., eds. *The Letters of Franklin K. Lane: Personal and Political.* Boston: Houghton Mifflin Co., 1922.

Lansing, Robert. *The Peace Negotiations: A Personal Narrative.* Boston: Houghton Mifflin Co., 1921.

————. *The War Memoirs of Robert Lansing.* New York: Bobbs-Merrill Co., 1935.

MacDonald, William. "Great Britain and the Economic War." *The Nation* 107 (3 August 1918):117–19.

McAdoo, William G. *Crowded Years: The Reminiscences of William Gibbs McAdoo.* Boston: Houghton Mifflin Co., 1931.

Moulton, Harold G. *The Reparation Plan.* New York: McGraw-Hill Book Co., 1924.

Moulton, Harold G., and Pasvolsky, Leo. *War Debts and World Prosperity.* Washington: The Brookings Institution, 1932.

National Foreign Trade Council. *European Economic Alliances: A Compilation of Information on International Commercial Policies After the European War and Their Effect Upon the Foreign Trade of the United States.* New York: National Foreign Trade Council, 1916.

Phelps, Clyde William. *The Foreign Expansion of American Banks.* New York: Ronald Press Co., 1927.

Redfield, William C. *With Congress and Cabinet.* New York: Doubleday, Page & Co., 1924.

Requa, Mark L. *The Relation of Government to Industry.* New York: Macmillan, 1925.

Salter, James A. *Allied Shipping Control: An Experiment in International Organization.* London and New York: Oxford at the Clarendon Press, 1921.

Sarnoff, David. *Looking Ahead: The Papers of David Sarnoff.* New York: MacGraw-Hill Book Co., 1968.

Seymour, Charles, ed. *The Intimate Papers of Colonel House.* 4 vols. Boston: Houghton Mifflin Co., 1926–1928.

Smith, George O., ed. *The Strategy of Minerals.* New York: D. Appleton and Company, 1919.

Stimson, Henry L., and Bundy, McGeorge. *On Active Service in Peace and War.* New York: Octagon Books, 1971.

Strong, Josiah Edward. "Steel-Making Minerals." *Foreign Affairs: An American Quarterly Review* 4 (July 1926):601–12.

Temperley, H. W. V., ed. *A History of the Peace Conference at Paris.* 6 vols. London: Frowdy, Hodder, and Stoughton, 1920–1924.

"The New Radio Legislation." *The Wireless Age* No. 4 (January 1917): 226–40.

Tribolet, Leslie B. *The International Aspects of Electrical Communications in the Pacific Area.* Baltimore: The Johns Hopkins University Press, 1929.

Tumulty, Joseph P. *Woodrow Wilson as I Know Him.* New York: Doubleday, Page & Co., 1921.

Vanderlip, Frank A. *What Happened to Europe?* New York: Macmillan, 1919.

———. *What Next in Europe?* New York: Harcourt, Brace & World, Inc., 1922.

Viner, Jacob. "National Monopolies of Raw Materials." *Foreign Affairs: An American Quarterly Review* 4 (July 1926):585–600.

Wallace, Benjamin Bruce, and Edminister, Lynn Ramsey. *International Control of Raw Materials.* Washington: The Brookings Institution, 1930.

Welles, Sumner. "Is America Imperialistic?" *The Atlantic Monthly* 134 (September 1924):412–23.

Williams, Benjamin H. *Economic Foreign Policy of the United States.*
New York: MacGraw-Hill Book Co., 1929.
Young, Owen D. "Freedom of the Air." *Saturday Evening Post* 202
(16 November 1929):16, 193–94.

II. Secondary Sources

A. Articles

Abrahams, Paul. "American Bankers and the Economic Tactics of
Peace." *The Journal of American History* 46 (December 1969):572–83.
Braisted, William R. "China, the United States Navy, and the Beth-
lehem Steel Company, 1909–1929." *Business History Review* 42
(Spring 1968):50–66.
Buhite, Russell D. "Nelson Johnson and American Policy Toward China,
1925–1928." *Pacific Historical Review* 35 (November 1966):451–65.
Burks, David D. "The United States and the Geneva Protocol of 1924:
'A New Holy Alliance'?" *American Historical Review* 44 (July 1959):
891–905.
Carlton, David. "Great Britain and the Naval Disarmament Conference
of 1927." *Political Science Quarterly* 83 (December 1968):573–98.
———. "The Anglo-French Compromise on Arms Limitation, 1928."
Journal of British History 8 (1969):141–62.
Chandler, Alfred D., Jr. "The Beginnings of 'Big Business' in American
Industry." *Business History Review* 33 (Spring 1959):1–31.
Chandler, Alfred D., Jr., and Galambos Louis. "The Development of
Large-Scale Economic Organizations in Modern America." *Journal
of Economic History* 30 (March 1970):210–17.
Costigliola, Frank C. "The Other Side of Isolationism: The Establish-
ment of the First World Bank, 1929–1930." *The Journal of American
History* 59 (December 1972):602–20.
Cuff, Robert D. "Woodrow Wilson and Business-Government Relations
During World War I." *Review of Politics* 31 (July 1969):385–407.
DeNovo, John. "The Movement for an Aggressive American Oil Policy
Abroad, 1918–1920." *American Historical Review* 61 (July 1956):
854–76.
Eis, Carl. "The 1919–1930 Merger Movement in American Industry."
Journal of Law and Economics 12 (October 1969):267–98.
Falkus, M. E. "United States Economic Policy and the 'Dollar Gap' of
the 1920's." *The Economic History Review* 24 (November 1971):
599–623.
Fry, M. G. "The North Atlantic Triangle and the Abrogation of the
Anglo-Japanese Alliance." *Journal of Modern History* 39 (March
1967):46–64.

Glad, Paul W. "Progressives and the Business Culture of the 1920's." *Journal of American History* 52 (June 1966):75–89.

Hawley, Ellis W. "Secretary Hoover and the Bituminous Coal Problem." *Business History Review* 42 (Autumn 1968):247–70.

———. "Herbert Hoover, the Commerce Secretariat, and the Vision of an 'Associative State,' 1921–1928." *Journal of American History* 61 (June 1974):116–40.

Heald, Morrell. "Business Thought in the Twenties: Social Responsibility." *American Quarterly* 13 (Summer 1961):126–40.

Himmelberg, Robert F. "The War Industries Board and the Antitrust Question in November 1918." *Journal of American History* 52 (June 1965):59–74.

———. "Business, Antitrust Policy, and the Industrial Board of the Department of Commerce, 1919." *Business History Review* 42 (Spring 1968):1–23.

Hogan, Michael J., "Informal Entente: Public Policy and Private Management in Anglo-American Petroleum Affairs, 1918–1924." *Business History Review* 48 (Summer 1974):187–205.

———. "The United States and the Problem of International Economic Control: American Attitudes Toward European Reconstruction, 1918–1920." *Pacific Historical Review* 44 (February 1975):84–103.

Kane, N. Stephen. "Bankers and Diplomats: The Diplomacy of the Dollar in Mexico, 1921–1924." *Business History Review* 47 (Autumn 1973):335–52.

Kaufman, Burton I. "United States Trade and Latin America: The Wilson Years." *Journal of American History* 58 (September 1971):342–62.

———. "Organization for Foreign Trade Expansion in the Mississippi Valley, 1900–1920." *Business History Review* 46 (Winter 1972): 444–65.

———. "The Organizational Dimension of United States Economic Foreign Policy, 1900–1920." *Business History Review* 46 (Spring 1972):17–44.

Kirwin, Harry W. "The Federal Telegraph Company: A Testing of the Open Door." *Pacific Historical Review* 22 (August 1953):271–86.

Koistinen, Paul A. C. "The 'Industrial-Military Complex' in Historical Perspective: World War I." *Business History Review* 41 (Winter 1967):378–403.

———. "The 'Industrial-Military Complex' in Historical Perspective: The Inter-War Years." *Journal of American History* 56 (March 1970): 819–39.

Leffler, Melvyn P. "The Origins of Republican War Debt Policy, 1921–1923: A Case Study in the Applicability of the Open Door Interpretation." *Journal of American History* 59 (December 1972):585–601.

———. "Political Isolationism, Economic Expansion, or Diplomatic

Realism: American Policy Toward Western Europe, 1921–1933." *Per-spectives in American History* 8 (1974):413–61.

May, Henry F. "Shifting Perspectives on the 1920's." *Mississippi Valley Historical Review* 43 (December 1956):405–27.

Nordhauser, Norman. "Origins of Federal Oil Regulation in the 1920's." *Business History Review* 47 (Spring 1973):53–71.

Reed, Peter M. "Standard Oil in Indonesia, 1898–1928." *Business History Review* 32 (Autumn 1958):311–37.

Rhodes, Benjamin. "Reassessing 'Uncle Shylock': The United States and the French War Debt, 1917–1929." *The Journal of American History* 55 (March 1969):787–803.

Sklar, Martin J. "Woodrow Wilson and the Political Economy of Modern United States Liberalism." *Studies on the Left* 1 (1960):17–47.

Snyder, J. Richard. "Coolidge, Costigan and the Tariff Commission." *Mid-America* 50 (April 1968):131–48.

Stratton, David H. "Behind Teapot Dome: Some Personal Insights." *Business History Review* 21 (Winter 1957):385–402.

Urofsky, Melvin I. "Wilson, Brandeis and the Trust Issue, 1912–1914." *Mid-America* 49 (January 1967):3–28.

Vinson, John Chalmers. "The Annulment of the Lansing-Ishii Agreement." *Pacific Historical Review* 27 (February 1958):57–69.

————. "The Imperial Conference of 1921 and the Anglo-Japanese Alliance." *Pacific Historical Review* 21 (August 1962):257–67.

Wheeler, Gerald E. "Isolated Japan: Anglo-American Diplomatic Cooperation, 1927–1936." *Pacific Historical Review* 30 (May 1961): 165–78.

Wicker, Elmus R. "Federal Reserve Monetary Policy, 1922–1933: A Reinterpretation." *Journal of Political Economics* 73 (August 1956): 325–43.

Williams, William Appleman. "The Legend of Isolationism in the 1920's." *Science & Society* 19 (Winter 1954):1–20.

————. "China and Japan: A Challenge and a Choice of the Nineteen Twenties." *Pacific Historical Review* 26 (August 1957):259–79.

————. "A Note on American Foreign Policy in Europe in the 1920's." *Science & Society* 22 (Winter 1958):1–20.

B. Books

Adler, Selig. *The Isolationist Impulse: Its Twentieth Century Reaction.* New York: Oberland-Schuman, 1957.

————. *The Uncertain Giant, 1921–1941: American Foreign Policy Between the Wars.* New York: Macmillan, 1965.

Arndt, Hanna W. *The Economic Lessons of the Nineteen-Thirties.* New York: Oxford University Press, Inc., 1944.

Baran, Paul A., and Sweezy, Paul M. *Monopoly Capitalism: An Essay on the American Economic and Social Order.* New York: Monthly Review Press, 1966.

Bates, J. Leonard. *The Origins of Teapot Dome: Progressives, Parties and Petroleum, 1909–1921.* Urbana: University of Illinois Press, 1963.

Beers, Burton F. *Vain Endeavor: Robert Lansing's Attempts to End the Anglo-Japanese Rivalry.* Durham, N. C.: Duke University Press, 1962.

Bernstein, Barton J., ed. *Towards a New Past: Dissenting Essays in American History.* New York: Pantheon Books, Inc., 1968.

Birdsall, Paul. *Versailles Twenty Years After.* New York: Reynal & Hitchcock, 1941.

Boulding, Kenneth E. *The Organizational Revolution: A Study in the Ethics of Economic Organization.* Chicago: Quadrangle Books, Inc., 1968.

Braeman, John; Bremner, Robert H.; and Brody, David, eds. *Change and Continuity in Twentieth Century America: The 1920's.* Columbus: Ohio State University Press, 1968.

———. *Twentieth-Century American Foreign Policy.* Columbus: Ohio State University Press, 1971.

Brandes, Joseph. *Herbert Hoover and Economic Diplomacy: Department of Commerce Policy, 1921–1928.* Pittsburgh: University of Pittsburgh Press, 1962.

Buckley, Thomas H. *The United States and the Washington Conference, 1921–1922.* Knoxville: University of Tennessee Press, 1970.

Chandler, Alfred D., Jr. *Strategy and Structure: Chapters in the History of the Industrial Enterprise.* Cambridge, Mass.: The M. I. T. Press, 1962.

Chandler, Lester V. *Benjamin Strong, Central Banker.* Washington: The Brookings Institution, 1958.

Clarke, Stephen V. O. *Central Bank Cooperation, 1924–1931.* New York: Federal Reserve Bank of New York, 1967.

———. *The Reconstruction of the International Monetary System: The Attempts of 1922 and 1933.* Princeton: Princeton University Press, 1973.

Clay, Henry. *Lord Norman.* London: Macmillan, 1957.

Cochran, Thomas C. *The American Business System: A Historical Perspective, 1900–1955.* Cambridge, Mass.: Harvard University Press, 1957.

Coit, Margaret L. *Mr. Baruch.* Boston: Houghton Mifflin Co., 1957.

Corey, Lewis. *The House of Morgan.* New York: AMS Press, Inc., 1969.

Craig, Gordon A., and Gilbert, Felix, eds. *The Diplomats, 1919–1939.* 2 vols. New York: Atheneum Publishers, 1972.

Crozier, Michael. *The Bureaucratic Phenomenon.* Chicago: University of Chicago Press, 1964.

Cuff, Robert D. *The War Industries Board: Business-Government Rela-*

tions During World War I. Baltimore and London: The Johns Hopkins University Press, 1973.

Curry, Roy Watson. *Woodrow Wilson and Far Eastern Policy, 1913–1921.* New York: Bookman Associates, 1957.

DeNovo, John. *American Interests and Policies in the Middle East.* Minneapolis: University of Minnesota Press, 1963.

Diamond, William. *The Economic Thought of Woodrow Wilson.* Baltimore: The Johns Hopkins University Press, 1943.

Dorfman, Joseph. *The Economic Mind in American Civilization.* vols. 4, 5. New York: The Viking Press, 1959.

Ellis, L. Ethan. *Frank B. Kellogg and American Foreign Relations, 1925–1929.* New Brunswick, N. J.: Rutgers University Press, 1961.

————. *Republican Foreign Policy, 1921–1933.* New Brunswick, N. J.: Rutgers University Press, 1968.

Fausold, Martin L. and Mazuzan, George T., eds. *The Hoover Presidency: A Reappraisal.* Albany: State University of New York Press, 1974.

Feis, Herbert. *Petroleum and American Foreign Policy.* Commodity Policy Studies, No. 3. Stanford: Food Research Institute of Stanford University, 1944.

————. *The Diplomacy of the Dollar: First Era, 1919–1932.* Baltimore: The Johns Hopkins University Press, 1950.

Fischer, Fritz. *Germany's War Aims in the First World War.* New York: W. W. Norton & Co., Inc., 1967.

Fowler, W. B. *British-American Relations, 1917–1918: The Role of Sir William Wiseman.* Princeton: Princeton University Press, 1969.

Galambos, Louis. *Competition & Cooperation: The Emergence of a National Trade Association.* Baltimore: The Johns Hopkins University Press, 1966.

Gelfand, Lawrence E. *The Inquiry: American Preparations for Peace, 1917–1919.* New Haven and London: Yale University Press, 1963.

Gibb, George Sweet, and Knowlton, Evelyn H. *History of Standard Oil: The Resurgent Years, 1911–1927.* New York: Harper & Brothers, 1956.

Glad, Betty. *Charles Evans Hughes and the Illusions of Innocence: A Study in American Diplomacy.* Urbana: University of Illinois Press, 1966.

Graebner, Norman A., ed. *An Uncertain Tradition: American Secretaries of State in the Twentieth Century.* New York: McGraw-Hill Book Co., 1961.

Griswold, Alfred Whitney. *The Far Eastern Policy of the United States.* New York: Harcourt, Brace & Co., 1938.

Haber, Samuel. *Efficiency and Uplift: Scientific Management in the Progressive Era, 1890–1920.* Chicago: University of Chicago Press, 1964.

Hawley, Ellis W. *The New Deal and the Problem of Monopoly: A Study in Economic Ambivalence.* Princeton: Princeton University Press, 1966.

Hays, Samuel P. *The Response to Industrialism, 1885–1914.* Chicago: University of Chicago Press, 1957.

————. *Conservation and the Gospel of Efficiency: The Progressive Conservation Movement, 1890–1920.* Cambridge, Mass.: Harvard University Press, 1959.

Hicks, John D. *Republican Ascendancy, 1921–1933.* New York: Harper & Brothers, 1960.

Howeth, Linwood S. *History of Communications-Electronics in the United States Navy.* Washington: GPO, 1963.

Huthmacher, J. Joseph, and Susman, Warren I., eds. *Herbert Hoover and the Crisis of American Capitalism.* Cambridge, Mass.: Schenkman Publishing Co., Inc., 1973.

Iriye, Akira. *After Imperialism: The Search for a New Order in the Far East, 1921–1933.* Cambridge, Mass.: Harvard University Press, 1965.

Israel, Jerry. *Progressivism and the Open Door: America and China, 1905–1921.* Pittsburgh: University of Pittsburgh Press, 1971.

————, ed. *Building the Organizational Society: Essays on Associational Activities in Modern America.* New York: The Free Press, 1972.

Jacobson, Jon. *Locarno Diplomacy: Germany and the West, 1925–1929.* Princeton: Princeton University Press, 1972.

Kaufman, Burton I. *Efficiency and Expansion: Foreign Trade Organization in the Wilson Administration, 1913–1921.* Westport, Conn.: Greenwood Press, Inc., 1974.

Kennan, George F. *American Diplomacy, 1900–1950.* Chicago: University of Chicago Press, 1951.

Kolko, Gabriel. *The Triumph of Conservatism: A Reinterpretation of American History, 1900–1916.* New York: The Free Press, 1963.

Lawrence, James. *The World's Struggle with Rubber, 1905–1931.* New York: Harper & Brothers, 1931.

Leuchtenburg, William E. *The Perils of Prosperity, 1914–1932.* Chicago: University of Chicago Press, 1958.

Levin, N. Gordon, Jr. *Woodrow Wilson and World Politics: America's Response to War and Revolution.* New York: Oxford University Press, Inc., 1968.

Lewis, Cleona. *America's Stake in International Investments.* Washington: The Brookings Institution, 1938.

Lief, Alfred. *The Firestone Story: A History of the Firestone Tire & Rubber Company.* New York: Whittlesey House, 1951.

Link, Arthur S. *Woodrow Wilson and the Progressive Era, 1910–1917.* New York: Harper & Row, Pubs., 1954.

———. *Wilson: The New Freedom.* Princeton: Princeton University Press, 1956.

———. *Wilson the Diplomatist: A Look at His Major Foreign Policies.* Baltimore: The Johns Hopkins University Press, 1957.

Lloyd, Craig. *Aggressive Introvert: A Study of Herbert Hoover and Public Relations Management, 1912–1932.* Columbus: Ohio State University Press, 1973.

Loth, David. *Swope of G. E.: The Story of Gerard Swope and General Electric in American Business.* New York: Simon & Schuster, Inc., 1958.

Maclaurin, W. Rupert. *Invention and Innovation in the Radio Industry.* New York: Macmillan, 1949.

Mayer, Arno J. *Wilson vs. Lenin: Political Origins of the New Diplomacy, 1917–1918.* Cleveland: The World Publishing Company, 1964.

———. *Diplomacy of Peacemaking: Containment and Counterrevolution at Versailles, 1918–1919.* New York: Vintage Books, 1969.

McConnell, Grant. *Private Power & American Democracy.* New York: Alfred A. Knopf, Inc., 1966.

Mintz, Ilse. *Deterioration in the Quality of Foreign Bonds Issued in the United States, 1920–1930.* New York: National Bureau of Economic Research, 1951.

Morgan, E. Victor. *Studies in British Financial Policy, 1914–1925.* London: Macmillan, 1952.

Morgenthau, Hans. *In Defense of the National Interest: A Critical Examination of American Foreign Policy.* New York: Alfred A. Knopf, Inc., 1951.

Murray, Robert K. *The Harding Era: Warren G. Harding and His Administration.* Minneapolis: University of Minnesota Press, 1969.

———. *The Politics of Normalcy: Governmental Theory and Practice in the Harding-Coolidge Era.* New York: W.W. Norton & Co., Inc., 1973.

Nash, Gerald D. *United States Oil Policy, 1890–1964.* Pittsburgh: University of Pittsburgh Press, 1968.

Nelson, Ralph L. *Merger Movements in American Industry, 1895–1956.* Princeton: Princeton University Press, 1959.

Nicolson, Harold. *Dwight Morrow.* New York: Harcourt, Brace & Co., 1935.

Noggle, Burl. *Teapot Dome: Oil and Politics in the 1920s.* Baton Rouge: Louisiana State University Press, 1962.

O'Connor, Harvey. *Mellon's Millions: The Life and Times of Andrew W. Mellon.* New York: Blue Ribbon Books, 1933.

Osgood, Robert E. *Ideals and Self-Interest in America's Foreign Relations*. Chicago: University of Chicago Press, 1953.

Parrini, Carl P. *Heir to Empire: United States Economic Diplomacy, 1916–1923*. Pittsburgh: University of Pittsburgh Press, 1969.

Perkins, Dexter. *Charles Evans Hughes and American Democratic Statesmanship*. Boston: Little, Brown and Company, 1956.

Prothro, James Warren. *The Dollar Decade: Business Ideals in the 1920's*. Baton Rouge: Louisiana State University Press, 1954.

Pusey, Merlo J. *Charles Evans Hughes*. 2 vols. New York: Macmillan, 1951.

Radosh, Ronald, and Rothbard, Murray N., eds. *A New History of Leviathan: Essays on the Rise of the American Corporate State*. New York: E. P. Dutton & Co., Inc., 1972.

Rothbard, Murray N. *America's Great Depression*. Princeton: D. Van Nostrand, Co., Inc., 1963.

Smith, Daniel M. *Aftermath of War: Bainbridge Colby and Wilsonian Diplomacy, 1920–1921*. Philadelphia: American Philosophical Society, 1970.

Smith, Rixey, and Beasley, Norman. *Carter Glass, A Biography*. New York and Toronto: Longmans, Green & Co., Inc., 1939.

Smith, Robert F. *The United States and Revolutionary Nationalism in Mexico, 1916–1932*. Chicago: University of Chicago Press, 1972.

Soule, George. *Prosperity Decade: From War to Depression, 1917–1929*. New York: Rinehart & Co., 1947.

Staley, Eugene. *Raw Materials in Peace and War*. New York: Council on Foreign Relations, 1937.

Stein, Herbert. *The Fiscal Revolution in America*. Chicago: University of Chicago Press, 1969.

Tillman, Seth P. *Anglo-American Relations at the Paris Peace Conference of 1919*. Princeton: Princeton University Press, 1961.

Tulchin, Joseph. *The Aftermath of War: World War I and U.S. Policy Toward Latin America*. New York: New York University Press, 1971.

Vinson, John Chalmers. *The Parchment Peace: The United States and the Washington Conference, 1921–1922*. Athens, Ga.: University of Georgia Press, 1955.

Weinstein, James. *The Corporate Ideal in the Liberal State*. Boston: The Beacon Press, Inc., 1968.

Wicker, Elmus R. *Federal Reserve Monetary Policy, 1917–1933*. New York: Random House, Inc., 1966.

Wiebe, Robert H. *Businessmen and Reform: A Study of the Progressive Movement*. Cambridge, Mass.: Harvard University Press, 1962.

———. *The Search For Order, 1877–1920*. New York: Hill & Wang, Inc., 1967.

Williams, William Appleman. *The Tragedy of American Diplomacy.* New York: Dell Publishing Co., 1972.

―――. *The Contours of American History.* Chicago: Quadrangle Books, Inc., 1966.

Williamson, Harold F. et al. *The American Petroleum Industry: The Age of Energy, 1899–1959.* Evanston, Ill.: Northwestern University Press, 1963.

Wilson, Joan Hoff. *American Business & Foreign Policy, 1920–1933.* Lexington, Ky.: University of Kentucky Press, 1971.

―――. *Ideology and Economics: U. S. Relations with the Soviet Union, 1918–1933.* Columbia: University of Missouri Press, 1974.

Wolfers, Arnold. *Britain and France Between the Two Wars: Conflicting Strategies of Peace From Versailles to World War II.* New York: W. W. Norton & Co., Inc., 1966.

C. Unpublished Materials

Chalk, Frank. "The United States and the International Struggle for Rubber, 1914–1941." Ph.D. diss., University of Wisconsin, 1970.

Costigliola, Frank C. "The Politics of Financial Stabilization: American Reconstruction Policy in Europe, 1924–1930." Ph.D. diss., Cornell University, 1972.

―――. "Anglo-American Rivalry in the 1920's." Paper presented at the annual meeting of the Organization of American Historians, Denver, 1974.

Hawley, Ellis W. "Herbert Hoover and Economic Stabilization, 1921–1922." Paper presented at the Second Herbert Hoover Centennial Seminar, Herbert Hoover Presidential Library, West Branch, Iowa, April 1974.

―――. "Techno-Corporatist Formulas in the Liberal State, 1920–1960: A Neglected Aspect of America's Search For A New Order." Paper presented at a Conference on Twentieth Century Capitalism, Harvard University, September 1974.

Hughes, Brady A. "Owen D. Young and American Foreign Policy, 1919–1929." Ph.D. diss., University of Wisconsin, 1969.

Klachko, Mary. "Anglo-American Naval Competition, 1918–1922." Ph.D. diss., Columbia University, 1962.

Leffler, Melvyn P. "The Struggle for Stability: American Policy Toward France, 1921–1933." Ph.D. diss., Ohio State University, 1972.

―――. "Herbert Hoover, the 'New Era,' and American Foreign Policy." Paper presented at the Second Herbert Hoover Centennial Seminar, Herbert Hoover Presidential Library, West Branch, Iowa, April 1974.

Noring, Nina J. "American Coalition Diplomacy and the Armistice, 1918–1919." Ph.D. diss., University of Iowa, 1972.

Seidel, Robert Neal. "Progressive Pan Americanism: Development and

United States Policy Toward South America, 1906–1931." Ph.D. diss., Cornell University, 1973.

Van Meter, Robert H., Jr. "The United States and European Recovery, 1918–1923: A Study of Public Policy and Private Finance." Ph.D. diss., University of Wisconsin, 1971.

———. "Herbert Hoover and the Economic Reconstruction of Europe, 1918–1921." Paper presented at the First Herbert Hoover Centennial Seminar, Herbert Hoover Presidential Library, West Branch, Iowa, February 1974.

Wilson, Joan Hoff. "Hoover's Agricultural Policies, 1921–1928." Paper presented at the Second Herbert Hoover Centennial Seminar, Herbert Hoover Presidential Library, West Branch, Iowa, April 1974.

Zieger, Robert H. "Herbert Hoover, The Wage-Earner, and the 'New Economic System,' 1919–1929." Paper presented at the Second Herbert Hoover Centennial Seminar, Herbert Hoover Presidential Library, West Branch, Iowa, April 1974.

Index

British Western Telegraph Company,
111–25 *passim*
Brown, F. J., 115, 116, 124
Brussels Conference, 33, 34
Bullard, William, 133, 133n10
Bureau of Foreign and Domestic Commerce, 16, 31, 82, 106, 193
Buying pools, 190, 193, 194, 205, 206,
207

C

Cable industry, 109, 215
Cables: British, 106–7, 117–18; ex-German, 110, 118, 119
Canada, 113, 219
Caribbean Petroleum Company, 166,
167, 169
Carlton, Newcomb, 113, 124
Cartels, 188, 190, 191, 200, 204, 207
Castle, William R., Jr., 127, 201
Central America, 81, 130, 141, 145. *See
also* Latin America; South America
Ceylon, 188, 191
Chamberlain, Austin, 198, 199
Chamber of Commerce of the United
States, 97, 98
Child, Richard Washburn, 43, 44, 46,
49
Chile, 111, 113, 145, 188
China, 11, 84–96 *passim*, 104, 146–53
passim, 158, 214
China financial consortium, 11, 84–96
passim, 182, 183, 212
Churchill, Winston: and stabilization of
pound sterling, 73–74, 75, 76; favors
Anglo-American cooperation in oil
policy, 178–79; on rubber policy, 192,
199; attacks U.S. war debt policy,
218, 219, 220; on Anglo-American relations, 220
Colby, Bainbridge, 36, 90, 161
Colon Development Company, 166,
167, 168
Colonial Office, Great Britain, 179, 192
Commercial Cable Company, 117, 118–27 *passim*
Congress, U.S., 24, 34, 40, 51, 53, 114,
130, 131, 135, 142, 201, 205, 206, 207
Coolidge, Calvin, 39, 41, 69, 126, 157,
183
Coolidge administration, 5, 6, 57, 80
Cooperation: between business and government, 2, 3, 8, 18, 19, 41, 209, 212;
among business, 2, 3, 18, 41, 79–80,
83, 105, 109, 129, 132, 136–37, 148,
149, 150, 158, 162–63, 174, 190, 191,
193, 205–6, 207, 209, 211; govern-

ment support for, among business,
18, 19, 40–41, 93, 96–97, 99, 113,
211–12; between business and government in reconstruction policy, 29,
30–31; between bankers and government in regulating foreign investment, 78, 81, 82, 83, 86, 95, 99, 100,
101, 103, 204; lack of, among business, 92–93, 97–98, 103–4, 113, 123–24, 163, 195–96, 214–15; between
business and government in communications policy, 109, 132, 133–34, 136–37, 142, 154, 155; between
business and government in oil policy,
161–62, 164; between business and
government in resource policy, 190,
191, 193, 204, 205, 206
Cooperation, international: and parallel
developments in domestic economy,
2, 17–18, 209; Hoover on, 3–4, 42; vs.
state-management and competition,
4, 7–9, 209–11; and Open Door
policy, 5, 16–17, 212; in European reconstruction, 13, 20–21, 29, 34, 37,
45, 96, 212–14; in postwar plans of
Wilsonians, 16; Republican support
for, 41–42; in Austrian reconstruction, 60, 61, 62, 64–65, 66, 212; in
Dawes Plan and bankers loan to Germany, 71; in restoring gold standard,
76; in regulating foreign investment,
78, 84, 85, 86, 95–96, 104; in communications policy, 114–15, 125, 129,
137–39, 140, 142–43, 145–46, 146–49, 150–53, 157–58; in oil policy,
159–60, 169–70, 177; in resource
policy, 186, 191, 195, 196–97, 199,
208, 214; in stabilizing pound sterling, 213–14; flaws in structure of,
214–17; in Young Commission, 223;
in Bank for International Settlements,
223; mentioned, 1–5, 9–11, 211–12.
See also Anglo-American cooperation
Costa Rica, 166, 167, 168, 169
Craige, Robert, 201, 202, 219, 220
Culbertson, William S., 17, 203
Curzon, Lord, 56, 147, 178

D

Daniels, Josephus, 132, 133, 134, 135,
142, 145, 148, 189n8
Davis, Norman, 13, 24, 25, 28, 29, 34,
35, 36, 90
Dawes Commission, 68, 69, 70, 76, 77,
221
Dawes Plan, 68, 69, 70, 71, 72, 104,
221, 222